Governing Finance in Europe

Governing Finance in Europe

A Centralisation of Rulemaking?

Edited by

Adrienne Héritier

European University Institute (EUI); Robert Schuman Centre for Advanced Studies (RSCAS), Florence, Italy

Magnus G. Schoeller

Centre for European Integration Research (EIF), Department of Political Science, University of Vienna, Austria; Robert Schuman Centre for Advanced Studies (RSCAS), Florence, Italy

Cheltenham, UK • Northampton, MA, USA

Published by
Edward Elgar Publishing Limited
The Lypiatts
15 Lansdown Road
Cheltenham
Glos GL50 2JA
UK

Edward Elgar Publishing, Inc.
William Pratt House
9 Dewey Court
Northampton
Massachusetts 01060
USA

A catalogue record for this book
is available from the British Library

Library of Congress Control Number: 2020940523

This book is available electronically in the **Elgar**online
Social and Political Science subject collection
http://dx.doi.org/10.4337/9781839101120

ISBN 978 1 83910 111 3 (cased)
ISBN 978 1 83910 112 0 (eBook)

Printed and bound in Great Britain by TJ International Ltd, Padstow

Contents

Figures and tables

Contributors

Fabio Bulfone is postdoctoral researcher at the Max Planck Institute for the Studies of Societies in Cologne.

Joseph Ganderson is a researcher at the European Institute, London School of Economics and the Department of Social and Political Sciences, European University Institute, Italy.

Adrienne Héritier is Emeritus Professor of Social and Political Sciences at the European University Institute, Italy.

Johannes Karremans is postdoctoral researcher at the Political Science Department of the University of Salzburg.

Heikki Marjosola is Assistant Professor of Financial Law at the University of Helsinki.

Magnus G. Schoeller is a researcher at the Centre for European Integration Research, Department of Political Science, University of Vienna, Austria.

Agnieszka Smoleńska is a researcher at the Law Department, European University Institute and Senior EU Affairs Analyst at Polityka Insight.

Magnus Strand is Associate Professor of European Law at Uppsala University, Sweden. The present work has been carried out as part-time professor at the European University Institute, Italy.

Acknowledgements

This research would not have been possible without important support from the following institutions. First and foremost, we acknowledge funding from the Swedish Research Council (Grant No 2016-01596) and the support of the University of Uppsala. Moreover, the Robert Schuman Centre of the European University Institute in Florence provided crucial administrative and infrastructural support, including the managing of funds and language editing, and also intellectual input such as critical and constructive discussions with the 'EUI Reading Group on Finance.' Finally, the book profited from valuable collaboration with the Hertie School of Governance Berlin.

1. Governing finance in Europe: a centralisation of rule-making?

Adrienne Héritier and Magnus G. Schoeller[1]

Vet du inte, min son, med hur lite visdom världen styrs?
Dost thou not know, my son, with how little wisdom the world is governed? (Axel
Oxenstierna, 1648)

1.1 INTRODUCTION

The governance of finance in Europe is embedded in international regulatory agreements. Especially since the financial crisis of 2008, international agreements have sought to introduce rules to ensure that micro-risks (failures to maintain financial contracts) and macro-risks (contagion, leading to system-stability risks) are reduced. The implementation of international regulations in European regulations and, as a result, in national regulations, has had important repercussions on the regulatory structure of the European Union. Did these changes lead to a centralisation reflected in a shift of formal rule-making and the supervision of its implementation from the national to the supranational level? If so, why did this happen and through which processes? Who wins and who loses from this shift? Finally, what are the implications for political accountability in rule-making?

This book's answers to these questions will be provided from different research perspectives and different theoretical backgrounds: political science, law, the sociology of finance and economics. This is crucial in order to grasp the complicated processes that are triggered by regulation and its impact in this most dynamic and globally interlinked of markets. We specify the conditions under which different paths of political, social and economic development are embarked upon leading to different outcomes – that is, centralisation, decentralisation or fragmentation – and their effects. Specifying the condi-

[1]   We would like to thank the Swedish Research Council for generously funding this research project under the title "A Centralisation of Rulemaking in Europe? The Legal and Political Governance of the Financial Market" (Grant No 2016-01596) and the direction of Carl Fredrik Bergström.

tions means that the answers to our research questions are not immediately self-evident. European financial regulation and its impact differ according to the political, legal and economic situations of member states. Importantly, however, they are also influenced by factors such as competition between global financial regulatory powers, self-regulation by private actors and technological innovation. These factors may not only foster the centralisation of financial regulation but they may also constitute counter-forces leading to decentralisation or fragmentation.

We consider our question on centralisation from four broad perspectives: from a *vertical international* perspective, that is, European regulation in the context of international regulatory agreements; a *horizontal international perspective*, that is, regulatory competition between regional powers and its impact on European rule-making; *hybrid regulation*, that is, the interaction between private and public actors in regulation and its impact; and *technological innovation*, that is, the impact of technological innovation on financial regulation. Linking the international (vertical and horizontal) perspectives and their impact on regulatory structure in the EU is an area that so far has been little investigated and so is a particular focus of our analysis. Moreover, given that the self-regulation of actors in financial markets has historically been of paramount importance, the interaction between private self-regulation and the public regulation of financial markets constitutes a crucial feature of the operation of financial markets. Equally, technological innovation has been another crucial factor influencing trading in financial markets and its regulation. The acceleration of these technology-driven changes due to digitalisation has raised important challenges for regulation, which we will investigate theoretically and empirically. In the conclusion, the analytical and empirical insights gained in the individual chapters of this book will be linked to see whether there are contradictions, confirmations/reinforcements or complementarities of findings.

The *vertical international perspective*: There has been much pressure to harmonise financial regulation in Europe on regional financial market regulation from international agreements and regulatory bodies. This pressure translates into a complex political process at the EU level, and in turn European regulation translates differently into member state regulation depending on specific national economic, political, institutional, legal and social factors. This means the outcomes in regulatory structure and regulatory policy substance are not necessarily uniform and do not necessarily lead to a centralisation of rule-making.

The *horizontal international perspective*: There is regulatory competition between large financial regulatory powers such as the EU[1] and the US. The attempts by these financial powers to impose their own regulation on the rest of the world or to ensure its extraterritorial application is a typical feature of regulatory competition. This may lead to a fragmentation of the regulatory structure internationally, and in consequence to regulatory arbitrage by the regulated. Within a financial power, however, regulatory competition may lead to more internal centralisation of regulatory structures to better coordinate regulatory activities in view of external competition.

The *public/private interaction perspective*: Self-regulation by private actors and private and public co-regulation have always been important features of financial regulation. Self-regulation rules have frequently emerged in new markets, with public actors subsequently intervening step by step, leading to a form of hybrid regulatory governance structure.

The *technological innovation perspective*: Given the dynamic features of financial markets and the rapid innovation of ever more financial products based on new technologies, the question arises of the implications for regulation of these new instruments. How, for instance, do regulators deal with trillions of daily financial transactions in high-frequency trading in derivatives? Is 'regtech', an instrument developed by private actors, able to ensure compliance with public regulation or would mere principle-based regulation be the answer? The implications of these contrasting approaches for the regulatory structure are very different given that regtech leads to a harmonisation of detailed rules while principle-based regulation leaves latitude to member states when implementing the principles stated in the legislation.

All our answers to, or hypotheses on, the questions raised from these four different perspectives will be derived from theoretical arguments developed in political science (including policy analysis and political economy), law, the sociology of finance and economics. The hypotheses will then be subjected to empirical assessment by collecting data on the large bodies of legislation resulting from MiFID, MiFIR II and the capital markets union (CMU), drawing on archival material, press analyses, existing data collections and interviews with financial market actors.

Hence, *Governing Finance in Europe: A Centralisation of Rule-making?* offers an innovative and generalisable theorisation of factors driving and impeding the centralisation of rule-making in Europe and its consequences in terms of policy effects and political accountability.[2] In doing this, it provides the first comprehensive theoretical account of regulatory centralisation in all its multiple aspects at the regional and international levels. By focusing on international pressure, international competition between financial powers, hybrid governance by public/private actors and technological innovation, the book grasps the complex dynamics of rule-making and their impacts on regulatory structure, policy effects and political accountability. This theoretical framework is applied to two major instances of EU financial legislation that so far have been largely under-researched from our perspective, namely

MiFID II and the capital markets union, the two most important EU legislative programmes in recent decades.

1.2   THEORETICAL APPROACHES

What are the drivers of centralisation of regulatory competences in EU financial governance, and what are the forces acting against such centralisation? This chapter discusses various approaches to conceptualising this question and presents possible answers, that is, hypotheses. We start with well-established theoretical arguments drawn from political science regarding legislative processes and their outcomes in the context of higher level regulatory mandates (in particular, developed in Europeanisation research), move on to less well-known arguments from political science and law regarding rival regulatory powers, turn to new arguments drawn from the literature on regulation and the sociology of finance regarding public–private interaction in regulation, and end with little-known arguments regarding the impact of technological innovation on regulation.

We define centralisation as an intentional uploading of formal legislative rule-making and rule supervision to the supranational level. Correspondingly, we define decentralisation as an intentional devolving of legislative rule-making and the supervision of financial activity under this legislation to the national level. Furthermore, we define regulatory fragmentation as an unintended parallel rule-making and supervision of rules by various bodies at the same level or at different levels, supranational and national, in which different regulatory or supervisory regimes overlap and share fuzzy borders.

When defining centralisation, moreover, the content of rule-making needs to be taken into account. Centralisation as an intentional uploading of formal rule-making and supervision to the supranational level only implies centralisation in the implementation phase at the national level if the content of the rules is prescriptive in detail. If the rules are vague, and therefore offer many possibilities for their interpretation, we do not expect centralisation to ensue after their implementation.

1.2.1   Research Perspective One: Vertical International Perspective

From the *vertical international perspective*, we ask: how does the impact of international agreements, such as ISDA or the Basel accords, on EU legislation and its implementation in member states affect the regulatory structure at the EU and member-state levels? In particular, since the financial crisis of 2008 there has been much pressure on regional financial market regulation from international agreements and regulatory bodies to harmonise financial regulation in Europe. This pressure has translated into a complex political process at the EU level, and in turn EU regulation has been implemented differently in member state regulations depending on each state's specific national economic, political, institutional, legal and social conditions. This means that the outcomes in terms of regulatory structure and policy substance are not necessarily uniform and that centralisation of rule-making is not necessarily observed. How do we account for such different outcomes of EU legislation adopted in the context of international agreements?

The answer to this question mainly builds on the literature on Europeanisation in which the factors and processes that determine the outcome of European legislation in member state legislation and its implementation are analysed (Héritier et al. 1994). In general terms, the literature distinguishes three channels through which higher level legislation influences lower level legislative and implementation activities: a rational-actor bargaining process within institutional rules (Héritier and Farrell 2009); socialisation (Schimmelfennig 2000); and diffusion (Börzel and Risse 2012). According to the rationalist/ institutionalist approach, actors seek to maximise their preferences over outcomes within the restrictions of existing institutional rules (Héritier 2007). Using a sociological institutionalist or constructivist approach, Börzel and Risse (2012) emphasise the power of ideas and their diffusion as important channels through which European legislation is translated into national legislation. The argument is that some ideas have become so powerful and strong that actors willingly adopt them, that is, their preferences over outcomes converge. In our case, centralisation is the outcome.

Since the short- and medium-term material costs and benefits of financial regulation play a preeminent role in financial regulation, we follow a rationalist institutionalist approach. We assume that a change of preferences under the influence of normative arguments (socialisation) and copying others if pronounced material interests are negatively affected are less plausible. This does not mean that we discard ideational approaches per se. Instead, we wish to investigate how much explanatory traction one approach, the rational institutionalist approach, holds when explaining the outcomes of regulatory structure in an area where short- and medium-term material interests play a paramount role.

We further assume a certain latitude in the content of European legislation and identify actors' preferences, the given institutional rules and economic conditions as factors which predict the likely impact of European legislation on member state legislation. The same explanatory approach is used to further explain the outcome of the implementation of national legislation in actual practice on the ground. The outcome of implementation is accounted for by studying the interaction of a different set of actors, including *de facto* veto players with diverse preferences, in the specific institutional context. According to this explanatory approach, one would expect that if legislative mandates are incomplete contracts[3] the outcomes of European legislation being adopted and implemented in member states will lead to different results, that is, in our case, not to centralisation but to decentralisation or fragmentation.

Using this rational institutionalist political science explanation, we argue that the main *causal factors* determining the outcome (centralisation, decentralisation or fragmentation) are, first, the *nature of the goals and instruments* in the international agreements or standards in question. Precisely formulated objectives linked to monitoring and peer review exert more pressure on European actors when implementing international agreements. By contrast, vaguely formulated goals do not exert much pressure on them.

Second, European *actors' preferences* regarding the goals defined in an international agreement matter. If European actors, such as the Commission, the European supervisory authorities, member states and the ECB, have the same preferences as the actors that formulated the goals in the international agreement, the implementation of the international agreement at the European level is likely to happen. However, if we assume precise goals and that European actors have divergent outcome preferences, implementation will depend on the outcome of a political conflict between the international and European levels, political conflict at the European level, and subsequently political conflicts on transposing European legislation into national legislation at the national level. Different outcomes are likely.

Third, the *institutional conditions* under which political decisions on implementing international agreements at the European level are made matter. Assuming the relevant European actors have divergent preferences, the number of formal veto-players when implementing international agreements makes a difference. If there is discretion in implementation and a high number of veto-players at the European level, the outcome is unlikely to be centralisation.

Fourth, it also matters whether there are important *de facto veto players with divergent preferences* at the European level which can bring political weight to bear if international agreements/standards are to be implemented at the European or national level. Among these are industry associations, investors associations and public opinion. As the 'varieties of capitalism' literature (see, among many others, Hall and Soskice 2001) has shown, the power of *de facto* veto players varies according to institutional political economic arrangements, thereby including or excluding them from decision-making at the national level. We therefore propose *a decision-making rule hypothesis (assuming heterogeneous preferences)*:

H1.1 Under unanimous-decision and de facto consensus rules, legislation will lead to a decentralised regulatory structure in the formal legislative outcome.

The underlying causal mechanism is that actors opposing a centralised regulatory structure under a unanimity rule will veto it. Given that there are no *ex ante* control and sanctioning mechanisms, national veto players do not fear any consequences if they insist on realising their particular preferences instead of transposing the goal of regulatory centralisation. Therefore, they (threaten to) veto any transposition into national law that does not fully accommodate their particular preferences. As preferences diverge, there is no space for agreement. Therefore, the international agreement will either not be transposed into European and national law or a particularistic solution will be found. Given that this happens in other member states as well, the outcome will be a decentralised or fragmented regulatory structure. As Helleiner and Pagliari (2011, pp. 179, 186) underline, since the financial crisis there has been a domestic politicisation of financial regulation with legislators, political leaders and domestic societal groups participating in regulatory debates. Politicisation makes different outcomes more plausible.

By contrast, we propose that:

H1.2 Under majority rule, legislation will lead to a centralised regulatory structure.

The underlying causal mechanism builds on the fact that if a majority of formal decision-making actors support centralisation, they can impose it on the other decision-makers. Knowing the institutional rule, actors can anticipate the outcome of a vote. Those supporting the transposition of an international agreement into EU law – or any other centralising measure at the EU level – will therefore seek to build a winning coalition. If they succeed, EU legislation will be adopted and opposing actors have no choice other than to implement the centralising measures at the national level.

Including *de facto* veto players that are not formal decision-makers, we further propose *a de facto veto player hypothesis*:

H2 In the absence of formal and de facto veto players, the implementation of European legislation at the national level will lead to a de facto centralised structure.

The causal mechanism set into motion reflects the interaction among implementing actors of various natures – that is, bureaucrats, interest associations, target groups – that concur on the centralising goal of the legislation and contribute their respective resources to obtaining the legislative objective. A centralisation of the regulatory structure will follow. In doing this, they will not encounter any resistance. If this is the case in all member states, the result will be a centralised regulatory structure in the EU.

Another relevant argument and finding in Europeanisation research is that politically and economically powerful member states are crucial in determining whether regulatory centralisation goals are adopted or not (Héritier et al. 1994). If these states already have centralised regulatory structures, they tend to support such structures being adopted in European legislation since it saves them the transaction costs involved in regulatory adaptation (see also Mattli 1999).

Hence, we suggest a *power/adjustment cost hypothesis*:

H3 If centralised regulatory structures proposed by the EU are compatible with those in large powerful member states, centralisation is more likely.

The underlying causal mechanism is as follows. Powerful member states with centralised regulatory structures support a Commission proposal for centralisation in order to save the transaction costs of structural adaptation. Indeed, member states actively seek to upload their regulatory regimes and regulatory structures to the European level by proposing them to the Commission and, if taken on board by the Commission, they subsequently support them in the political process (Héritier et al. 2001).[4] Otherwise, they veto the proposal or they threaten to do so. They will also have the power resources to compensate weaker member states if they adopt their regulation. Less powerful member states, instead, lack the power to do any of this. Even under formal unanimity, they would not have a *de facto* veto.

Next to the institutional rule governing the decision-making process, the specific features of the legal instrument employed for regulation constitute important factors determining the outcome. Legal instruments may contain vague or precise provisions and may or may not be linked to formal sanctions. Assuming diverse preferences of actors over outcomes – that is, centralisation, decentralisation or fragmentation – we submit a *regulatory content hypothesis*:

H4.1 If the legislative provisions are vague (be they directives, regulations, standards or guidelines), they lead to a decentralised or fragmented regulatory structure.

H4.2 If the legislative provisions are precise and linked to sanctions in the case of non-compliance, they lead to a centralised regulatory structure.

The causal mechanism underlying this claim is that a vagueness of the international agreement to be translated into European legislation allows national veto players or reluctant member state governments to frame their claims in the decision-making process as consistent with the international agreement and the subsequent European legislation. They may thus adopt a deviant regulation or not adopt it all. At the aggregate European level, this results in decentralisation. Given that there are no control and sanctioning mechanisms, national veto players do not fear any consequences if they insist on realising their particular preferences (instead of transposing the centralising goal). As a result, they may successfully prevent a uniform transposition into European and national law. The outcome will be a decentralised or fragmented regulatory structure.[5]

When considering European legislation in the context of international agreements, a further conclusion may be drawn from multi-level governance studies (Putnam 1988; Tsebelis 1990; Hooghe and Marks 2001). The existence of an international agreement may offer the Commission a window of opportunity to take action and define a dominant role for itself in the regulation in question. Newman and Posner (2016) show that reform-minded actors may successfully use international agreements as a normative resource to strengthen their positions in the European decision-making process in order to pursue their regulatory aims. Our argument is that the Commission uses the legislative and administrative requirements posed by the international agreement to strengthen its position in the legislative bargaining process at the European level.[6] Therefore, we submit an *institutional empowerment hypothesis*:

H5 Under the conditions required by international agreements, in the absence of powerful veto players the Commission will be able to increase its institutional power in financial regulation, which equals a centralisation of regulatory structure.

The mechanism causing this outcome is the following. By virtue of its right of legislative initiative, the Commission uses the international agreement to be adopted as a window of opportunity to propose a policy measure. In the draft it is likely to propose a strong institutional role for itself in implementing the legislation. Moreover, in shaping its position, the Commission can move faster than the Council of Ministers, which has to coordinate the various positions of the member states before proposing a measure. If in the subsequent political decision-making process the Council and the EP are not able to fend off these claims by the Commission, the latter will obtain additional institutional powers in the execution of the policy.[7]

In conclusion, from the vertical research perspective on European legislation in the context of international agreements, we argue that legislation and its implementation are subject to a variety of factors influencing European regulatory structures: national formal and *de facto* veto-players; the specificity or vagueness of the regulatory content and the type of legal instrument used; member state wishes to upload their own regulatory structure to the European level; and attempts by the Commission to increase its institutional power. Given the actors' diverse preferences and power and differing institutional decision-making rules, specific constellations of these factors as described in the hypotheses may lead to more centralisation, decentralisation or fragmentation.

European legislation is not only influenced by international agreements as in the vertical international perspective but – from a horizontal perspective – is situated in an environment of possible competition among other large powers engaged in regulating finance.

1.2.2   Research Perspective Two: The Horizontal International Perspective

The horizontal international perspective asks whether regulatory competition between states or regional polities affects the structure of European financial regulation, and if so, how. Or more specifically, does competition with the US,[8] and increasingly the UK, favour a centralisation, decentralisation or fragmentation of the EU's regulatory structure?

We assume that all financial powers seek to transfer their own regulatory standards to 'the rest of the world' because it offers them economic advantages and saves them the costs of regulatory adaptation. In order to develop our argument, we consider the following relevant factors.

First, we focus on the *preferences of the relevant actors* – that is, the US, the UK and the EU – as to regulatory centralisation. We assume that they all prefer centralisation over decentralisation and fragmentation but they strive for centralisation on their own terms. If their regulatory provisions differ, given the wish to centralise (each on its own terms), regulatory competition will follow.

Second, we consider the *size of the home markets* of the relevant actors (Simmons 2001; Drezner 2008). The larger the home market of a public actor, the greater its influence over the rest of the world since it has leverage by being able to grant access to its market. Regulatory power not only derives from the size and attractiveness of the home financial market but also from "being the home country for internationally important investors and institutions" (Helleiner and Pagliari 2011, p. 176). Cohen (2006) calls this 'financial intervention power'. It allows a financial centre to define regulations and impose them on others.

These factors lead to the following *regulatory competition hypothesis*:

H6 Regulatory competition between leading financial powers prompts regulatory centralisation in the other actors' internal regulatory structures.

Applying this to the concrete actors in our analysis, the underlying causal mechanism is that regulatory competition from any of the regional powers strengthens political forces within a polity striving for a more unified and centralised regulatory approach. This is because the competitive pressure from the other polities seeking to impose their regulatory provisions on the rest of the world prompts internal policy reactions. This in turn incentivises political forces, for instance in the EU, to increasingly support a Commission-coordinated regulatory response to US regulation, leading to more centralisation of EU regulation. A centralised response (as opposed to member-state-specific decentralised responses) will create one large home market, which gives the EU and its member states more leverage in the competition with the US (Kalyanpur and Newman 2019). Thus, in the post-crisis era the EU regulatory authorities started acting unilaterally to reduce the EU's "dependence on and vulnerability to US regulation" (Helleiner and Pagliari 2011, p. 177). Most recently, the Commission and the European Securities and Markets Authority (ESMA) have emphasised that with Brexit ESMA needs supervisory instruments that enable it to react swiftly in view of "the large, liquid and interconnected capital market next door, which is not part of, or subject to, its regulatory requirements" and have called on national regulators to implement European regulation evenly "… to minimise the risks of regulatory arbitrage as a result of relocations from the UK to the EU27" (*Financial Times* 2019a).

A consequence of rivalling regulatory powers is that private actors, that is, financial firms, are tempted to engage in regulatory arbitrage or regulatory venue shopping in order to obtain the most advantageous regulatory regime for themselves. Commercial forces thereby drive the diffusion of the regulation of a regional financial power. Thus, the U.S. Security and Exchange Commission (SEC) is presently under pressure to adapt its regulations on funding investment research to those adopted under the EU's MiFID II. Stakeholders such as the Council of Institutional Investors would like to see the SEC let all managers (not only those investing on behalf of EU investors) implement the MiFID II rules (*Financial Times* 2019b).

A possible reaction of financial powers to contain regulatory arbitrage is that they may engage in a coordination of their regulatory provisions if one actor takes upon itself the costs of leadership to achieve a negotiated coordination. Coordination will be achieved if all parties profit from the coordination. The repercussion on the internal regulatory structure of the actors involved is centralisation, as only a coherent actor can successfully negotiate with other superpowers.

We therefore submit a *regulatory arbitrage hypothesis*:

H7 A high degree of transnational regulatory arbitrage by financial firms will lead to more coordination between two public regulatory actors if one of the parties takes a leading role in such coordination. This in turn exerts pressure for more regulatory centralisation within each regional polity.

The underlying causal mechanism starts with private actors' tolerance of competing regulatory regimes. If there is such tolerance, competition will increasingly take the form of regulatory arbitrage. Regulatory actors seek to fight regulatory arbitrage and therefore intervene in a more coordinated and thereby centralising way. One of the parties needs to take on a leadership role to bring such coordination about. An actor engages in leading if the costs of leadership are less than its individual gains that can be achieved through coordinated action (Schoeller 2019, pp. 30–32). Negotiating partners follow this leadership if they perceive the gains from coordination to be superior to the status quo of competing regulation. The repercussion on the internal regulatory structure of the actors involved is an internal centralisation of regulatory structure as a precondition for a successful negotiation with the other superpowers.

Thus, at present, in the case of central counterparty (CCP) clearing houses, which were introduced by the G20 to coordinate and manage the risks of over-the-counter derivative dealing, there is a multitude of requirements for clearing houses, which creates compliance conflicts. The US first issued clearing rules and then the EU followed suit and has issued its own rules. In response, the US Commodity and Futures Trading Commission is calling for a coordination of US and EU rules (*Financial Times* 2019c).

In conclusion, from the horizontal international perspective, the relevant factors driving centralisation are regulatory competition between regional financial powers and regulatory arbitrage by firms fuelled by market mechanisms.

The European regulatory structure is not only impacted by international agreements (research perspective one) and competition with other financial superpowers (research perspective two) but also by the century-old interaction and collaboration among private and public actors in regulating finance, to which we turn next.

1.2.3   Research Perspective Three: Transnational Public/Private Regulation

The regulation of finance has had a long tradition of self-regulation by private financial actors alongside public regulation or in co-regulation with public regulators. New markets trading with innovative financial instruments emerge for purposes such as to offer access to capital to smaller companies and investors or to avoid the regulations on existing financial instruments (Goodhart 1986). New market actors may engage in self-regulation because the regulator responsible does not engage in regulation. As sociologists of finance (such as

MacKenzie 2008) show in their research on the development of stock markets, markets and firms initially engage in self-regulation, which is then frequently joined with or entirely replaced by public regulation. MacKenzie (2004) and Fenton-O'Creevy et al. (2007; see also Baker 1984) describe how in the trading pits of Chicago traders originally engaged in face-to-face trading based on mutual trust in a thin market with few players relying on informal rules, which were then gradually formalised. Knorr-Cetina and Bruegger (2002) and MacKenzie (2019) describe how actors thus created rules that defined the conditions for access to the stock market, the roles of diverse actors in the market and the market's operating rules. As markets grew deeper and the number of players and trading options increased, these informal networks broke down. However, even under such conditions actors still seek to create rules of mutual reciprocity or networks, seeking to challenge the anonymity of counter-parties in order to understand who they are trading with (Fenton-O'Creevy et al. 2007; MacKenzie 2004).[9] Even if markets operate on the basis of advanced technology such as algorithm-based high-frequency trading, virtual social rules of obligations and rights emerge, and actors rely on a social heuristics structure to manage risks in an attempt to obtain extra information about who they are dealing with (Fenton-O'Creevy et al. 2007; Knorr-Cetina and Preda 2011; Riles 2011).[10]

Gradually, observing the developments in self-regulation, public regulatory actors take on a more active role in the regulation of these markets if they consider that there are micro-risks for investors and macro-risks to the system's financial stability.[11] Ronit and Schneider (2000) distinguish between the private legal authority that governments delegate to private actors to regulate markets and the legal authority that private actors develop on their own. Pistor (2013) goes beyond this distinction and describes the hybrid nature of money. She argues that it does not make sense to differentiate between markets and private actors on the one hand and public regulators on the other. Instead, they need to be considered joint forces. She mentions the example of collateralised debt obligations (CDOs), which were jointly created by Freddie Mac, a public actor, together with the Joint Bank of Boston and Salomon Brothers, a private actor (Pistor 2017). Along similar lines, Dorn emphasises that the capital markets union (CMU) brings a form of powers shared by public and private actors (Dorn 2016). Likewise, Fenton-O'Creevy et al. point out that the hybrid character of finance regulation is reflected in the fact that regulators are *in* the market but also *outside* the market structure.

In view of the extensive existence of private self-regulation in financial markets, for regulators the question arises of how they should deal with social rules emerging in markets, that is, virtual rules of rights and obligations that emerge in market transactions in order to have more information about who you are dealing with (private legal authority, according to Ronit and Schneider

2000). Should they get rid of existing self-regulation or build on it? Should they collaborate or co-regulate with private actors?

The response would seem to depend on the overall theoretical economic orientation of public regulators. The neoclassical school has a preference for a stochastic equilibrium model in which market competition defines the prices of financial instruments and the market by itself produces a new equilibrium in the case of market disturbances. It also considers emerging social self-regulation rules with some reservation because these rules define the conditions for market access and operating in the market.

Regulators in the theoretical school of new economics, by contrast, show a preference for building on existing self-regulation rules. They will only intervene if the social rules lead to excessive rent-seeking and fraudulent behaviour in self-regulated governance structures with fixed market roles.[12] Similarly, if the regulators perceive macro-risks or system stability risks deriving from private self-regulation arrangements, they will want to intervene. The result is hybrid public/private regulation and moderate regulatory decentralisation.

In a two-step argument, this leads to the following *self-regulation hypothesis*:

H8 Self-regulation prompts (centralised) public regulation.

In a first step,

H8.1 New financial instrument markets prompt self-regulation by new market actors,

or alternatively

H8.2 New market actors join existing self-regulating communities of private actors with fixed market roles (which regulate access and market operations).

The underlying causal mechanism is as follows. The dynamics in new markets using new financial instruments are characterised by high uncertainty. In order to reduce the risks linked to this uncertainty regarding transaction partners, private actors develop minimal social rules which actors abide by in their own interest (H8.1). Alternatively, they seek to join pre-existing private self-regulation governance arrangements where fixed rules have been established regarding the conditions for market access and market operations. Financial industry groups engage in such self-regulation through the creation of private standards, individual financial exchanges, clearing houses and firms that set regulatory standards worldwide, which are subsequently endorsed by public authorities (Porter 2005; Helleiner and Pagliari 2011).

In a second step, this regulatory structure may call forth public intervention and regulatory centralisation under the following conditions:

H8.3 If self-regulation with fixed market roles is characterised by excessive rent-seeking, there will be public intervention, that is, structural centralisation.

H8.4 If self-regulation with fixed market roles creates system-stability risks, this will be followed by public intervention leading to a centralised regulatory structure.

The underlying causal mechanism which can be observed reveals self-regulating rules on financial platforms with fixed market roles that lead to rent-seeking by the market position-holders. This is because the established rules of access to the financial platform and the costs of operating in it, as defined by the owners of the platform, are high for those seeking access to it. If public regulators con-sider them excessive, they will intervene in order to correct market distortions. Furthermore, if self-regulated new markets are considered to create overall system-stability risks, public regulators will intervene and create a process of regulatory centralisation.

An important explanation of why there may be a process of centralisation in financial markets and corresponding regulatory centralisation is also offered by a legal theory of finance which emphasises the close link between financial instruments and law (Pistor 2013). Law gives authority to means of payment and vindicates financial instruments and financial contracts in general. State-backed money, that is, money guaranteed by a central public actor, is the asset of last resort. At the same time, by delegating rule-making to different stakeholders, that is, private actors as in the self-regulation mentioned above, law and politics also facilitate regulatory pluralism. As a result, in a first instance this may lead to a process of regulatory fragmentation of financial markets. Since legal reforms and legal contractual financial instruments create credible commitments and allow for a scaling of financial transactions into the periphery, both domestically and globally, this also means that in the case of a crisis all actors, but particularly those on the periphery, "will face the full force of the law" (Pistor 2013, p. 325). This is because near the apex, that is, the public backstop of the money hierarchy (Mehrling 2017), on account of the power-based politics of financial markets, actors "are most likely to benefit from another lifeline" (Pistor 2013, p. 325), and correspondingly a flexible interpretation of their contracts. "This will lead over time to a greater concen-tration of finance at the apex where the ultimate backstop resides" (Pistor 2013, p. 325; see also Mehrling 2017). Assuming a flexibility of law (Pistor 2013), or law as incomplete contracts, as in Héritier (1999), and assuming a scarcity of liquidity, this leads to the following *hierarchy of money hypothesis*:

H9 In the case of a crisis/liquidity squeeze, the most powerful actors will successfully negotiate a position close to the top of the hierarchy/apex, which will lead to a centralisation of regulatory structure.

The causal mechanism is as follows. In the case of a liquidity crisis, large private players which have the power to threaten a withdrawal of their resources and/or are relevant to the stability of the system have more clout in negotiating solutions with the sovereign backstop actors. Since contracts are incomplete and negotiable, they may obtain supportive actions by public actors. However, in return for being 'saved', they have to accept more central control of their market behaviour, that is, regulatory centralisation.

Financial regulatory structures in Europe are not only affected by the implementation of international agreements, rivalling regulatory financial powers and public–private interaction, but also to an important extent by technical innovations in the development of financial instruments and business models.

1.2.4   Research Perspective Four: Technological Innovation and Regulation

Historically, important technological changes have led to profound changes in financial market transactions and forms of market organisation. The history of new technologies allowing simpler financial services to increase productivity and to gain a competitive edge in the market is well known (see, for instance, Knorr-Cetina and Preda 2011). Such transformations now appear to be accelerating. This arises in particular via the application of technological digital innovation to financial activity (fintech). Equally, however, the regulatory technology has altered (regtech), both in terms of alleviating the asymmetry of information between the regulated and the regulator and of shifting from 'formal regulation to functional regulation' (with implications for the preferred structure of regulation; see below).

Sociological theorists such as Knorr-Cetina and Preda (2011) analyse the impact of changing technological instruments on market transactions over the decades: from the telephone to the computer screen to automated algorithms and robot-based trading, which is used in particular in high-frequency trading in foreign exchange markets. These different technological devices have enabled new organisational forms of trading, typically from 'fixed market role platform models' to public order books accessible to all on the internet for bids and offers ("all-to-all" trading, as in MacKenzie 2018). Such technologically driven changes in market structure, organisation and behaviour have been described as a passage from network coordination with direct interaction and contracting with other individual actors (Knorr-Cetina and Preda 2011) to scopic coordination, under which markets are watched on a worldwide joint screen and trade takes place reacting to the screen, which in turn changes the market. In high-frequency trading this happens at a speed in which dealers' decisions are based on implicit cognitive processes because *ex ante* explicit considerations would be much too slow and could not follow. Since algorithms have taken on the role of dealers making trading decisions and human beings merely watch and modify these algorithms, a new epistemic class of mathematicians has emerged who understand these algorithms and their design. Trading based on algorithms accelerates trading, as we see in high-frequency trading (Knorr-Cetina and Preda 2011; see also Chapter 2).

These technological advances imply important changes in the functioning of markets and as a result pose new challenges for the regulation of these markets. New technologies enable the creation of a multitude of new financial products, which are being marketed in new ways by fintech firms and digitalised financial service providers. Sheridan (2017, p. 417) describes the main features of fintech business as "a disruptive innovation occurring free from legacy technological systems and with asynchronous compliance".[13] An important implication is an increasing disintermediation – or less organisational intermediation – in trading. Thus, the number of proprietary trading firms has increased, replacing trading on a public trading floor with big banks.

What do these technology-driven changes in market dynamics and market organisation imply for regulators? They are faced with a situation in which on the one hand they would like to encourage digitally based financial innovations and the new fintech enterprises that have developed them, but on the other hand they have to ensure that there are no fraudulent practices or rent-seeking (micro-regulation) and that no systemic-stability risks result from these new market actors marketing new financial products (macro-regulation). Since the financial crisis of 2008, regulators have mainly been focusing on the too-big-to-fail risk of large financial institutions and the possible abuses deriving from an implicit government guarantee of them. The regulatory approach resulting from this has been mostly strict requirements for banks, such as minimum capital and liquidity requirements and restrictions on proprietary trading.

In the case of fintechs and technologically enabled finance in economic function areas as diverse as payment systems, lending, capital raising, investment, trading, clearing, settlement and money itself, we are faced with decentral finance and decentral risks of small firms (Minto et al. 2017, p. 434). Nevertheless, due to the global interlinkedness of financial transactions, these decentralised financial activities may pose macro-risks which – through contagion effects – may imply system-stability risks. As Magnusen (2017) argues, some fintechs, being small disaggregated actors, are more vulnerable to economic shocks than large financial institutions, the effects of which may be contagious for other small firms. Fintechs are hard to monitor and their activities are hard to constrain because there is little systematic information about them and also because fintech markets do not engage in collective action or cooperate.

What may be observed is that established financial firms in the market start interacting with fintechs to their mutual advantage. The established players cooperate with fintechs, profiting from their flexible introduction of new financial technologies. Fintechs profit from the cooperation with established financial actors by getting support in regulatory questions and having access to the established players' customer networks (Nicoletti 2017, pp. 177–178). This creates a complex network of actors, which renders supervision more difficult (Minto et al. 2017, p. 432).

The new complexity of financial markets raises concerns to which regulators have to react. In view of the pace of large financial innovations taking place about every ten years (from the dematerialisation of stocks and bonds to digitised certificates in the 1980s and the introduction of blockchains in 2010 (SIBOS 2016), regulators are faced with considerable challenges in dealing with digitalised financial services and automated robots and their impacts on customers and markets.[14] There are basically four options for regulators in view of these developments. The LSE School of Management and Finance advocates regulation by principle (Black 2005; Black et al. 2007), defining targets but leaving the choice over how to realise these targets up to the regulated. Principle-based regulation is supposed to offer flexibility for firms, facilitate innovation and thereby increase competitiveness. Regulators too enjoy more flexibility under principle-based regulation. The regulator can insist on improved firm conduct to enhance substantive compliance instead of just box-ticking. This may be advantageous for stakeholders too. The outcome is a decentralised or fragmented structure of regulation.

The second option is to build on already existing self-regulating rules established by private actors and control their implementation. In the markets for the digitally-based new financial products of fintechs, we may observe the initial steps of new players entering into contact with established private platforms in order to market their products while in turn accepting certain rules, such as capital requirements and clearing processes. The public regulator, which has to accept this first step of fintechs joining self-regulated platforms, monitors their behaviour for micro-fraudulent behaviour or possible macro-effects of system-stability risks. The outcome is a decentralised structure of regulation.

The third option is that regulators engage in a collaborative approach with the new players, balancing openness to innovation and disruptive technologies with protecting the interests of consumers, investors and privacy protection. The sandbox experiments applied by the Financial Conduct Authority to fintechs are a case in point. Using this regulatory technique, the regulator may grant regulatory exemptions for a certain period to a start-up's new financial instrument. A question which arises is for how long and, if successful, how to scale up to a higher level (Arner et al. 2016).

The fourth option is regtech, a digitally based in-time observation of financial market transactions monitoring their compliance with existing regulations. Regtech is a category of fintech firms specialised in technologies that facilitate monitoring, reporting and compliance with regulatory requirements (Minto et al. 2017, p. 431). Financial transactions worldwide are tracked in real time (comparable to observing global weather systems). Regtech developed post-crisis because of the high fines that were imposed on financial firms and the costs of regulation and compliance. Therefore, an increase in the type and volume of data that have to be reported (such as most recently under MiFID II) has been an incentive to automate compliance and monitoring processes. For instance, in a 'smart contract', blockchain technologies allow "self-executing pieces of software code embedded into a blockchain system" to "automatically pay out an insurance claim" (*Financial Times* 2018c). Using artificial intelligence, the law is an inherent part of the code in the instruments, thereby regulating them. Moreover, the distributed ledger technology underlying blockchains cannot be different in different countries "because the technology is by definition borderless" (*Financial Times* 2018c). The outcome is a centralised structure of regulation.

The technologically driven changes in market actors, structure and organisation and the possible regulatory options lead us to the following hypotheses.

Assuming that the regulators have little information regarding the structures and operations of fintechs (Donald 2018), the degree of uncertainty about the nature of a new financial instrument introduced by fintechs is crucial when explaining regulators' responses. We therefore distinguish between different types of uncertainty: (a) unclear substance of the instrument and/or the business model introduced; (b) unclear legal nature; (c) unclear effects regarding cross-sectoral risks that call for a public good provision by regulation; and (d) reduced uncertainty linked to compliance due to the use of regtech, a financial instrument developed by fintechs.

Hence, in a first step, with each hypothesis developed, the degree of uncertainty about the nature of the new financial instrument at stake has to be specified.

Unclear substantive nature of new instrument and/or business model
If the substantive nature of a new financial instrument and/or a new business model used by a fintech is unclear to the regulator, either technically or in terms of business activity, regulators may interact with private actors directly in order to collaborate in the development of potential regulatory approaches. This may happen on the basis of a public-led or private-led initiative. It can take the form of innovation hubs created by governments in which "regulated

and unregulated entities (i.e. unauthorised firms) engage with the competent authority to discuss fintech-related issues (share information and views, etc.) and seek clarification on the conformity of business models with the regulatory framework or on regulatory licensing requirements" (ESA/DP/201/02, see ESA 2018). Alternatively, public–private cooperation may take the form of regulatory sandboxing: "Regulatory sandboxes take the idea of innovation hubs a step further by creating an environment where supervision is tailored to innovative firms or services" (European Commission 2018). If a bespoke regulatory solution is found in the course of this cooperation between the regulator and fintech representatives in a member state, there remains a scaling problem. That is, the bespoke solution does not apply widely. Hence, it leads to a fragmentation of regulatory structure within the EU.

From an analytical viewpoint, the advantage offered by sandboxing and innovation hubs to regulators is that they learn more about the technicalities of the new instruments and the business rationale of the new activity.[15] Industry respondents also support the possibility of sandbox regulation, as it allows them to obtain a degree of regulatory support,[16] or may even grant them influence in the actual shaping of a pertinent regulation (EC fintech action plan 2018). Regulatory authorities are keen to stress that regulatory sandboxes do not involve the disapplication of regulatory obligations, but they could involve the exercise of supervisory powers or levers for proportionality that already exist. According to the ESMA surveys (2018/2019) of national competent authorities (NCAs), most national supervisors consider existing EU legislation flexible enough to be applied to the authorisation of new fintech products and services (ESMA 2019, p. 22). We conclude that:

H10 If the substantive nature of a new financial instrument and/or a new business model used by a fintech is unclear, the regulator may take recourse to bespoke regulatory solutions developed in cooperation with fintechs. The result will be a fragmented regulatory structure.

Unclear legal nature of the new financial instrument and/or business model

The unclear legal nature of a newly introduced financial instrument, such as initial coin offerings (ICOs) or cryptocurrencies, consists in uncertainty as to whether they fall within the scope of existing regulatory structures. In our case, this specifically concerns the extent to which such new fintech services are captured by the definitions provided in EU regulation, for example whether they are 'services for consideration' or 'financial instruments'. From a legal point of view, a number of interpretative strategies may be pursued by the regulatory authorities. As a first option, they may pursue a functional approach, whereby in the light of uncertainty stemming from innovation, legal concepts are interpreted broadly so as to incorporate the innovation in existing legal categories in order to prevent regulatory arbitrage and ensure that the objectives of the specific regulatory instrument are attained. As an alternative option, regulatory authorities may adopt a restricted narrow interpretation of the existing framework with a view to restricting the competence at EU level or developing a bespoke regime for the new entities (Marjosola, Chapter 5 in this volume; Möllers 2010; Gikay 2018; Lehmann 2019). Pursuing either such interpretative strategy with regard to cryptocurrencies and ICOs would lead to two possible structural regulatory outcomes, both subject to verification by EU courts.

In the concrete case of EU regulation, for example, a fintech innovation is legally considered to be a financial instrument. This would mean that the regulation is set under centralised European legislation but responsibility for implementation lies with member states. Since MiFiD II and MiFIR leave some latitude to member states in their interpretation of proportionality and flexibility in the authorisation of products and services, such an interpretation would be likely to lead to a decentralised fracturing of regulation.

H11.1 If the regulator considers a new financial product to be a financial instrument falling under existing regulation, fragmentation will be avoided. The resulting regulatory structure will be shaped according to the existing legislation and thus reproduce the existing structure (centralised vs. decentralised).

H11.2 If a new financial product is not considered a financial instrument falling under existing legislation, locally limited bespoke (self-)regulations will emerge leading to a fragmented regulatory structure.

Cross-sectoral risk protection/public good provision

Regulation often seeks to ensure the provision of a specific public good (Drahos 2004) which under normal market conditions would be under-supplied or not produced at all. In the case of the financial sector, the objectives of regulation relate to ensuring financial stability in markets, restoring incentives where risk-taking attitudes in markets are distorted as a result of perverse incentives or (re)establishing information symmetry so as to protect specific vulnerable actors (e.g. creditors). However, financial activity – and in particular financial activity which involves a high degree of uncertainty such as fintech (Pacces 2010) – may also fall within the scope of cross-sectoral regulations which have been put in place to ensure public goods such as security or individual privacy.

Given the cross-sectoral risk stemming from innovative financial instruments or services that require risk protection as an inclusive public good for all, we assume that providers prefer no regulation over regulation. This might apply in areas such as cybersecurity, cloud outsourcing and data protection. In such areas, regulators would prefer centralised harmonised regulation in order to provide comprehensive risk protection. Since such risks extend across sectors, they require coordination among many regulatory authorities, which requires horizontal rules at the international level. While such rules exist, for instance, in private data protection and anti-money laundering, they do not exist on a wide basis with respect to cross-sectoral risks stemming from innovative financial instruments. However, if relevant cross-sectoral risk rules *are* already in place, such as in the case of data protection, regulators may engage in rule-stretching. We therefore propose:

H12 If regulators are certain that fintech activities imply cross-sectoral risks and they can build on pre-existing cross-sectoral rules protecting public goods, they will adopt centralizing measures based on these rules.

Regtech
Financial firms may offer regtech as a big data-driven artificial intelligence (AI) service based on machine learning and smart contracts. Regtech is designed partly to help financial firms deal with regulators' data requirements. However, in view of the mass of data and the dynamics of data inflows, regulators also consider using regtech instruments themselves as a possible aid to authorise processes, assess risks and control the regulatory compliance of financial firms in a new way. Instead of conducting investigative compliance control through manual sampling, universal real-time compliance control is designed into smart contracts inherent in the financial instrument (Cook 2018). Regtech lends itself to the application of large standardised regulatory requirements but not to situations with complex financial ecosystems and cooperation between diverse market participants and regulators (Donald 2018).

Assuming that regulators suffer from work overload[17] and that there are pertinent regtech offers from fintechs, and further assuming that the regulatory provisions require detailed harmonised rules, we expect that:

H13.1 The low uncertainty about the application of new financial instruments and their compliance with rules due to the use of regtech offers regulators real-time insight in regulatory compliance and triggers automatic enforcement of the relevant rules. This leads to a centralisation of regulatory structure.

Moreover, the use of regtech instruments requires a large amount of resources to be employed. These comprise not only material capacities but also institutional (competences) and non-material (expertise) resources. If the regulator can afford to use regtech to implement harmonised uniform rules, it leads to a strengthening of regulatory compliance and enhances the central control

Table 1.1   *Research perspectives and hypotheses*

Research Perspective	Hypothesis	Independent Variable (Values)	Conditions	Dependent Variable
1. Vertical (international)	H1 Decision-making rule	Unanimity/*de facto* consensus vs. (qualified) majority	Heterogeneous preferences	
	H2 Veto players	Presence/absence of de jure/*de facto* veto players	Heterogeneous preferences	
	H3 Power/adjustment costs	Compatibility of regulatory structures between powerful MS and COM proposal	Pre-existence of domestic regulatory structures	
	H4 Regulatory content	Vagueness vs. preciseness/bindingness of provisions	Heterogeneous preferences	
	H5 Institutional empowerment	Presence/absence of international agreement	Absence of powerful veto players	
2. Horizontal (international)	H6 Regulatory competition	Presence/absence of regulatory competition		CENTRALISATION DECENTRALISATION FRAGMENTATION
	H7 Regulatory arbitrage	High/low degree of transnational regulatory arbitrage	One party assuming leadership on coordinational efforts	
3. Transnational (public/private)	H8 Self-regulation	1. Presence/absence of new instruments (H8.1) or market actors (H8.2) 2. Presence/absence of excessive rent-seeking (H8.3) or systemic risk (H8.4)		
	H9 Hierarchy of money	Presence/absence of liquidity squeeze (crisis)	Flexibility/ incompleteness of law	

Governing finance in Europe

Research Perspective	Hypothesis	Independent Variable (Values)	Conditions	Dependent Variable
	H10 Substantive nature	Clarity/ambiguity of new financial instrument (substantive certainty)		
	H11 Legal nature	Presence/absence of existing legislation (legal certainty)		
	H12 Cross-sectoral risks	Presence/absence of cross-sectoral risks	Pre-existence of cross-sectoral rules protecting public goods	
4. Technological innovation	H13 Regtech	Presence/absence of regtech (H13.1) Capacity (material, institutional, non-material) to make use of regtech (H13.2)	Work-overload of regulators Regulatory provisions at t1 requiring harmonised rules	

capacity of regulators. Once instituted, the technology might actually save the cost of employing human resources.

H13.2 If regulators are endowed with rich material, institutional (compe-tences) and non-material (expertise) resources, they will make use of regtech, which will result in a centralised regulatory structure.

Table 1.1 provides an overview about the research perspectives and hypotheses of this book. In the following empirical chapters, the hypotheses developed in this theory chapter will be subjected to an empirical plausibility probe by collecting data on the large bodies of legislation resulting from the MiFID II and the capital markets union (CMU). The empirical areas of the MifiD, MIfiR II and the capital markets union are used because they have been of eminent practical importance in European financial regulation in recent decades. Each area provides a universe of cases from which the authors of the individual chapters select certain measures as their concrete cases in order to probe the plausibility of the relevant hypotheses developed above. The chapters draw on archival material, press analyses, existing data collections and interviews with financial market actors.

NOTES

1. Since the 1970s, the EC/EU has increasingly strengthened its role by adopting legislation seeking to harmonise member states' regulation of financial markets.
2. We do not share the notion of 'financial market exceptionalism' which argues that financial markets are protected from regulation by the efficient capital market hypothesis. According to this view, regulators trusting in the correct pricing mechanisms of markets capturing all relevant information need not interfere in the regulation of micro aspects of financial markets. Other exceptional features of financial markets are seen in the – compared to other sectors – extremely high information barrier against regulators and the public alike understanding financial market transactions and the enormous amount of resources at the disposal of market players compared to regulators (Donald 2018).
3. That is, contracts not defined in all their details but leaving room for interpretation in the course of their application.
4. It is a common practice of large member states to offer to 'second' expert personnel to the relevant Commission DG to 'write' a legislative draft (Héritier et al. 2001).
5. In one strand of discussion on the rigidity of international agreements, there is a claim that divergent national or regional standards may be desirable if their mutual equivalence is recognised (Drezner 2008; Rodrik 2009). In the case of negative spillovers of diverse standards, this impact is contained by "international financial charters with limited aims" (Rodrik 2009).
6. The underlying causal mechanism is that pre-existing non-binding international agreements may serve as focal points to save the transaction costs of information and negotiation, and if they are used politically by reform-minded actors at lower

levels this leads to a centralisation of the regulatory structure at these levels. Moreover, as Porter argues, in informal trans-governmental networks of technocratic officials, the interests of regulators are influenced by their frequent social interactions and may eventually converge if they remain technocratic in nature and operate outside the pressure of domestic politics (Porter 2005).

7. An example of such an attempt by the Commission is the single supervision mechanism under the European Banking Union. The Commission first proposed that the supervision competences should be allocated to itself. In the face of stiff political opposition from both the EP and the member states, the task was given to the ECB.

8. Of course, the international regulatory polity now goes clearly beyond the regulatory powers of Europe and the United States, but includes China, India and other centres of wealth. However, because the US and the EU are the pace-setters in financial regulation and also for practical research purposes, this project focuses on the two 'traditional' financial powers and to some extent on the UK.

9. For example, Fenton-O'Creevy et al. (2007) describe how in foreign currency exchange markets a rule of behaviour emerged according to which actors cannot always only ask for the price of a quote but never buy, because the transactions would then only flow in one direction. Hence, the social rule emerged that you have to buy at some point.

10. Another example mentioned by Fenton-O'Creevy et al. is the self-regulation which emerged in the Hong Kong Stock Exchange. In view of listing requirements, public Chinese companies seeking access to the Hong Kong Stock Exchange address 'reputational intermediaries' to go to market, such as Goldman Sachs or McKinsey. These firms 'lend their reputation' to new companies when they access the Hong Kong stock market. They help them when submitting an initial public offering, offering advice as to the appropriate governance structures in order to reassure potential investors. For 'lending their reputation' to incoming quotable companies, the established financial firms charge a fee.

    Some players in new markets using high frequency trading (HFT) also apply what is called material self-regulation (MacKenzie 2018). Some firms have introduced a device to slow down trading (a 'speed bump') to reduce the advantage of HFT traders.

11. We can presently observe such developments in the activities of some fintechs, such as initial coin offerings and bitcoin networks.

12. Fixed market roles in private self-regulatory governance define rules of access and the costs of participating in the operation of trading platforms.

13. A disruptive innovation implies an actor entering with a new technology competing successfully with established market actors (such as, potentially, distributed ledger technology) (Sheridan 2017, p. 418). Legacy-free technology presents an advantage for fintechs when competing with investment banks with established computer systems. Asynchronous compliance means that the operations of fintech companies are faster than financial service regulation (Sheridan 2017, p. 419).

14. Following their distinction of the economic functions of fintechs, that is, lending and capital raising, investment and trade, and clearing and settlement, Minto, Voelkerling and Wulff (2017, p. 436) require distinctive regulatory actions.

15. During the public consultation on fintechs conducted by the Commission, some national authorities considered that regulatory sandboxing is not part of their supervision task, while others welcomed it.

16. Support is particularly needed when it comes to regulatory provisions regarding market infrastructure, that is, central clearing counterparties and central security depositories (ESMA 2019, p. 29).
17. The Financial Conduct Authority (FCA), for instance, is responsible for the supervision and regulation of 56,000 financial firms (N. Cook, FCA 2017. Webinar Regulating RegTech, 17 October, "Powering Innovation in Financial Services").

BIBLIOGRAPHY

Arner, Douglas W., Janos Barberis and Ross P. Buckey. 2016. 'FinTech, RegTech, and the Reconceptualization of Financial Regulation'. *Northwestern Journal of International Law & Business* 37 (3): 371–414.

Baker, Wayne E. 1984. 'The Social Structure of a National Securities Market'. *The American Journal of Sociology* 89 (4): 775–811.

Black, Julia. 2005. 'The Emergence of Risk Based Regulation and the New Public Management in the UK'. *Public Law* Autumn 2005: 512–549.

Black, Julia, Martyn Hopper and Christa Band. 2007. 'Making a Success of Principles-Based Regulation'. *Law and Financial Markets Review* 1 (3): 191–206.

Börzel, Tanja A. and Thomas Risse. 2012. 'From Europeanisation to Diffusion: Introduction'. *West European Politics* 35 (1): 1–19.

Cohen, Benjamin J. 2006. 'The Macrofoundations of Monetary Power'. In *International Monetary Power*, edited by David M. Andrews, 31–50. New York, NY: Cornell University Press.

Conac, Pierre-Henri. 2017. 'Algorithmic Trading and High Frequency Trading'. In *Regulation of the EU Financial Markets: MiFID II and MiFIR*, edited by Guido Ferrarini and Danny Busch, 469–486. Oxford, UK: Oxford University Press.

Cook, Nicholas. 2018. 'What will the Regulator of the Future Look Like?' Financial Conduct Authority, IFGS 2018 Panel, 27 March 2018.

Donald, David C. 2018. 'Information, and the Regulation of Inefficient Markets'. In *The Political Economy of Finance Regulation*, edited by E. Augouleas and D.C. Donald, 38–62. Cambridge, UK: Cambridge University Press.

Dorn, Nicholas, ed. 2016. *Controlling Capital: Public and Private Regulation of Financial Markets*. New York, NY: Routledge.

Drahos, Peter. 2004. 'The Regulation of Public Goods'. *Journal of International Economic Law* 7: 321–339.

Drezner, Daniel W. 2008. *All Politics Is Global: Explaining International Regulatory Regimes*. Princeton, NJ: Princeton University Press. http://www.books24x7.com/marc.asp?bookid=30589.

Dür, Andreas. 2011. 'Fortress Europe or Open Door Europe? The External Impact of the EU's Single Market in Financial Services'. *Journal of European Public Policy* 18 (5): 619–635. https://doi.org/10.1080/13501763.2011.586792.

ESMA. 2019. 'ESMA Report on the Licensing of FinTech Firms across Europe', 12 July. https://www.esma.europa.eu/sites/default/files/library/esma50-164-2430_licensing_of_fintech.pdf (accessed 17 April 2020).

European Commission. 2018. 'FinTech Action Plan: For A More Competitive And Innovative European Financial Sector', 8 March. Brussels: European Commission.

European Supervisory Authorities (ESA). 2018. 'Report FinTech: Regulatory Sandboxes and Innovation Hubs', p. 7. https://esas-joint-committee.europa.eu/

Publications/Reports/JC202018207420Joint20Report20on20Regulatory20Sandb oxes20and20Innovation20Hubs.pdf (accessed 18 April 2020).

Fenton-O'Creevy, Mark, Nigel Nicholson, Emma Soane and Paul Willman, eds. 2007. *Traders: Risks, Decisions, and Management in Financial Markets*. Oxford, UK: Oxford University Press.

Financial Times. 2018. 'Fintech Vulnerable to Dishonesty and Corruption, Warns Senior British Judge', 21 March 2018. https://www.ft.com/content/d5cd22ae-2c66 -11e8-9b4b-bc4b9f08f381 (accessed 18 April 2020).

Financial Times. 2019a. 'Mifid II's Transparency Rules Go Global', 20 January 2019. https://www.ft.com/content/f2a46c41-4bd4-3580-92a0-3dd0bae8daf3 (accessed 18 April 2020).

Financial Times. 2019b. 'We Must Rethink Our Clearing House Rules', 24 January 2019. https://www.ft.com/content/ebed650e-1fbc-11e9-a46f-08f9738d6b2b (accessed 18 April 2020).

Financial Times. 2019c. 'ESMA Calls for Extra Powers to Deal with Brexit Uncertainty', 13 February 2019. https://www.ft.com/content/50ec9252-2f91-11e9 -8744-e7016697f225 (accessed 18 April 2020).

Gikay, A.A. 2018. 'European Consumer Law and Blockchain Based Financial Services: A Functional Approach Against the Rhetoric of Regulatory Uncertainty'. *Tilburg Law Review* 24 (1): 27–48.

Goodhart, Charles. 1986. 'Financial Innovation and Monetary Control'. *Oxford Review of Economic Policy* 2 (4): 79–102.

Hall, Peter A. and David Soskice, eds. 2001. *Varieties of Capitalism: The Institutional Foundations of Comparative Advantage*. Oxford, UK: Oxford University Press.

Helleiner, Eric and Stefano Pagliari. 2011. 'The End of an Era in International Financial Regulation? A Postcrisis Research Agenda'. *International Organization* 65 (1): 169–200.

Héritier, Adrienne. 1999. *Policy-Making and Diversity in Europe: Escaping Deadlock*. Cambridge, UK: Cambridge University Press.

Héritier, Adrienne. 2007. *Explaining Institutional Change in Europe*. Oxford, UK: Oxford University Press.

Héritier, Adrienne and Henry Farrell, eds. 2007. 'Contested Competences in Europe: Incomplete Contracts and Interstitial Institutional Change'. *West European Politics*, Special Issue 30 (2). Routledge, Taylor and Francis.

Héritier, Adrienne, Dieter Kerwer, Christophe Knill, Dirk Lehmkuhl, Michael Teutsch and Anne-Cécile Douillet. 2001. *Differential Europe: The European Union Impact on National Policymaking. Governance in Europe*. Lanham, MD: Rowman & Littlefield.

Héritier, Adrienne, Susanne Mingers, Christophe Knill and Martina Becka. 1994. *Die Veränderung von Staatlichkeit in Europa Ein regulativer Wettbewerb: Deutschland, Großbritannien und Frankreich in der Europäischen Union*. Wiesbaden: VS Verlag für Sozialwissenschaften. http://nbn-resolving.de/urn:nbn:de:1111-201306291199 (accessed 18 April 2020).

Hooghe, Liesbet and Gary Marks. 2001. *Multi-Level Governance and European Integration. Governance in Europe*. Lanham, MD: Rowman & Littlefield.

Kalyanpur, Nikhil and Abraham L. Newman. 2019. 'Mobilizing Market Power: Jurisdictional Expansion as Economic Statecraft'. *International Organization* 73 (1): 1–34.

Knorr Cetina, Karin and Urs Bruegger. 2002. 'Traders' Engagement with Markets'. *Theory, Culture & Society* 19 (5–6): 161–185.

Knorr-Cetina, Karin and Alex Preda, eds. 2011. *The Sociology of Financial Markets*. Reprint. Oxford, UK: Oxford University Press.

Lehmann, M. 2019. 'Global Rules for a Global Market Place? – The Regulation and Supervision of FinTech Providers'. European Banking Institute Working Paper Series 2019, 45.

MacKenzie, Donald. 2004. 'The Big, Bad Wolf and the Rational Market: Portfolio Insurance, the 1987 Crash and the Performativity of Economics'. *Economy and Society* 33 (3): 303–334.

MacKenzie, Donald. 2008. *An Engine, Not a Camera: How Financial Models Shape Markets*. First MPI Press paperback ed. Inside Technology. Cambridge, MA: MIT Press.

MacKenzie, Donald. 2018. '"Making", "Taking" and the Material Political Economy of Algorithmic Trading'. *Economy and Society* 47 (4): 501–523.

MacKenzie, Donald. 2019. 'Market Devices and Structural Dependency: The Origins and Development of "Dark Pools"'. *Finance and Society* 5: 1–19.

Magnuson, William. 2017. 'Regulating Fintech'. *Vanderbilt Law Review* 71 (4): 1167–1226.

Mattli, Walter. 1999. *The Logic of Regional Integration: Europe and Beyond*. New York, NY: Cambridge University Press.

Mehrling, Perry. 2017. 'Finance and Its Discontents'. *Finance and Society* 2 (2): 138–150.

Minto, Andrea, Moritz Voelkerling and Melanie Wulff. 2017. 'Separating Apples from Oranges: Identifying Threats to Financial Stability Originating from FinTech'. *Capital Markets Law Journal* 12 (4): 428–465.

Möllers, T.M.J. 2010. 'Sources of Law in European Securities Regulation: Effective Regulation, Soft Law and Legal Taxonomy from Lamfalussy to de Larosière'. *European Business Organization Law Review* 11 (3): 379–407.

Newman, Abraham and Elliot Posner. 2016. 'Transnational Feedback, Soft Law, and Preferences in Global Financial Regulation'. *Review of International Political Economy* 23 (1): 123–152. https://doi.org/10.1080/09692290.2015.1104375.

Nicoletti, Bernardo. 2017. *The Future of FinTech: Integrating Finance and Technology in Financial Services*. London, UK: Palgrave.

Pacces, Alessio M. 2010. 'Consequences of Uncertainty for Regulation: Law and Economics of the Financial Crisis'. *European Company and Financial Law Review* 7 (4). https://doi.org/10.1515/ecfr.2010.479.

Pistor, Katharina. 2013. 'A Legal Theory of Finance'. *Journal of Comparative Economics, Law in Finance* 41 (2): 315–330. https://doi.org/10.1016/j.jce.2013.03.003.

Pistor, Katharina. 2017. 'From Territorial to Monetary Sovereignty'. *Theoretical Inquiries in Law* 18 (2). http://www7.tau.ac.il/ojs/index.php/til/article/view/1498 (accessed 18 April 2020).

Porter, Tony. 2005. *Globalization and Finance*. Cambridge, UK: Polity.

Posner, Elliot. 2009. 'Making Rules for Global Finance: Transatlantic Regulatory Cooperation at the Turn of the Millennium'. *International Organization* 63 (4): 665–699.

Putnam, Robert D. 1988. 'Diplomacy and Domestic Politics: The Logic of Two-Level Games'. *International Organization* 42 (3): 427–460.

Quaglia, Lucia. 2015. 'The Politics of "Third Country Equivalence" in Post-Crisis Financial Services Regulation in the European Union'. *West European Politics* 38 (1): 167–184.

Riles, Annelise. 2011. *Collateral Knowledge: Legal Reasoning in the Global Financial Markets. Chicago Series in Law and Society*. Chicago, IL: University of Chicago Press.

Rodrik, Dani. 2009. 'A Plan B for Global Finance'. *The Economist*, 2009. https://www.economist.com/finance-and-economics/2009/03/12/a-plan-b-for-global-finance (accessed 18 April 2020).

Ronit, Karsten and Volker Schneider. 2000. 'Private Organizations and Their Contribution to Problem-Solving in the Global Arena'. In *Private Organisations in Global Politics*, edited by Karsten Ronit and Volker Schneider, 1st edn, 1–33. New York, NY: Routledge.

Schimmelfennig, Frank. 2000. 'International Socialization in the New Europe: Rational Action in an Institutional Environment'. *European Journal of International Relations* 6 (1): 109–139.

Schoeller, Magnus G. 2019. *Leadership in the Eurozone: The Role of Germany and EU Institutions*. London, UK: Palgrave Macmillan.

Sheridan, Iain. 2017. 'MiFID II in the Context of Financial Technology and Regulatory Technology'. *Capital Markets Law Journal* 12 (4): 417–427. https://doi.org/10.1093/cmlj/kmx036.

SIBOS. 2016. 'When RegTech Meets FinTech: The Day after Tomorrow – How Technology Disruption Intersects with Regulation in Securities'. Geneva, Switzerland: SIBOS.

Simmons, Beth A. 2001. 'The International Politics of Harmonization: The Case of Capital Market Regulation'. *International Organization* 55 (3): 589–620.

Tsebelis, George. 1990. *Nested Games: Rational Choice in Comparative Politics. California Series on Social Choice and Political Economy* 18. Berkeley, CA: University of California Press.

Veer, Reinout A. van der and Markus Haverland. 2018. 'Bread and Butter or Bread and Circuses? Politicisation and the European Commission in the European Semester'. *European Union Politics* 19 (3): 524–545.

Zeitlin, Jonathan, ed. 2015. *Extending Experimentalist Governance? The European Union and Transnational Regulation*. 1st ed. Oxford, UK: Oxford University Press.

PART I

Vertical research perspective: European legislation in the context of international agreements

2. MiFID II between European rule-making and national market surveillance: the case of high-frequency trading

Johannes Karremans and Magnus G. Schoeller

2.1 INTRODUCTION

In line with the spirit of the regulatory reforms initiated after the outbreak of the global financial crisis in 2008, the EU reviewed its 'Markets in Financial Instruments Directive' (MiFID). As this was an action coordinated at the international level, this initiative allows us to look into the theoretical propositions developed in our first research perspective, that is, the 'vertical perspective'. The revised legislative package, MiFID II, entered into force in January 2018 and consists for the most part in extending public oversight of those areas of the financial market that between the 1980s and 2000s mostly operated in the dark. More precisely, one of the key objectives of MiFID II was to introduce reporting obligations in market segments that until recently operated directly between buyers and sellers or on alternative trading venues (see Chapter 6 for two illustrative case studies).

The lack of public oversight in the pre-crisis era was related not only to the predominance of the neoliberal paradigm in the international political economy and financial markets, but also to an exponential growth in the number and complexity of financial instruments. Technological progress played an important role in this growth as it allowed for a significant increase in the speed and volume of simultaneous transactions. Public oversight was therefore not only discouraged by the idea that markets would best regulate themselves but also by the technical difficulty of bringing complex expanding markets under regulatory control.

In an effort to reform financial market regulation in Europe, MiFID II addressed this challenge as it introduced European legislation into an area of the financial markets in which technological innovation plays a defining role, namely *high-frequency-trading* (HFT) transactions. HFT is a specific form of 'algorithmic trading' that is distinguished by the speed and intensity with which transactions occur. Using algorithms and elaborate software, firms engaging in HFT trade financial assets at the milli- or even nanosecond level. As public oversight in this sphere requires the development of equally advanced software to track and store information about these transactions, the implementation of such public regulation is a costly and burdensome enterprise. This raises the political question of how such costs should be distributed, not only between public and private actors but also between the national and supranational levels.

In addition to addressing the technological challenge of regulating transactions happening in nanoseconds, MiFID II's rules on HFT also extended the reach of European legislation into an area in which different member states have different traditions of market surveillance. Particularly in the years following the eurozone crisis, member states increasingly started developing conflicting views on the regulation of finance, with HFT being one of the most heated issues. These conflicting views were strongly related to the role HFT played in their national economies. Being home to some of the main HFT traders, the Dutch government, for instance, was a strong advocate of limiting public regulation of HFT (*The Economist* 2013). Countries like Italy and France, by contrast, tended to be staunch proponents of strict HFT regulation (*Financial Times* 2013).

Among the many legislative provisions in MiFID II aimed at expanding public oversight, those on HFT constitute an ideal case study for discussing our questions of whether and how the recent reforms of financial regulation in Europe constitute a centralisation of rule-making. On the one hand, in fact, the rules seem to constitute an unambiguous case of centralising legislative power in EU financial regulation, as prior to MiFID II HFT had been entirely unregulated in the EU. On the other hand, however, and as our analysis will show, the new legislation also leaves considerable leeway for member states to implement it according to their views on HFT, particularly when it comes to market surveillance.

Based on our theoretical conjectures on the driving forces behind centralisation in the context of international agreements, in the following pages we seek to explain the emergence of the EU's regulation of HFT and to explore the challenges and consequences of its implementation. To do this, we rely on original evidence from legislative texts, European Parliament (EP) documents and debates, the European Commission's[1] stakeholder consultation prior to proposing MiFID II, the guidelines and policy documents released by the European Securities and Markets Authority (ESMA), (financial) media reports and semi-structured elite interviews. Our analysis is divided into two parts, with the first part focusing on the emergence of HFT regulation in the EU and the second examining the challenges related to the implementation of the new rules.

With regard to the emergence of the EU's HFT regulation, we argue that the G20-led agenda on better regulation of financial markets and the rapid growth of financial technology (fintech) in conjunction with the financial crisis of 2008 opened a window of opportunity for the EU institutions to advance the centralisation of HFT regulation at the European level. Concerning the implementation of the new regulation, our argument is that it represents a centralisation of rule-making when it comes to defining the technical standards which firms and trading venues are required to adhere to when reporting on their activities. Regarding market surveillance, however, we argue that the new rules might very well lead to patterns of decentralisation. In particular, this second part of our argument relies on original interview material that shows how differently Dutch and Italian regulators view HFT and its implications.

2.2   THE EMERGENCE OF HIGH-FREQUENCY-TRADING REGULATION IN THE EU

MiFID II in general and its HFT rules in particular constitute an under-explored area of financial market research, especially in the political science literature. While lawyers and economists have provided extensive analyses regarding the content of the new provisions (e.g. Busch 2016; Busch and Ferrarini 2017; Ferrarini and Moloney 2012; Sheridan 2017), we still know very little about the political forces and dynamics that led to the unprecedented HFT regulation.

In terms of its content, the MiFID II rules on HFT are very much in line with the broader aim of increasing the transparency of financial markets. First, MiFID II provides a legal definition of HFT based on the specific technological infrastructure, system-determination and high message intraday rate of orders, quotes and cancellations. Second, HF traders are required to establish internal systems and controls according to technical standards specified by the ESMA. Third, they must notify the competent authorities of their activities, both in their home country and at the trading venue. Fourth, HFT firms need to provide detailed information about their algorithmic trading strategy, activities, and compliance and risk measures, either on a regular basis or ad hoc whenever the competent authority asks for it. Moreover, they are subject to reporting requirements regarding all executed and deleted orders. Fifth, MiFID II stipulates specific requirements for HF traders that pursue a market-making strategy, such as an obligation to provide liquidity on a continual and regular basis. Finally, trading venues are also required to have internal systems and controls to ensure that HFT does not lead to disorderly markets. These measures include an 'order-to-trade' ratio, possible limitations of trading volumes and a 'flagging' system that allows venues to identify HF traders and their orders (see Busch 2016; Gomber and Nassauer 2014, p. 15f).

The Commission presented the legislative proposal for MiFID II on 20 October 2011 after having conducted an extensive review of the preceding MiFID I legislation, which included a large stakeholder consultation. However, as we will show below, much of the specific HFT legislation was introduced by the EP in the course of an ordinary legislative procedure. The legislative process was accompanied by an extensive impact assessment, related studies and yet another stakeholder consultation carried out by the EP (Ferrarini and Moloney 2012, p. 560). The EP adopted its amendments to the Commission's proposal in a first reading on 26 October 2012, and debates in the Council were held from February 2013. On 15 April 2014 the EP eventually adopted a compromise struck with the Council in trialogue negotiations, which was followed by the Council's decision on 13 May 2014, so that the final act could be signed on 15 May 2014.[2] After the original starting date had been postponed by a year due to technical issues related to its implementation by financial firms, MiFID II finally entered into force on 3 January 2018.

The new EU regulation of HFT is clearly in line with the G20 goal of regulating and supervising all actors and practices that could jeopardise financial stability. Therefore, the G20 agenda kicked off in Pittsburgh in 2009 provided a legitimate background for the EU to advance its own regulation in this area.[3] Indeed, there are at least four reasons for considering HFT a systemic risk factor. First, due to the large volume of orders in HFT[4] there is a risk of overloading the system, leading to malfunctioning of the markets. Moreover, the fast placing and removing of orders may result in an instable order book and therefore lead to uncertainty for other market participants. Second, there is a risk of HFT amplifying volatility and therefore leading to over-reactions in the markets. Third, given that the contribution of HFT to capital formation is virtually insignificant and other market participants lack the same access to the order book, investors may switch to dark markets in order to avoid interaction with HF traders. Finally, due to its technological advantage regarding the speed and volume of transactions, HFT may be particularly well-suited to market manipulation or other abusive techniques (see Recital 62, MiFID II; Conac 2017, p. 472).

Although the EU regulation of HFT is thus perfectly in line with the G20 targets, it is not a direct response to the G20 agreement (Interview 1). Indeed, the terms 'algorithmic' and 'high-frequency trading' do not even appear in the Pittsburgh summit statement. Only at the G20 Seoul summit in November 2010 did leaders agree to mandate the International Organization of Securities Commissions (IOSCO) to develop recommendations on how to deal with "the risks posed to the financial markets by the latest technological developments".[5]

At that time, however, the European Commission had already started its review of MiFID (see above). Therefore, when the IOSCO's recommendations were endorsed at the G20 summit in Cannes in November 2011, the Commission had already concluded a large stakeholder consultation (Commission 2010) and officially proposed MiFID II, including its new provisions on HFT (Commission 2011).[6]

Following our first theoretical conjecture, we expect the decision-making rule (qualified majority voting vs. unanimity) to have an important impact on the final regulatory structure in the legislative outcome (*H1.1* and *H1.2*, 'decision-making rule hypotheses'). To the extent that we can assume heterogeneous preferences regarding HFT regulation, this conjecture is corroborated by the case of MiFID II. While we cannot find evidence that member state governments, an EU institution or a significant share of stakeholders were completely against the regulation of HFT, preferences did diverge as to *how* the emerging practices should be regulated (see below, and also Interview 1).[7] At the same time, no single member state or national veto player could have blocked the legislation on its own as it was shaped under co-decision. This gave the Commission, the EP and the supporting member state governments in the Council an opportunity to build a winning coalition in favour of centralising regulatory legislation on HFT at the EU level.

Within our first (vertical) research perspective, we also conjecture that *de facto* veto players – that is, powerful non-legislative actors such as interest associations, target groups and national supervisory authorities – can foster centralisation or decentralisation (*H2*, '*de facto* veto player hypothesis'). While this regards primarily the implementation of regulatory legislation at the national level (see below), powerful interest groups may also exert influence in the early phases of the decision-making process. As a matter of fact, stakeholders were consulted early and multiple times in the making of MiFID II. Not only did the Commission launch a major stakeholder consultation, but the Committee of European Securities Regulators (CESR), predecessor of the European Securities and Markets Authority (ESMA), and the EP also consulted the industry (Ferrarini and Moloney 2012, pp. 559f). This may have prevented more radical HFT regulatory proposals such as an introduction of minimum holding periods for orders or an obligation to provide constant liquidity to the markets. However, although the market response to the Commission may have been hostile in some respects (see Ferrarini and Moloney 2012, p. 584), most stakeholders did not oppose the regulation itself or its centralisation. On the contrary, they largely recognised the need to regulate HFT and supported individual provisions such as the requirement for HFT firms and trade venues to put in place specific risk controls and for co-location facilities to be offered on a non-discriminatory basis.[8]

In the theory chapter, we furthermore expected centralisation at the EU level to be more likely if the proposed legislation is compatible with that in large member states (*H3*, 'power/adjustment costs hypothesis'). Indeed, France and Germany[9] already introduced national regulations in 2012 and 2013 respectively. The national legislation in these two large member states therefore predates EU legislation. In particular, the French regulatory regime is restrictive with regard to HFT, as the French regulatory authority (AMF) holds a critical view of HFT. In 2015, the AMF sanction commission decided on a €5 million sanction on high-frequency traders. This decision was interpreted as a *de facto* ban on HFT in France, given that the usual behaviour of high-frequency traders was judged to be a violation of French law (Conac 2017, pp. 473, 484f). Indeed, as an EU official explained, the French pushed HFT legislation "because they were concerned that this high-frequency trading was a way of manipulating the markets. So they were concerned that these people needed to have clear rules on transparency, on governance, to ensure that they would not disturb the markets too much" (Interview 1).

In Germany, by contrast, the national law on HFT anticipated the main features of MiFID II. For instance, the definition of HFT in MiFID II, Art. 4(40) mirrors the German definition and both laws require HF traders to notify their competent authorities, introduce internal systems and controls, and flag orders generated by algorithmic trading (see Conac 2017, p. 473; Sheridan 2017, p. 422). According to our interviews, it is indeed plausible that this congruence between the German and EU legislation is not a mere coincidence but is causally linked: "Before coming forward with legislative proposals there are some member states that are consulted. And those that have pre-existing legislation are probably the ones the Commission is speaking to most actively" (Interview 1).

Moreover, we conjectured in our theory chapter that in the absence of powerful veto players the Commission may use an international agreement to increase its institutional power by centralising regulation at the European level (*H5*, 'institutional empowerment hypothesis'). The evidence we find partly confirms this hypothesis but at the same time draws a more differentiated picture. It is true that MiFID II, and therefore also HFT regulation, stands in the broader context of the G20 targets set in Pittsburgh (Gomber and Nassauer 2014, p. 6; Kennedy 2017, p. 3; Moloney 2012, p. 328). However, there is no mention of HFT in the G20 summit document and neither does the Commission refer to the G20 in direct connection with HFT. Hence, we argue that the window of opportunity used by the Commission to introduce its HFT regulation was not only opened from the outside by the G20 agenda[10] but also from the inside by the combination of the rapid and unpredictable rise of fintech and the financial crisis of 2008 (see Chapters 6 and 7). Already in its public consultation on the MiFID review in December 2010, the Commission

made it clear that in its view HFT could pose a threat to the orderly functioning of markets and should therefore be regulated (Commission 2010, p. 15).
In its official legislative proposal, the Commission explicitly mentions the
emergence of HFT as one of the reasons for the initiative (Commission 2011,
pp. 2, 177f). In addition, the relevant recital in the final directive relates the
regulation of HFT to the sudden growth of fintech:

> Technical advances have enabled high-frequency trading and an evolution of busi-
> ness models. [...] Yet that trading technology also gives rise to a number of potential
> risks [...]. It is appropriate to subject high-frequency algorithmic trading techniques
> [...] to particular regulatory scrutiny.[11]

The necessary political salience and legitimacy of HFT regulation was sup-
plied by the financial crisis. Although the Commission did not claim a direct
causal link between HFT and the crisis, it brought the issues 'crisis', 'consumer
(investor) protection' and the 'rise of fintech' into close semantic connection.
Thus, in its legislative proposal the Commission argued that

> the financial crisis has exposed weaknesses in the regulation of instruments other
> than shares, traded mostly between professional investors. Previously held assump-
> tions that minimal transparency, oversight and investor protection in relation to this
> trading is more conducive to market efficiency no longer hold. Finally, rapid inno-
> vation and growing complexity in financial instruments underline the importance of
> up-to-date, high levels of investor protection. (Commission 2011, p. 2)

Hence, as opposed to our conjecture, it was not only an international agreement but also internal developments that provided the Commission with the
opportunity to foster the centralisation of HFT regulation. As an EU official
put it:

> Some of the proposals that came out after the crisis were led by the international
> agenda. But in fact the international agenda was also influenced by what was
> happening in Europe. [...] So you cannot say that the European agenda has been
> completely driven by the G20, because the European agenda has also influenced the
> G20 agenda [...]. Because this was in fact something that was made as a response
> to the crisis [...]. So you had the excuse of the crisis to come up with solutions for
> things that people already knew that MiFID I was not perfect at [...]. The structure
> of markets was not effective because you had platforms that were popping up
> outside the MiFID scope, where you had no supervision, no investor protection, no
> transparency. So the crisis was the excuse to sort out a number of bottlenecks that
> MiFID I had, that people were basically aware of. (Interview 1)

Finally, we conjectured that it is the Commission which advances regulatory
centralisation at the EU level. However, a crucial finding of our analysis is that
it was actually the *EP* which acted as 'policy entrepreneur' (Kingdon [1984]

2003) by using the increased salience caused by the financial crisis and its role as formal co-decider to make HFT a central issue in the revised directive (see below; EP debate of 25 October 2012[12]). This finding is in line with recent research suggesting that the EP strategically invests resources in salient policy issues in order to appear as the unique supporter of public interest (Meissner and McKenzie 2018). In fact, the Commission's original legislative proposal mentions HFT in the recitals but does not propose regulatory provisions specific to HFT (although many of the provisions on algorithmic trading would also apply to HFT). It was the EP which introduced HFT as a stand-alone subject of EU regulatory legislation. First, it introduced a specific definition of high-frequency trading (Amendment Art. 4(30a,b)), which was absent in the Commission's proposal. Although the final content of the definition mirrors the German legislation (Conac 2017, 473; Art. 4(40) MiFID II) rather than the EP's amendments, HFT thus became a separate regulatory item in MiFID II. Moreover, the EP introduced crucial provisions on specific storing requirements for HFT firms (Amendment Art. 17(2a) > Art. 17 (2) MiFID II), the testing of algorithms (Amendments Art. 51(3), 51(7ec) > Art. 48(6), 48(12g) MiFID II) and extra fees for market participants using HFT techniques (Amendment Art. 51(5a) > Art. 48(9) MiFID II). Although some of the amendments on HFT did not survive the legislative procedure – for example, the 500-millisecond holding period for orders – the EP succeeded in introducing HFT and making it one of the most salient issues in MiFID II (see the EP debate of 25 October 2012;[13] Euractiv 2012[14]).

Hence, the EU's HFT regulation came about as a reaction by the EU institutions to the rapid growth of fintech and the related systemic risks. The global financial crisis together with the G20 reaction kicked off at Pittsburgh in 2009 gave these measures a high level of saliency and legitimacy. They therefore opened a window of opportunity for the Commission to advance its own regulatory agenda. However, as this analysis shows, the entrepreneurial force behind the specific HFT regulation (going beyond the more general regulation of algorithmic trading) was the EP. Based on the Commission's legislative proposal, the EP introduced HFT as a stand-alone object of regulatory legislation and increased its salience as one of the most important parts of MiFID II. This allowed the EP, once again, to present itself as a promoter of the common good in the EU.

In the next section, we turn to the question of how the new legislation has been implemented in the member states. While the emergence of the new legislation is a clear case of centralisation, a closer look at its implementation draws a more differentiated picture.

2.3   THE IMPLEMENTATION OF HIGH-FREQUENCY-TRADING REGULATION IN THE EU

As under MiFID II HFT is understood as a subset of algorithmic trading, the first rule of concern for firms dealing in HFT is the obligation to notify their activities both to the competent authority of the firm's home member state and to the authority of the member state of the trading venue at which the firm engages in algorithmic trading.[15] While the national competent authorities provide firms and trading venues with the precise information about the format with which the order data is to be stored, the technical standards for firms and trading venues to implement systems for information storage are indicated in the Commission's delegated regulation of 2016, which also assigns to the ESMA the authority to clarify further specification of these standards. As delegated regulations apply directly and do not need to be transposed in national legislation, the technical standards defined by the Commission and the ESMA can directly be adopted by all firms operating in the EU's jurisdiction. Therefore, in terms of the technical standards to which firms must store information on their HFT activities, we can expect centralised patterns of implementation. In other words, we can expect the technical standards to which information on HFT transactions is stored to be the same across the whole EU.

With regard to how public authorities use and interpret the information stored by firms, however, we expect a different dynamic. Under MiFID II, in fact, member states have the responsibility to appoint a national authority that is responsible for carrying out market supervision. Furthermore, MiFID II does not contain further specifications as to how member states should carry out supervision, leaving them a considerable degree of autonomy (Conac 2017) and increasing the potential for decentralised patterns. As anticipated in the introduction, the regulation of HFT is a policy area in which different member states have different and contraposing interests. These contrapositions run largely parallel to different conceptions of how public authorities should intervene in financial markets, with the UK, Ireland and various northern European countries tending to favour financial innovation and light-touch regulation and continental European countries like France and Italy tending to favour a more restrictive regulation of the financial sector (Quaglia 2012). Consequently, as market supervision falls under the responsibility of national authorities, we expect that the veto power of member states increases, leading to a fragmentation of the criteria for interpreting certain market practices as abuses. In other words, we expect that the more autonomy member states have in carrying out market supervision, the more the information stored by firms is used and interpreted in different ways, leading *de facto* to a decentralised and fragmented implementation of the HFT provisions.

Our overall expectation, therefore, is that the implementation of HFT provisions features a mix of centralised and decentralised patterns. In the following pages, we will explore these patterns following our '*de facto* veto player' (*H2*) and 'legal content' (*H4.1* and *H4.2*) hypotheses presented in Chapter 1. More precisely, in the case of the implementation of technical standards, these hypotheses lead us to expect centralising patterns. The fact that these standards are defined by a delegated regulation bypasses the potential veto power of member states. In addition, the ESMA's role in providing further clarification of these standards presumably reduces the possibilities for diverse interpretations. In the case of market surveillance, by contrast, considering the lack of clear provisions as to how national authorities should carry out market supervision and the different views of member states on HFT, it is plausible to expect different national authorities to develop different criteria for defining and sanctioning market abuses. Our two hypotheses therefore lead us to expect that the autonomy left to the member states to implement market surveillance may lead to a decentralised regulatory structure.

To explore our conjectures, we rely on evidence coming from two main empirical sources, one focused on the European level, the other on the national level. The former consists in the information and policy documents available on the ESMA's website. The latter consists in interviews with members of national regulatory authorities coming from two opposing fronts regarding financial regulation (Quaglia 2012), namely the Italian *Commissione Nazionale per la Societá e la Borsa* (CONSOB – Italian financial markets authority) and the Dutch Authority for Financial Markets (AFM). The selection is based on the contraposing positions that Italy and the Netherlands have towards financial markets in general and HFT in particular. In other words, these interviews provide an assessment of the implementation of MiFID II from the perspective of regulators coming from two different hemispheres of European governance. As we shall see, one sees innovation in financial markets as a challenge and the other as an opportunity. By looking jointly at these three different sources, we are able to map both the forces pushing towards centralisation and – if any – the forces triggering decentralisation.

As anticipated, the implementation of MiFID II's provisions on HFT is a shared responsibility between private and public actors. The implementation of technical standards is mostly a burden to be carried by the former. The responsibilities of private actors are, in fact, already implicitly visible in various MiFID II articles in which, as already outlined in section 2.2, the rules with which firms dealing in HFT are expected to comply are stated. These obligations bring a considerable amount of cost to firms, as they are not only obliged to report their transactions to both their national authority and the national authority of the trading venue, but must store detailed information about the "nature of [their] algorithmic trading strategies, details of the trading parameters or limits to which the system is subject [and] the key compliance and risk controls that [they have] in place".[16] The storage of such detailed information is burdensome, particularly when considering the technical standards which such information must meet.

While the national competent authorities provide firms and trading venues with precise information about the format in which the order data is to be stored, the Commission's delegated regulation of 25 April 2016 indicates the technical standards to which firms and trading venues must implement systems for information storage. These technical standards are also further clarified by a report and guidelines published by the ESMA (ESMA/2015/1464; ESMA/2016/1452). Broadly speaking, these technical standards oblige investment firms and trading venues to put in place a complex system storing information on transactions happening within fractions of seconds. This involves carrying out various tasks. The first consists in synchronising the respective business clocks, which is essential for identifying and distinguishing transactions happening in milli- or nanoseconds. The second task is to develop a complex system for storing information regarding the venue, trading date time, quantity, quantity currency, price, price currency, up-front payment, up-front payment currency and instrument details.[17] In addition, when required, information should also be provided about how the transaction changed the market positions of the parties involved.

The most difficult technical standard to implement is arguably the storage of information on algorithmic transactions using micro- or millisecond granularity, depending on the case. This means storing the time of the transaction as the exact micro/millisecond in which it happened. While investment firms are burdened with the task of implementing highly sophisticated data storage systems, trading venues are required to monitor the trading activities being carried out on their platforms and to interfere in the transactions whenever there is a need to contain the growth and the pace of them. More specifically, trading venues are expected to reduce the number of unexecuted trades and to set certain minimum price movements for financial instruments.

Besides being technically challenging, these requirements burden private actors with considerable costs, in terms of both technical infrastructure and personnel (Kindermann et al. 2016). For this reason, there were serious concerns in the private sector about whether the kick-off date for MiFID II (3 January 2018) would "go well" (Kennedy 2017, 3), in the sense that it would not disrupt markets. So far, the kick-off of MiFID II has not caused disruption but it has started provoking significant changes in the markets, as since January 2018 dealing in HFT entails substantial investment in developing reporting systems. Therefore, the burdens on firms introduced by MiFID II are undoubtedly producing winners and losers, with firms capable of sticking to the new requirements on the one hand, and firms for which the technical or personnel costs may become unbearable on the other (e.g. *Financial Times* 2018).

As was underscored by the national regulators we interviewed (Interviews 2, 3), the Commission's delegated regulation and the related report and guidelines published by the ESMA have an important function of harmonising the technical standards across the whole EU jurisdiction. The definition of technical standards in delegated regulations, in fact, ensures that they directly apply to all member states and do not need to be transposed into national legislation. Consequently, as there is almost no room for interpretation bias by national legislators, these technical standards are implemented consistently in all EU member states. The importance of delegated regulations for achieving homogeneous implementation was also acknowledged by our interviewees from the Dutch (Interview 2) and Italian (Interview 3) regulatory authorities, both when confronted with the question of whether EU legislation is helping their supervision of transnational markets and when asked about the extent to which such legislation establishes a common European framework. The two regulators not only both responded affirmatively to these questions but also underlined the positive impact of delegated regulations:

> [...] we are happy with the idea that now not more and more directives are implemented, but regulation is coming that has a direct impact, so you do not have to implement that in the national legislation. And for us that is very helpful because you do not have to change your national law, and you do not have expectation differences. [...] You skip the national interpretation, implementation, therefore you have less interpretation issues. (Interview 2)

> MiFID II/MiFIR and MADII/MAR introduced a comprehensive framework for the regulation, supervision and enforcement of risks related to algotrading and HFT and related market abuse practices. This goes from the introduction of a common definition of these trading techniques to the identification of specific obligations to be put in place by both investment firms and trading venues in terms of testing of the algorithm, IT controls, system capacity, flagging of orders, trading halts, etc, as well as the identification of specific market abuse practices linked to the use of HFT. In addition, it is noted that such requirements are mostly contained in delegated regulations issued by the European Commission, which are directly applicable in all EU member states and do not need to be transposed into national legislation. (Interview 3)

Both interviewees emphasised that the definition of technical standards through delegated regulations allows circumvention of the problem of national interpretation, thus reducing the *de facto* veto power of member states. Therefore, conforming with our '*de facto* veto player' (*H2*) and 'legal content' (*H4.1* and *H4.2*) hypotheses, the implementation of the technical standards constitutes the most centralising aspect of the HFT provisions contained in MiFID II.

In contrast to the detailed guidelines on the technical standards that private actors must comply with, MiFID II's provisions regarding how national competent authorities should carry out their supervision tend to be rather opaque (Conac 2017). As a result, member states have considerable leeway in carrying out supervision in the way and intensity they deem appropriate, but also in imposing additional requirements on firms engaging in HFT (Kindermann et al. 2016). This leeway may tap into different traditions in dealing with financial markets and their latest developments. Some member states, like the Netherlands, have made innovation in financial markets one of their main national economic interests (*The Economist* 2013). This also impacts on the views that regulators have on innovation, and algorithmic trading in particular. When asked about whether and how technological innovation and HFT constitute a challenge for market surveillance, our interviewee from the Dutch AFM responded by underscoring his organisation's positive stance towards the innovations brought by traders:

> Well, we are positive about traders. We think they are an essential part of the capital markets. And of course the trading behaviour, they put in a lot of orders, they do a lot of transactions – the high frequency traders – but on the other hand, they also give liquidity to the market. So to put it the other way round, if they are not in the market, it could be a quite empty market. [...] So we think that they are an important part of the capital markets and of course they should behave like everyone should behave. (Interview 2)

By contrast, when asked the same question, our interviewee from the Italian authority responded more negatively, highlighting the risks that HFT brings to the functioning and integrity of financial markets:

> The significant weight and increasing importance of algotraders and HFTs in recent years have raised increasing attention by regulators as to the risks and potential drawbacks in terms of market quality. [...] The technological developments, such as algotrading and HFT, have brought to light new risks for the orderly functioning, transparency and integrity of capital markets. In particular, from a supervisory point of view, the use of HFT makes it harder to detect abuses and irregularities, given the high level of complexity of the algorithms used and of the strategies implemented. (Interview 3)

Contrary to the Dutch case, the Italian regulators seem to view innovations in financial markets as a real challenge for their regulatory systems. Consequently, market surveillance may develop in different ways in different member states, particularly when considering that MiFID II leaves national regulators with sufficient autonomy to develop such divergences.

When asked about whether there have been instances of divergent market surveillance in different member states since the entry into force of MiFID II, our interviewees from both the Dutch and Italian authorities answered that so far this has not been the case. However, both interviewees clearly perceived the heterogeneity of the different views of their counterparts in other member states and saw this as a challenge for uniform market surveillance. From the Dutch perspective, for instance, problems can arise in particular with southern European countries, as they are not part of the Euronext group[18] and therefore have a highly different trading system:

> We are part of the Euronext group – but a lot of other countries are not. They have a different trading system. Different issues can then arise. So what in one trading system can be acceptable is possibly not acceptable in another trading system. I'm not sure if it is possible to solve that because then you should say every country needs to have the same trading system and that's not what we want. (Interview 2)

When asked further about possible divergent views that different national authorities may have about HFT, our interviewee from the Dutch AFM again emphasised the different views that may emerge between countries that are part of Euronext and countries that are not, and that these differences run largely parallel to the differences between northern and southern European countries:

> I think some of the southern European countries are more critical about it, but that's also because the trading system. [...] The trading system in Spain is very different to our trading system. It is also for Italy, but not for France because they're part of the Euronext system. [...] For us, I think our trading system, [...] especially Euronext, is quite familiar with the fact that HFT exists and we react on that. (Interview 2)

It is interesting to note from this quote how – in the configuration of divergent national interests – France is at times aligned with the Mediterranean countries (e.g. Wasserfallen and Lehner 2017) and at other times with the continental northern European countries (e.g. Quaglia 2012). The quote therefore seems to indicate that France is truly an in-between case, featuring characteristics of both the southern and the northern political economies.

On this same set of questions about possible divergent views among member states, our interviewee from CONSOB acknowledged the fact that such potential indeed exists, but stated that this threat has largely been tackled by the policy dialogues between national authorities and the ESMA (Interview 3). When asked about the kind of problems that could emerge from inconsistent application across member states, the CONSOB interviewee clearly pointed to regulatory arbitrage and to the risk of misapplication in some member states that may in turn lead to risk contagion. In addition, another potential problem indicated by the Italian regulator is the applicability of EU requirements to third-country firms using HFT. This problem may become particularly concrete once the United Kingdom has left the EU.

The different views on the supervision of financial markets are thus divided into two hemispheres of European governance, with the Dutch regulators being an example of the north-west and the Italian regulatory authority of the Mediterranean countries. The different perspectives on the challenges in the (mis)application of EU rules between Dutch and Italian authorities, therefore, is strongly linked to different views that national regulators have on the benign or malign characteristics and effects of HFT. As we have seen, when asked about the role that HFT plays in the spread of market abuses or irregularities, a clear contrast emerges between the Italian authorities pointing towards the relation between HFT and new risks to the integrity of capital markets and the Dutch authorities underlining instead the essential role that HFT traders play in the functioning of financial markets. These different national attitudes to HFT are likely to persist under MiFID II, as national authorities have the autonomy to investigate the legal conformity of the activities of the firms and venues operating in their jurisdictions (Conac 2017). Consequently, it is likely that in jurisdictions like the Netherlands the authorities will be more laissez faire and less likely to sanction certain misconducts, while in jurisdictions like Italy HFT may turn out to be more restricted. Therefore, for HFT market surveillance we find our '*de facto* veto player' (*H2*) and 'legal content' (*H4.1* and *H4.2*) hypotheses corroborated, as diverse stances on the risks related to HFT and the relative vagueness of EU provisions lead to decentralising patterns.

However, it is important to note the role that the ESMA has played in managing these differences so far. During the first years of implementation, ESMA provided an important forum for national regulators to compare their different views at the European level, which then led the ESMA to provide its set of responses to some of the controversies that emerged between national regulators (Interviews 2, 3). This is also in line with recent accounts of how the ESMA developed as a centralised European rule-maker in the post-crisis period (Spendzharova 2017). Since its foundation in 2008, in fact, the ESMA has fully exploited its role as the European standard setter in financial market regulation, while at the same time acting as a forum for national authorities to discuss their different points of view.

The decentralising effects of national diverging views on HFT may thus be tempered by the fact that effective investigation requires cross-border cooperation, and that the ESMA acts as a coordinator of such cooperation. The transnational nature of the markets in which HFT takes place means that in order to obtain a complete picture of a certain market activity information needs to be collected from different jurisdictions. Both the Dutch and Italian regulators, in fact, underlined that today there is a European system of mapping and tracking financial cross-border transactions in which every day each national authority sends a report on the activities in its national financial market to the ESMA, which in turn sends a report back with a complete European overview (Interviews 2, 3). In the long run, this cooperation might trigger a standardi-sation of market surveillance across the EU, which may be facilitated by the fact that the heads of the national authorities jointly constitute the ESMA's board of supervisors and are therefore responsible to the Commission for the correct functioning of financial markets under the framework of MiFID II. As the national regulators also underscored during our interviews, the frequent interactions between the ESMA and national regulators may very well lead towards generating a (centralised) European view on the surveillance of market malpractices.

2.4 CONCLUSION

MiFID II's provisions on HFT need to be seen as an extension of the G20 Pittsburgh agenda, with both the European Commission and the EP seeking to expand the scope of EU regulation to a type of trading that accounts for a large share of trades in European financial markets. Against a background of technological innovation and the lessons drawn from the financial crisis, the EU therefore has forcefully advanced the centralisation of financial regulation with regard to HFT. By drawing partly on existing legislation in Germany, the EU developed a common framework for the regulation of HFT in which firms are obliged to store and report information on their trades to the national competent authorities, which in turn are in charge of conducting market sur-veillance. Surprisingly, when it came to incorporating HFT regulation into MiFID II, it was the EP rather than the Commission which acted as policy entrepreneur centralising the regulation of HFT at the European level.

While the regulation of HFT constitutes a case of centralisation of rule-making, given that HFT was previously unregulated at the European level, regarding its implementation a more complex story needs to be told. As HFT relates to the economic interests of the member states in different ways, it also generates different views among public authorities on the extent to which it is a potential source of threat. As a result, we find that there are patterns of both centralisation and decentralisation in the implementation of EU regulation of HFT: a centralisation of rule-making, including the definition and implementation of technical standards; a decentralisation of the imple-mentation of the new rules and surveillance of adherence to them. The former has been achieved through European legislation and delegated regulations that are directly applicable in all member states, and by placing the burden of implementation on firms dealing in HFT; the latter is triggered by national authorities' diverging views on HFT.

From our analysis, it emerges that not only do different member states have diverging ways of looking at HFT but also that these differences may result in different ways of conducting market surveillance, which – in the regulators' view – may in turn lead to regulatory arbitrage or risk contagion. At the same time, however, we have also found that the ESMA is playing an important role in coordinating these differences by bringing together the diverging points of view of the national authorities and thus generating a common European view on market surveillance with regard to HFT. The extent to which this activity will suffice to prevent market surveillance within the EU being fragmented is still an open question.

NOTES

1. Hereafter, 'the Commission'.
2. See   https://oeil.secure.europarl.europa.eu/oeil/popups/ficheprocedure.do ?reference=2011/0298(COD)&l=en (accessed 22 February 2019).
3. See Newman and Posner (2016) for the theoretical underpinning of this argument.
4. According to the ESMA (2014), the market share covered by HFT varies between 24% and 40%, depending on the measurement approach.
5. The Seoul Summit Document, https://www.g20germany.de/Content/DE/ StatischeSeiten/Breg/G7G20/Anlagen/G20-seoul-gipfel-dokument-en___blob= publicationFile&v=1.pdf (accessed 30 January 2019).
6. Hence, our hypotheses on the difference between vague and precise international agreements do not apply to the EU's HFT regulation.
7. See, e.g. the respective EP debates (http://www.europarl.europa.eu/sides/getDoc .do?pubRef=-//EP//TEXT+CRE+20121025+ITEM-017+DOC+XML+V0//EN& language=EN accessed 30 January 2019), the contributions by national parliaments (http://www.connefof.europarl.europa.eu/connefof/app/exp/COM(2011)0656 accessed 30 January 2019) and the stakeholder responses to the Commission's consultation on the review of MiFID (Commission 2010). Even national authorities were in favour of regulating HFT at the European level. The Netherlands Authority for the Financial Markets (AFM), for instance, took a rather sceptical view regarding a strict regulation of HFT but it acknowledged that some degree of regulation was needed and, while taking into account the specific properties of the market structure in single countries, "given the international nature of the financial markets, this process should take place at not lower than European level. Unilateral national measures are useless and therefore undesirable".
8. A notable exception was BNP Paribas, which argued that "high-frequency trading should not be regulated at all". Moreover, one interviewee vaguely recalled fierce lobbying by the finance industry against HFT regulation, and explicitly referred us to the position of the Association for Financial Markets in Europe (AFME). However, when we examined their responses to the Commission's consultation, we found no evidence of fierce opposition, but general approval of the regulatory proposal as such and concerns or disagreement only in relation to single provisions. The interviewee also provided an explanation for this apparent contradiction: "I think probably they would prefer to kill it [the legislative proposal], but they understood that they would not be able to kill it, and [...] so they

tried to soften. Whenever they find out that they cannot avoid having something, they simply try to soften it. And it does make sense, because basically then you would be in damage control mode. You will try to ensure that you will have at least something that makes sense and that you can work with."

9. France and Germany are the EU's most powerful member states in terms of economic and market size, population and voting weight in the Council (see, e.g. Krotz and Schild 2013; Schoeller 2018). One may speculate on the extent to which their powerful position in EU financial market regulation will increase with the exit of the United Kingdom and thus the City of London.

10. The G20 Pittsburgh agreement can instead be seen more as an enabling factor (or necessary condition) in that it legitimised the agenda of reform-minded actors in the EU to introduce stricter regulation of the financial markets (MiFID II and MiFIR), of which HFT regulation became a part (for the theoretical underpinning of this argument, see Newman and Posner 2016).

11. Directive 2014/65/EU of the European Parliament and of the Council of 15 May 2014 on markets in financial instruments and amending Directive 2002/92/EC and Directive 2011/61/EU Text with EEA relevance. link https://eur-lex.europa.eu/legal-content/EN/ALL/?uri=CELEX%3A32014L0065 (accessed 8 April 2020).

12. http://www.europarl.europa.eu/sides/getDoc.do?pubRef=-//EP//TEXT+CRE+20121025+ITEM-017+DOC+XML+V0//EN&language=EN (accessed 30 January 2019).

13. http://www.europarl.europa.eu/sides/getDoc.do?pubRef=-//EP//TEXT+CRE+20121025+ITEM-017+DOC+XML+V0//EN&language=EN (accessed 30 January 2019).

14. https://www.euractiv.com/section/uk-europe/news/eu-lawmaker-turns-screw-on-ultra-fast-trading/ (accessed 6 February 2019).

15. Article 17, paragraph 2, MiFID II Directive.

16. Article 17, paragraph 2, MiFID II Directive.

17. ESMA, Guidelines on transaction reporting, order record keeping and clock synchronisation under MiFID II, ESMA/2016/1452, corrected on 7 August 2017.

18. Euronext is the largest stock exchange in continental Europe, and operates markets in Amsterdam, Brussels, London, Lisbon, Dublin, Oslo and Paris. It was founded in 2000 by a merger of the exchanges in Amsterdam, Paris and Brussels.

BIBLIOGRAPHY

Busch, Danny (2016) 'MiFID II: regulating high frequency trading, other forms of algorithmic trading and direct electronic market access,' *Law and Financial Markets Review*, 10:2, 72–82.

Busch, Danny and Guido Ferrarini (eds) (2017) *Regulation of the EU Financial Markets: MiFIDII and MiFIR*, Oxford: Oxford University Press.

Commission (2010) Public Consultation: Review of the Markets in Financial Instruments Directive (MiFID), 8 December 2010, Directorate General Internal Market and Services, Brussels.

Commission (2011) Directive of the European Parliament and of the Council on markets in financial instruments repealing Directive 2004/39/EC of the European Parliament and of the Council (Recast), 20 October 2011, Brussels.

Conac, Pierre-Henri (2017) 'Algorithmic trading and high-frequency trading,' In: Busch, Danny and Guido Ferrarini (eds) *Regulation of the EU Financial Markets: MiFIDII and MiFIR*, Oxford: Oxford University Press, 469–485.

ESMA (2014) 'Economic report on high-frequency trading activity in EU equity markets,' Number 1, 2014.

Ferrarini, Guido and Niamh Moloney (2012) 'Reshaping order execution in the EU and the role of interest groups: from MiFID I to MiFID II,' *European Business Organization Law Review*, 13, 557–597.

Financial Times (2013) 'Italy introduces tax on high-speed trade and equity derivatives,' 1 September.

Financial Times (2018) 'Goldman to treble Swedish office as post-Mifid equities hub,' 4 May.

Gomber, Peter and Frank Nassauer (2014) 'Neuordnung der Finanzmärkte in Europa durch MiFID II/MiFIR,' White Paper Series No. 20.

Kennedy, Steven (2017) 'Making history,' *ISDA Quarterly*, 3:3, 3.

Kindermann, Jochen, Fox Darren, Colston Nicholas, Stalin Charlotte and Penny Miller (2016) 'Algo and high frequency trading under MiFID2 – a few more pieces in the puzzle,' Simmons & Simmons elexica. http://www.elexica.com/en/legal-topics/asset-management/25-algo-and-high-frequency-trading-under-mifid2, accessed 11 March 2019.

Kingdon, John W. [1984] (2003) *Agendas, Alternatives, and Public Policies*, 2nd edition, New York: Longman.

Krotz, Ulrich and Joachim Schild (2013) *Shaping Europe: France, Germany, and Embedded Bilateralism from the Elysée Treaty to twenty-First Century Politics*, Oxford: Oxford University Press.

Lehner, Thomas and Fabio Wasserfallen (2019) 'Political conflict in the reform of the eurozone,' *European Union Politics*, 20:1, 45–64.

Meissner, Katharina L. and Lachlan McKenzie (2018) 'The paradox of human rights conditionality in EU trade policy: when strategic interests drive policy outcomes,' *Journal of European Public Policy*, 26:9, 1273–1291. DOI: 10.1080/13501763.2018.1526203.

Moloney, Niamh (2012) 'MiFID II: reshaping the perimeter of EU trading market regulation,' Guest Editorial, *Law and Financial Markets Review*, 6:5, 327–330.

Newman, Abraham and Elliot Posner (2016) 'Transnational feedback, soft law, and preferences in global financial regulation,' *Review of International Political Economy*, 23:1, 123–152.

NRC Handelsblad (2018) Nog geen uitzondering voor flitshandelaren, 7 March.

Quaglia, Lucia (2012) 'The "old" and "new" politics of financial services regulation in the European Union,' *New Political Economy*, 17:4, 515–535.

Schoeller, Magnus G. (2018) 'The rise and fall of Merkozy: Franco–German bilateralism as a negotiation strategy in eurozone crisis management,' *Journal of Common Market Studies*, 56:5, 1019–1035.

Sheridan, Iain (2017) 'MiFID II in the context of financial technology and regulatory technology,' *Capital Markets Law Journal*, 12:4, 417–427.

Spendzharova, Aneta (2017) 'Becoming a powerful regulator: the European Securities and Markets Authority (ESMA) in European financial sector governance,' TARN Working Paper 8/2017.

The Economist (2013) 'Electronic trading. Dutch fleet. The home of the world's first stock exchange is now a high-frequency heartland,' 20 April.

Wasserfallen, Fabio and Thomas Lehner (2017) 'Mapping contestation on economic and fiscal integration: evidence from new data,' EMU Choices Working Paper, University of Salzburg, 23.

INTERVIEWS

Interview 1 (2019) European Parliament, senior official, 1 July, Brussels, Belgium.
Interview 2 (2019) Dutch Authority for the Financial Markets (AFM), official, 3 July, The Hague, the Netherlands.
Interview 3 (2019) Commissione Nazionale per la Societá e la Borsa (CONSOB – Italian financial markets authority), official, 2 July, Rome, Italy.

3. The internal and external centralisation of Capital Markets Union regulatory structures: the case of Central Counterparties

Fabio Bulfone and Agnieszka Smoleńska

3.1 INTRODUCTION

The aim of this chapter is to study if, how and to what extent the recent reforms of the regulatory framework for central counterparty clearing houses (CCPs) have led to a centralisation of the supervisory authority over the EU financial sector. The reform of the CCP regulation, known as the European Market Infrastructure Regulation (EMIR) was part of the Capital Markets Union (CMU) project. The CMU is a package of regulatory reforms unveiled in 2015 as one of the flagship projects of the Juncker Commission. It has the ambitious goal of deepening, integrating and diversifying the EU financial market, focusing in particular on non-banking segments like bond issuance, corporate bond securitisation, public equity investment, venture capital and credit intermediation by specialised non-bank financial firms (i.e. leasing companies and consumer finance companies) (Quaglia et al. 2016). Implementation of the various CMU proposals has indeed led to a reshaping of the regulatory framework for many financial activities, marking a landmark moment in EU financial regulation. At the same time, this regulatory activity has been contentious, as it has required strengthened cross-border intra-EU and extra-EU regulatory and supervisory cooperation. This is particularly true for the regulation of CCPs, which – as market infrastructure – are a key node of internal market integration, making them an ideal vantage point from which to study regulatory and supervisory centralisation in a horizontal and vertical perspective (Smoleńska 2017). In doing so, we will assess the plausibility of four hypotheses presented in the introduction to this volume, those dealing with regulatory outcomes depending on the compatibility of EU Member States' regulatory structures and international agreements (hypothesis 3), the Commission's power of initiative as a driver of centralisation (hypothesis 5), regulatory competition between financial powers (hypothesis 6) and the impact of regulatory arbitrage on supervisory and regulatory centralisation (hypothesis 7).

CCPs are financial market infrastructure tasked with reducing risk in financial transactions by interposing themselves between the two counterparties in a derivative contract (i.e. acting as buyer to the seller and seller to the buyer). They have recently come to occupy a pivotal position in financial markets as a consequence of the commitment made by G20 leaders in 2009 at the Pittsburgh Summit that over-the-counter (OTC) derivatives should be centrally cleared to increase transparency and reduce systemic risk. Prior to the G20 statement calling for their direct supervision, CCPs were not regulated, being treated as private insurances used by the parties in a transaction. The G20 commitment was transposed into EU legislation in 2012 with the EMIR regulation – one of the first post-crisis reforms of the EU financial regulatory framework. EMIR granted a number of competences in the regulation of CCPs to the European Securities Markets Agency (ESMA), one of the three European Supervisory Authorities (ESAs) established in 2010. Since then, the size of EU-based CCPs has grown. Between 2009 and 2015 the share of OTC interest-rate derivatives centrally cleared jumped from 36 to 60 per cent (Busch 2018, pp. 35–6). Centrally cleared interest rate swaps (IRS) witnessed even more impressive growth, going from 23.3 to 88.5 per cent of the total between 2007 and 2017 (Genito 2019, p. 939). As of 31 December 2017, the notional amount of outstanding OTC derivatives was more than EUR 500 trillion worldwide, of which interest rate derivatives represented more than 75 per cent and foreign exchange derivatives almost 20 per cent.

CCP operations are also contentious from a regulatory and supervisory perspective because of their extreme degree of geographical concentration. For example, in 2018 the UK housed three CCPs responsible for the clearing of 75 per cent of euro-denominated interest rate swaps, the largest category of OTC derivatives (House of Lords 2018), which is seen as problematic by the central bank of issuance, namely the ECB. Given the dramatic increase in transaction volume and their market infrastructure function, large UK-based CCPs like LCH Clearnet are perceived as having become 'too big to fail' as an insolvency of one of them would risk plunging the EU financial sector into crisis (Friedrich and Thiemann 2017). Consequently, while central clearing of OTC derivatives may indeed improve market resilience, the cross-border scope of their activity coupled with their uneven geographical distribution (i.e. concentration in London) makes CCPs a potential source of systemic risk (Genito 2019). This will be even more so when Brexit takes place as a large share of euro-denominated transactions will be located outside the formal jurisdiction of euro-area supervisors and of the central bank that issues the currency in which the bulk of transactions are made, that is, the ECB. This issue had already sparked controversy before the Brexit referendum, with the ECB unsuccessfully seeking to force the relocation of transactions in euros within its jurisdiction as early as 2010 under the ill-fated Location Policy (Marjosola 2015). While the EU courts have denied the ECB the competence to regulate CCPs and therefore to impose a forced relocation of euro-denominated clearing, the role of the issuing central bank in regulating CCPs has become the focal point of the EMIR review process. The outcome of the Brexit referendum in 2016 further contributed to creating a sense of urgency, as the withdrawal of the UK from the common regulatory framework increases the risk of supervisory loopholes. This dynamic, coupled with the persistently low level of investment in the EU, motivated the Commission to table a number of measures aimed at centralising supervision of CCPs as part of the CMU initiative.

In this chapter, we provide a legal analysis of the regulatory structure for CCPs put in place by the 2019 EMIR reform (EMIR 2019) coupled with a political science analysis of the factors which led to this regulatory outcome. As we detail below, the new rules give rise to a complex regime which differentiates between CCPs active in the EU market established in one of the EU Member States (intra-EU CCPs) and those that provide cross-border services in the EU but are based in third countries (extra-EU CCPs). While ESMA has acquired considerable direct supervisory powers over the extra-EU CCPs operating in the EU market (i.e. third-country CCPs such as those established in Hong Kong, Singapore and the US), national authorities retain supervisory powers over intra-EU CCPs (i.e. CCPs established in one of the EU Member States, such as LSH SA in France and Eurex Clearing in Germany). In other words, supervision has become more centralised for extra-EU than intra-EU CCPs. This differentiated regime has emerged despite the fact that in its initial proposal the Commission, flanked by the ECB, had called for the establishment of a single supervisory framework for intra-EU and extra-EU CCPs.

The remainder of the chapter is organised as follows. Section 3.2 locates our contribution within the framework developed in the volume's theoretical chapter, and in particular within the vertical international and horizontal international perspectives. Section 3.3 provides a detailed legal analysis of the EMIR framework as agreed by the European Parliament and the Council in spring 2019 (EMIR 2019). Particular attention is devoted to discussion of the emergence of a differentiated supervisory structure for EU-based and extra-EU CCPs. It will be shown that, while ESMA acquired direct supervisory powers over extra-EU CCPs, the supervision of intra-EU CCPs remains decentralised at Member State level. As far as the applicable rules are concerned, they are uniform and centralised for all CCPs (both intra- and extra-EU), given that EMIR is directly applicable across the EU and supplemented by ESMA technical standards. Section 3.4 details the political dynamics leading to this differentiated supervisory outcome. It highlights that both supervisory centralisation over extra-EU CCPs and the lack of centralisation over EU-based

CCPs result from a dual dynamic involving a state-centred 'neo-mercantilist'[1] battle (Howarth and Quaglia 2018, p. 1118) between different financial centres to attract financial investment outflowing from London in the context of Brexit and the bureaucratic competition between different EU authorities to strengthen their supervisory powers. Finally, section 3.5 concludes by providing reflections on and refinements of the hypotheses presented in the theoretical chapter.

3.2   RELEVANT HYPOTHESES, OPERATIONALISATION OF CONCEPTS AND RELEVANT ACTORS

In line with this volume's theoretical chapter, centralisation of regulatory structures is defined as an uploading of decision-making competences to the EU level via a strengthening of the existing powers or a broadening of the mandate of ESMA and/or the ECB vis-à-vis national competent authorities (NCAs). Instead, we define decentralisation as a process in which extensive powers are given to or retained by the NCAs of Member States. Fragmentation is defined as a situation in which unforeseen dynamics lead to a sub-optimal regulatory framework characterised by loopholes or supervisory conflicts.

We study regulatory structure outcomes bearing in mind that financial regulation is characterised by a high level of heterogeneity arising from the interaction between different regimes in place for different financial activities, such as banking and trading in financial instruments, and different supervisory cultures at the national level. Furthermore, to identify the structure it is necessary to consider its different components, that is, market access rules (the authorisation required), supervision (obtaining information, investigative powers and enforcement) and the oversight of equivalence regimes (specific powers to grant market access to third-country entities). In the EU, regulatory structures may be established on the basis of generally applicable regulations (MiFIR, EMIR) or may require transposition at the national level when they result from directives (AIFMD, UCITS). Finally, as is discussed in Chapter 4 of this volume, EU regulation may centralise regulatory structures by establishing a common framework of rules and yet leave their implementation (i.e. supervision) decentralised. In the following sections we will evaluate the impact of the 2019 EMIR regime, primarily focusing on the centralisation of the regulatory structure for supervision, given that full rule-centralisation already occurs under the generally applicable EU regulation.

The CCP market has two defining features – its important cross-border dimension and its geographical concentration in the UK – that make it a particularly interesting case to study two of the research perspectives presented in the theoretical framework: the vertical international and the horizontal international perspectives.

In line with the vertical international perspective, the regulation of CCPs at the EU level came about in response to international pressure for regulatory harmonisation stemming from the G20 Pittsburgh statement calling for mandatory clearing of derivatives traded through central counterparties and oversight of them. This commitment was subsequently transposed into EU law following a legislative proposal by the European Commission. Coherently with the vertical international perspective, this top-down pressure then had a differentiated impact on the Member States. One explanation for this is the heterogeneity of domestic regulatory, and also economic, structures. Furthermore, the process of implementing global commitments sparked different reactions from authorities at the EU level. The concomitant effect of these different dynamics led to a differentiated regulatory outcome with a co-existence of elements of centralisation, decentralisation and fragmentation. In the vertical international perspective, our legal and political analysis of EMIR 2019 helps us refine two hypotheses, which we discuss in the final section of this chapter:

Hypothesis 3. If centralised regulatory structures proposed by the EU are compatible with those in large powerful Member States, centralisation is more likely.

Hypothesis 5. Under the conditions required by international agreements, in the absence of powerful veto players the Commission will be able to increase its institutional power in financial regulation, which equals a centralisation of regulatory structure.

However, the Brexit referendum has made the CCP case perhaps even more relevant from the point of view of the second research perspective, which focuses on horizontal international competition between states and regional polities hosting large financial centres. In fact, as a result of the Brexit process, the UK will go from being home to the largest financial sector – and CCP market – in the EU to becoming an external (but highly integrated) financial powerhouse. We will show that the uncertainty surrounding this scenario has had a profound impact on the content of EMIR 2019. This allows us to assess the plausibility of two hypotheses:

Hypothesis 6. Regulatory competition between leading financial powers prompts regulatory centralisation in other actors' internal regulatory structures.

Hypothesis 7. A high degree of transnational regulatory arbitrage by financial firms will lead to more coordination between two public regulatory actors if one of the parties takes a leading role in such coordination. This in turn exerts pressure for more regulatory centralisation within each regional polity.

To assess the plausibility of these hypotheses, we focus on the preferences of some of the pivotal actors in the EU legislative process with due regard to the way in which they have been reshaped by the Brexit shock. These are: the European Commission, the European Parliament, the European Central Bank and the largest EU Member States – France and Germany. The European Commission has the exclusive right of legislative initiative, which it uses to set the agenda for legal reforms and to propose the content of future legislation. In the areas of integration considered, legislation is passed under the ordinary legislative procedure, that is, the European Parliament and a qualified majority of Member States in the Council must agree on the new rules. Within the Council, we focus on the preferences of France and Germany, as they are pivotal owing to the size of their economies and the weight of their votes within the Council. Furthermore, Paris and Berlin are two important EU financial centres housing the largest CCPs on the continent in terms of the notional value of daily OTC transactions (ESMA 2019b, p. 41). We therefore assume that no major regulatory reform of the EU financial framework for CCPs can be approved without their support. The relative weight of France and Germany has further increased as a result of the Brexit referendum, as the EU is losing what was arguably its most influential member on financial regulation matters (Moloney 2017). Over the course of the Great Financial Crisis, the European Parliament acquired important expertise in financial matters, which has enabled it to exert greater influence over the content of financial regulation in EU legislative processes. This activism came in response to growing concerns about financial regulation among EU voters. Although the preferences of the European Parliament are naturally as heterogeneous as those of its members, we assume that, due to the scope of their mandate, MEPs will focus on the institutional dimension of regulations. Hence, they will be particularly sensitive to the distribution of regulatory responsibilities among institutions and to issues of accountability. Finally, to the extent that the ECB has direct legislative competences with regard to the regulation of economic and financial matters in the EU, and as during the eurozone crisis it emerged as the most decisive EU institution, we consider expressed ECB preferences to be an important variable determining the distribution of powers within the regulatory structures. In particular, the ECB was active in the 2019 EMIR reform to the extent that its competences with regard to oversight of CCPs were affected, including via an amendment to its statute. For the most part, however, the ECB was a rule-taker in the processes we discuss.

We argue that supervisory centralisation can only come about when it matches the preferences of all these pivotal actors. This is also true when decisions are taken under qualified majority voting, as in the case of the EMIR, because notwithstanding voting rules the EU Council strives for consensus (in fact the voting results show that all the EMIR amendments were unanimously adopted by all the Member States). Until the Brexit referendum, the UK's resistance within the Council prevented supervisory centralisation for both intra-EU and extra-EU CCPs. The referendum and the consequent withdrawal of the UK from actively shaping EU regulations in the Council removed a veto player on supervisory centralisation. However, while the UK's departure catalysed sufficient support for the centralisation of supervision over extra-EU CCPs, Germany and other Member States in the Council opposed the centralisation of supervision over intra-EU CCPs, thereby leading to a decentralised outcome.

This chapter relies on a thorough analysis of EU legal rules, secondary sources, press releases, newspaper articles and official documents from the European Commission, the European Central Bank, the European Parliament, and the French, German and UK governments. This material is supplemented with interviews with three policymakers, namely a key financial adviser to the Juncker Commission (Interview 1), a policy advisor in the European Parliament (Interview 2) and an expert from the EU Council services (Interview 3).

3.3   CCP REGULATORY STRUCTURES UNDER THE EMIR FRAMEWORK

The EMIR 2019 reform put in place a complex regulatory structure with different regimes for CCPs established in the EU (intra-EU CCPs) and for those which provide services in the EU market but are established in third countries (extra-EU CCPs). In this section, we provide a detailed analysis of this two-pronged regulatory structure (see Table 3.1).

The first common EU regulatory framework for CCPs (EMIR) was established in 2012, making the oversight of CCP activities a matter of generally applicable EU regulation. The package was originally approved in July 2012 and came into force a month later (EMIR 2012). The EMIR 2012 regulation introduced mandatory clearing of OTC derivative transactions via CCPs. It defined a CCP as a "legal person that interposes itself between the counterparties to the contracts traded on one or more financial markets, becoming the buyer to every seller and the seller to every buyer" (Smoleńska 2017, p. 141). EMIR regulated the operation of and access to CCPs and introduced rules for access to the EU market by CCPs established in third countries.

EMIR introduced common rules for market entry for CCPs, that is, the conditions which such financial institutions need to fulfil to meet the requirements for authorisation. These included specific rules such as the level of capital requirements and governance standards. To allow for such a centralising effect, the legislative instrument chosen was a regulation. Furthermore, EMIR was adopted on the basis of Art. 114 TFEU, which grants the EU a general competence for regulating the internal market, rather than the service-specific Art. 53(1) TFEU, which was used in the case of MIFID (see Chapter 4 of this volume). The use of this legal basis allowed the regulation to have more far-reaching centralising effects, including granting specific supervisory competences to EU bodies.

Despite this centralisation of rules, however, supervision remained substantially decentralised, as national competent authorities retained responsibility for the application of the centralised regulatory requirements with regard to intra-EU CCPs. In terms of the locus of supervision, EMIR did not prescribe whether the domestic supervisor should be an independent agency or the central bank, which led to the emergence of heterogeneous supervisory architectures across the Member States. In half of the Member States, including France, domestic CCPs are supervised by the central bank, while in nine (including Germany, Austria and Poland) supervision rests with the designated financial market authority. With regard to extra-EU CCPs, EMIR established a general equivalence regime which allowed market access to third-country CCPs if their home supervision met the requirements established in EU rules. Under the equivalence regime, ESMA was responsible for 'recognising' third-country CCPs operating on EU territory on the basis of a decision adopted by the European Commission (Arts. 13 and 25 EMIR). In other words, extra-EU CCPs would formally continue to be supervised by their respective home authorities, with the role of ESMA confined to verifying that the conditions for continued recognition of the rules governing their behaviour, such as risk management, were "functionally equivalent" to EU rules. Specifically, ESMA had the competence to assess whether there was a cooperation agreement in place with the relevant supervisory authority, whether the CCP was authorised in the third country and in full compliance with the rules, whether the Commission adopted an equivalence decision and whether there was a risk of money-laundering related to the activity (since 2015). The 2012 EMIR foresaw no direct role for ESMA in the oversight of EU CCPs. The EU agency's role was therefore limited to collecting information about any new CCP authorisations and mediating when different national authorities disagreed over matters relating to the supervision of CCPs operating cross-border. Therefore, although EMIR brought some form of harmonisation, overall the regulatory structure remained decentralised for intra-EU CCPs and fragmented for third-country CCPs (with their activity not being fully captured by the regulatory structure).

The 2019 reform of EMIR strengthens supervisory centralisation, although in a differentiated manner. The regime for EU-based CCPs will continue to be decentralised with a key role for the relevant domestic supervisor. However, some partial elements of centralisation are introduced, such as the granting of a strengthened supervisory role for cross-border colleges (networks of supervisors) and an enhanced regulatory power for ESMA (the 'internal dimension' of the regulatory structure). Instead, centralisation replaces the fragmented regime for extra-EU CCPs in the 'external dimension' (see Table 3.1). Specifically, ESMA has acquired direct supervisory competences for the authorisation, supervision and enforcement of regulations with regard to central counterparties providing services in the EU market. The following sections outline these two distinct regulatory outcomes in more detail.

3.3.1   The Internal Dimension: The Supervision of EU-based CCPs

Following the 2019 EMIR reform, the regulatory structure for intra-EU CCPs will remain primarily decentralised with regard to the implementation of the rules, that is, national authorities will continue to supervise the CCPs established in the EU. However, despite the maintenance of a decentralised structure, the 2019 EMIR reform introduces a number of marginal central-ising features. Under the new rules, CCPs established in one of the Member States will continue to be supervised by the domestic authority on the basis of authorisations. Such authorisations are then valid across the entire EU territory (Art.10(5), 14 and Art. 22 EMIR; ESMA 2019). However, the reform compli-cates the regulatory structure by, to some extent, strengthening the suprana-tional dimension: first, by enhancing the role of the CCP supervisory colleges which were established under the 2012 EMIR regime, bringing together the various authorities in the jurisdictions where a CCP operates; second, by assigning ESMA new residual competences; and third, by specifying the role of central banks in CCP supervision as opposed to financial supervisors, thus intervening more intrusively in the decentralised structure. We explain these marginal features of centralisation below.

First, under the new regulatory regime the (centralised) supranational colleges gain more powers. While under the previous regime colleges were only to be consulted regarding the authorisation and ongoing supervision of intra-EU CCPs (i.e. they had no powers), under the 2019 EMIR if the com-petent authority deviates from the college's opinion it must explain why (Art. 19(4) EMIR, as amended). Thus, via the centralised colleges, various new authorities gain influence over the ongoing supervision of CCPs, including: (a) ESMA; (b) the competent authorities responsible for the supervision of large clearing members of the CCP; (c) the competent authorities responsible for the supervision of trading venues served by the CCP; (d) competent authorities supervising CCPs with which interoperability arrangements have been established; (e) competent authorities supervising central securities depositories to which the CCP is linked; (f) the relevant members of the ESCB responsible for the oversight of the CCP and the relevant members of the ESCB responsible for the oversight of CCPs with which interoperability arrangements have been established; and (g) the central banks issuing the most relevant EU currencies in which the cleared financial instruments are denominated. The inclusion of central banks within the colleges reflects awareness by the legislator of the impact CCP activities might have on monetary financial stability. The rules governing the operation of colleges are centralised and published by ESMA (ESMA 2019a).

Second, with the 2019 EMIR reform ESMA acquires some competences vis-à-vis the ongoing intra-EU CCP supervision. Specifically, a new dedicated CCP Supervisory Committee is established within ESMA, which brings together the national competent authorities but also includes full-time independent members of the Supervisory Committee appointed by members of ESMA's Board of Supervisors, subject to approval by the European Parliament. The CCP Supervisory Committee can assist national supervisors in the exercise of their tasks, such as the drafting of relevant supervisory decisions. EMIR thus allows for 'opt-in' centralisation of authority. While as a rule the role of ESMA with regard to supervision of intra EU-CCPs remains advisory, if the relevant national authority asks it to, the ESMA CCP Supervisory Committee can act as a *de facto* supervisor. Such 'opt-in' centralisation of supervision is allowed so national authorities may benefit from ESMA's resources or (centralised) expertise.

Third, the decentralised nature of the supervisory framework for intra-EU CCPs is qualified by the fact that, unlike EMIR 2012, EMIR 2019 regulates the institutional regulatory structure, delimiting the functions of the national central bank and the independent supervisor in crisis scenarios. A specific role is now foreseen for issuing central banks in crisis situations, meaning that although supervision remains decentralised in normal times in periods of instability – at least for euro area countries – the ECB will have a specific role in implementing crisis measures. The ECB has argued, however, that such a regulatory structure is fragmented as there is no harmonised role for the issuing central banks in *ongoing* supervision. Over the course of the legislative process the ECB has indeed argued that it should be endowed with a non-exhaustive list of measures and tools, and it was encouraged to do so by the CJEU judgment in the *Location Policy* case (Marjosola 2015; Draghi 2018).

Following the 2019 EMIR reform the regime for intra-EU CCP supervision remains formally decentralised, as the primary responsibility for decision-making and enforcement remains with the domestic regulators of each Member State. However, this decentralisation is qualified by: (a) parallel centralisation under cross-border supervision colleges; (b) opt-in centralisation through the CCP Supervisory Committee of ESMA; and (c) centralisation of the role of central banks in crises.

Table 3.1   The EU regulatory structure for CCPs after the 2019 reform

	Centralised	Decentralised	Fragmented
Intra-EU CCPs	substantive rules (EU regulation) supervisory colleges opt-in centralisation (ESMA) crisis role of central banks	supervision	ongoing supervision by central banks
Extra-EU CCPs	determination of the systemic nature of third country Tier 1 CCPs supervision of Tier 2 CCPs		oversight of non-systemic third-country CCPs (Tier 1)

3.3.2   The External Dimension: The Supervision of Extra-EU CCPs

EMIR 2019 creates a centralised supervisory structure for extra-EU CCPs operating in the EU. Specifically, the reform establishes a two-tier regime for third-country CCPs operating in the EU, with new supervisory powers being centralised in ESMA, and in particular in the newly-established CCP Supervisory Committee mentioned above. Under the 2012 EMIR regime, ESMA's powers of supervision over extra-EU CCPs operating in the EU territory were limited to monitoring the alignment of supervisory standards. After 2019, the regulatory and supervisory regime for extra-EU CCPs will be more centralised than that for intra-EU CCPs, as ESMA has been granted powers of direct supervision differentiating between different types of CCPs depending on their systemic importance in the EU market.

First, EMIR 2019 centralises in ESMA the competence for the determination of the systemic nature of CCPs. The conditions for determining this systemic relevance are established by EU regulations and include: the nature, size and complexity of the CCP; the potential effect a disruption to the CCP's activities would have on financial markets; the structure of the CCP's clearing membership, including access to information in this regard; the substitutability of the services provided by the CCP; and the CCP's interconnectedness with other EU financial structures (Art. 25(2a) EMIR). CCPs deemed non-systemic by ESMA (Tier 1 CCPs) continue to be supervised by third-country authorities as under the pre-reform regime. However, ESMA is assigned the competence to directly supervise 'systemically important' CCPs (Tier 2 CCPs). ESMA-supervised Tier 2 CCPs are also subject to stricter supervisory rules covering a wide array of issues, including margin requirements, liquidity risk control, collateral, settlement and the approval of interoperability arrangements under EMIR. Therefore, the new extra-EU CCP regulatory structure endows ESMA with a *Kompetenz-Kompetenz*, that is, the ability to determine – on the basis of specific criteria – whether or not it is the direct supervisor of a given extra-EU CCP operating in the internal market.

Second, the 2019 reform centralises supervision over extra-EU CCPs by endowing the newly-established Supervisory Committee with the same powers national authorities have over intra-EU CCPs. In addition to the general powers relating to fines and investigation, ESMA will now enjoy a special power to withdraw recognition with regard to the important (Tier 2) extra-EU CCPs, which would then require such entities to establish (relocate) in one of the EU Member States. Hence, under certain circumstances, Tier 2 CCPs might be obliged to relocate to a Member State and submit to the direct supervision of a national authority should they wish to continue to provide their services in the EU. We therefore observe a full centralisation of decision-making powers by ESMA vis-à-vis systemically important third-country CCPs.

A related example of centralisation of regulatory structure over extra-EU CCPs, which is nevertheless unlikely to be implemented, is included in the 'no-deal' Brexit planning foreseen by the European Commission in the case of a disorderly withdrawal of the UK from the EU. Contingency plans foresaw a centralised framework for the oversight of UK CCPs which, following the execution of Brexit, would immediately become third-country financial institutions from the perspective of the other EU Member States. The special EU regulations put in place foresaw that EU authorities would be granted special and unprecedented powers under the emergency rules which would govern financial transactions between the EU and the UK in the event of a no-deal Brexit. The dedicated Commission Delegated Regulation grants special monitoring powers to ESMA over systemically important CCPs (European Commission 2018).

To sum up, EMIR 2019 has created a differentiated CCP regulatory structure in the EU. Different rules apply to intra-EU CCPs and extra-EU CCPs. With regard to intra-EU CCPs, the supervisory structure remains decentralised despite a limited strengthening of the role of ESMA and of the cross-border supervisory colleges, together with some regulation of the oversight function of central banks. With regard to extra-EU CCPs, a centralised framework is established for CCPs considered systemically important in the internal market. Below, we assess the extent to which this regulatory outcome can be explained by (a) compatibility between centralised structures and the regulatory structures of the large Member States; (b) the European Commission's entrepreneurial behaviour in transposing an international agreement; and (c) regulatory competition between financial centres in the post-Brexit-referendum scenario.

3.4   THE POLITICAL DIMENSION: EXPLAINING THE EMERGENCE OF A DIFFERENTIATED SUPERVISORY REGIME

In 2015, the Commission launched a 'regulatory fitness' check of the EMIR legislation. The REFIT public consultation led the Commission to conclude that within the industry there was broad support for the EMIR regime, and that the existing regulatory framework only needed minor adjustments. Following some of the comments emerging from the consultation, in 2017 the Commission launched a legislative proposal, EMIR 'Refit', to streamline clearing and reporting obligations. The initiative was welcomed both by the CCP industry and the UK Treasury (House of Lords 2017).

However, the UK's decision to notify its intention to withdraw from the EU as a consequence of the June 2016 referendum led the Commission to change its approach to the regulation of CCPs. The possibility of having the largest providers to the EU financial sector of clearing services located outside the EU motivated a legislative proposal calling for a centralisation of the supervisory framework for both extra-EU CCPs and intra-EU CCPs in June 2017. The European Commission's communications accompanying the legislative proposal explicitly linked the prospect of Brexit with the need to centralise supervision over CCPs (Arriba-Sellier 2019). For instance, in a 2017 communication to the EP, the Parliament and the Council, the Commission stated that:

> … the foreseen withdrawal of the United Kingdom from the EU will have a significant impact on the regulation and supervision of clearing in Europe. At present, as much as 75% of euro-denominated interest rate derivatives are cleared in the UK. Derivatives denominated in some other Member States' currencies are also cleared in the UK. These transactions directly impact the responsibilities, including in the area of monetary policy, of the relevant EU and Member State institutions and authorities … specific arrangements based on objective criteria will become necessary to ensure that, where CCPs play a key systemic role for EU financial markets and directly impact the responsibilities, including financial stability and monetary policy, of EU and Member State institutions and authorities, they are subject to safeguards provided by the EU legal framework. This includes, where necessary, enhanced supervision at EU level and/or location requirements. (European Commission 2017a)

Despite the fact that above all Brexit affects the regulation and supervision of extra-EU CCPs (i.e. London's CCPs will transform from intra-EU CCPs to extra-EU CPPs if they continue to provide services in the internal market), in its initial legislative proposal the Commission called for the establishment of a centralised supervisory regulatory structure for both intra-EU and extra-EU CCPs. The fact that the regime which emerged in the end creates a differentiated regime leads us to analyse the negotiations and regulatory outcomes concerning the internal and external dimensions of supervisory centralisation separately in the following sections.

3.4.1   Explaining the Regime for Intra-EU CCPs: National Resistance to Supervisory Centralisation

The Commission's initial legislative proposal involved a centralisation of the supervision of intra-EU CCPs combining an extension of ESMA's supervisory powers with an expansion of the powers of the 'Central Bank of Issuance' (CBI). The CBI is the bank issuing the currency in which cleared transactions are denominated, that is, the ECB in the case of euro-denominated transactions (European Commission 2017b). The Commission explicitly linked the push for supervisory centralisation to a need to avoid regulatory arbitrage within the EU:

> First, the growing concentration of clearing services in a limited number of CCPs, and the consequential increase in cross-border activity, implies that CCPs in a small number of individual Member States are increasingly relevant for the EU financial system as a whole. Against this trend, the current supervisory arrangements relying mainly on the home-country authority ... need to be reconsidered. Second, diverging supervisory practices for CCPs ... across the EU can create risks of regulatory and supervisory arbitrage for CCPs and indirectly for their clearing members or clients.

Brexit made this threat of intra-EU regulatory arbitrage even more plausible as large financial centres like Paris, Frankfurt and Dublin entered into direct competition to attract financial investment outflows from London. Due to its geographical distribution (i.e. concentration in the UK), clearing is a particularly delicate market segment in this regard, as the Commission explicitly acknowledged:

> The departure of the United Kingdom from the Single Market reinforces the urgent need to further strengthen and integrate the EU capital market framework, including on central counterparties (CCPs), investment firms and markets for initial public offerings (IPOs). It also strengthens the need for further integration of supervision at EU level. (European Commission 2017c)

One should note that within our theoretical framework an enhancement of the supervisory powers of the central bank would equate to supervisory centralisation for the eurozone countries – even if the overall structure of independent supervisors remains decentralised – since EMU Member States share a common 'bank of issuance'. In the Commission's initial proposal, however, we find that two alternative projects for supervisory centralisation developed, one giving power to ESMA and the other to the central banks (i.e. the ECB for eurozone-based CCPs). The European Commission's original proposal leaning towards strengthening the role of central banks was accompanied by an ECB proposal to amend its statute to allow for such enhanced supervisory powers (Arriba-Sellier 2019, p. 713). Arguing that disturbances in the functioning of CCPs might impede the ability of the ECB to fulfil its mandate to maintain price stability, the ECB proposed being given direct supervisory powers over both intra-EU and extra-EU CCPs in the case in which the latter cleared significant amounts of euro-dominated transactions (European Central Bank 2017). The initiative was coordinated with the EMIR reform proposal put forward by the European Commission (Smoleńska 2017; Arriba-Sellier 2019). The UK reacted to the ECB's proposal with suspicion, seeing it as an attempt to revive Frankfurt's ambition to impose a relocation to the eurozone of UK-based CCPs clearing euro-denominated OTCs (House of Lords 2017).

Despite the Commission's strong push for supervisory centralisation, however, in the final agreement on the new EMIR legislation reached in 2019, the provisions leading to a strengthening of ESMA and the ECB's supervisory powers were considerably watered down (Interview 1). With regard to intra-EU CCPs, while all central banks (and therefore also the ECB) are granted some additional supervisory powers, as discussed above, these only apply to crisis situations. ESMA, meanwhile, gained limited supervisory powers and only at the request of national supervisors. The supervision of EU-based CCPs therefore remains essentially decentralised at the Member State level. We argue that two factors concurred in motivating this decentralised outcome. First, strong resistance emerged within the Council from Germany and other Member States to the uploading of supervisory authority to the EU level. Second, the European Parliament opposed strengthening the ECB's supervisory powers (Arriba-Sellier 2019; Interview 2).

Within the Council, Germany took a leading position in opposing the broadening of ESMA's supervisory powers over intra-EU CCPs in an effort to protect the prerogatives of domestic regulators. Other Member States, including Austria, Spain and Sweden, backed the German position (Reuters 2017; James and Quaglia 2019). During the negotiations, the German government even suggested formally splitting the draft legislation in two and discussing supervision of intra-EU and extra-EU CCPs separately (Brunsden and Stafford 2017). This came as little surprise as German authorities have always been somewhat reluctant to see supervisory and regulatory powers over domestic entities uploaded (see, for instance, Deutsche Bundesbank 2014; German Federal Government 2014; Moloney 2017). Already in 2011 during the negotiations on the first EMIR package, Germany presented a joint amendment with the UK stating that national competent authorities, and not EU agencies, should retain the power to authorise and supervise CCPs operating in their domestic markets (*Financial Times* 2011a). This view was also shared by the Deutsche Börse Group, owner of the German CCP European Commodity Clearing (ECC). According to Deutsche Börse:

> CCPs already today have established a supervisory college including all relevant European supervisory authorities. This well-functioning college structure, with well-established relationships and well-experienced NCAs, should be continued and not changed to direct supervision by ESMA. (Deutsche Börse Group 2017, p. 3)

Apart from this general concern about uploading supervisory and regulatory powers over domestic financial entities to the EU level, the German opposition to centralisation should be seen in the context of the competition to attract financial firms relocating from London after Brexit. In fact, over the course of Brexit negotiations (2016–2019), national supervisory authorities of countries hosting large financial centres, like Germany, France, Luxembourg and Ireland, engaged in a process of regulatory fine-tuning aimed at making their domestic markets more attractive to prospective foreign investors (Howarth and Quaglia 2018; Grossule 2019). This dynamic created strong incentives for regulatory and supervisory leniency, with a regulatory race to the bottom within the EU potentially ensuing (Friedrich and Thiemann 2017; Arriba-Sellier 2019). Of course, the implementation of this 'neo-mercantilist' strategy is conditional on the retention of ample supervisory powers by national supervisors. This in turn explains the strong resistance to supervisory centralisation over intra-EU CCPs coming from Germany. Even though France and the Netherlands were more supportive of a strengthening of ESMA's supervisory powers (Interview 1), vetoes by Germany and other Member States within the Council prevented the emergence of a consensus, therefore leading to a decentralised outcome.

The EU legislators also watered down the proposal to grant enhanced supervisory powers over CCPs to central banks (such as the ECB). In the agreement reached between the Council and the European Parliament, the scope of central bank supervisory powers was restricted to CCPs located in third countries and crisis scenarios, and even then with serious limitations (Arriba-Sellier 2019). The European Parliament also resisted the ECB's push for more supervisory powers for reasons related to the accountability of the supervisor (Interview 2). In fact, the European Parliament secured for itself considerable powers over the process of selection and oversight of the members of ESMA's CCP Supervisory Committee, powers that it does not have over the ECB. For this reason, the EP was more positive about strengthening the CCP Supervisory Committee than that of the ECB.

Disappointed with the marginal extension of its supervisory powers, the ECB withdrew its initial proposal for an amendment of its statute, blaming the failure on Member State reluctance to shift supervisory authority over EU-based CCPs away from national regulators (Brunsden and Jones 2019).

In a harshly-worded letter to the Council, the ECB complained that under the new framework it would not enjoy sufficient supervisory powers over CCPs established within the EU and would therefore lack power over a considerable amount of euro-dominated transactions (European Central Bank 2019).

3.4.2   Explaining the Regime for Extra-EU CCPs: The Role of the Commission as Policy Entrepreneur and the Neo-Mercantilist Competition Between Financial Centres after Brexit

The Brexit referendum, and the consequent spectre of the departure of a substantial part of the CCP industry from the EU, turned the regulation of extra-EU CCPs into a hotly-debated negotiating issue. In its initial proposal, the Commission planned to give ample regulatory powers over extra-EU clearing houses to ESMA and the relevant CBI. The proposal also envisaged a possibility for ESMA and the CBI to force the relocation of systematically important extra-EU CCPs (the so-called 'Tier 2') if they cleared a considerable amount of transactions in an EU currency. This proposal amounted to "a significant centralisation of financial supervision in critical areas" (Arriba-Sellier 2019, p. 709). The European Commission referred to Brexit and the ensuing risk of regulatory arbitrage as the main driver of the reformist initiative:

> there is a risk that changes to the CCP rules and/or regulatory framework in a third country could negatively affect regulatory or supervisory outcomes, leading to an un-level playing field between EU and extra-EU CCPs and creating scope for regulatory or supervisory arbitrage ... Moreover, a substantial volume of euro-denominated derivatives transactions (and other transactions subject to the EU clearing obligation) is currently cleared in CCPs located in the United Kingdom. When the United Kingdom exits the EU, there will therefore be a distinct shift in the proportion of such transactions being cleared in CCPs outside the EU's jurisdiction, exacerbating the concerns outlined above. This implies significant challenges for safeguarding financial stability in the EU that need to be addressed. (European Commission 2017d)

The UK was understandably very critical of the proposal, particularly the aspects of it related to a forced relocation of CCPs. Summarising the position of the cabinet, the UK Economic Secretary argued that "The Government does not support the inclusion of location requirements for substantially significant third-country CCPs in the proposal. A location policy is inconsistent with [a global approach to CCP regulation] and would risk fragmenting global derivatives markets" (House of Lords 2017).

However, after the Brexit referendum the UK *de facto* lost its veto power over financial regulation negotiations and in the final stages withdrew from the EMIR negotiations altogether. This is in stark contrast with the cases of earlier post-crisis reforms like Solvency II, AIFMD, EMIR 2012 and MIFID II, over which the UK had succeeded in exerting a decisive influence, leveraging its unparalleled regulatory expertise (for a detailed analysis, see City of London 2016). For instance, in the case of EMIR 2012 the negotiating effort by the UK Chancellor George Osborne prevented both the centralisation of supervision for intra-EU CCPs and the adoption of a regulatory design penalising UK-based CCPs vis-à-vis their eurozone counterparts (*Financial Times* 2011b). The UK was not alone in criticising the relocation policy requirement. Negative opinions on the forced relocation of euro-denominated derivatives also came from the US-based International Swaps and Derivatives Association (ISDA) and from FIA (FIA 2017; ISDA 2017).

Compared to the case of intra-EU CCPs, the decisive driver of supervisory centralisation was the fact that in the case of extra-EU CCPs both France and Germany supported a strengthening of ESMA's mandate. This support should again be seen in the context of the 'neo-mercantilist' competition between EU financial centres to attract firms relocating from London (Quaglia and Howarth 2018, p. 1118). France's position stemmed from a hope that the imposition of strict regulatory requirements would push UK-based CCPs to relocate in the EU. Already in 2009, a confidential document addressed to the Minister of Finance, Christine Lagarde, mentioned euro-denominated clearing as a strategically important segment for the euro area and for France, advising the government to ask for a forced relocation of these activities to the eurozone (James and Quaglia 2019, pp. 7–8). In June 2016, a few days after the Brexit referendum, the French President, François Hollande, explicitly called for a relocation of euro-denominated clearing to the EU (*Financial Times* 2016). For his part, the head of Banque de France suggested that LCH, the clearing house controlled by the London Stock Exchange, should develop interest rate clearing services in Paris (*Financial Times* 2018b). While Germany initially did not have a strong preference on the issue of CCP regulation, since 2016 and amid pressure from Deutsche Börse, the government started pleading for a forced relocation of euro-denominated clearing (Batsaikhan et al. 2017; James and Quaglia 2019). For instance, the Minister of Finance, Olaf Scholz, argued that "To minimise risk for financial stability, it is indispensable that [the central clearing of euro-derivatives clearing] is subject to strong regulation and supervision in full conformity with EU standards" (*Financial Times* 2018a). The French and German financial lobby groups Paris Europlace and Frankfurt Finance were also at the forefront of this effort to attract financial investment from London to increase competitiveness.

The joint support by the Commission, the European Parliament, France and Germany allowed ESMA to acquire considerable supervisory powers over extra-EU CCPs under the new EMIR regulation (Arriba-Sellier 2019). However, the system became more complex since ESMA was awarded more supervisory leverage over extra-EU CCPs than over intra-EU CCPs. Instead, an intervention by the Council and the European Parliament led to a mitigation of the initial proposal concerning the forced relocation of extra-EU CCPs, a move welcomed by both the UK authorities and UK-based CCPs (UK HM Treasury 2018).

Hence, while the removal of the UK as a veto player explains the enhanced supervisory centralisation over extra-EU CCPs, the lack of support within the Council for supervisory centralisation of intra-EU CCPs explains the decentralised outcome. These shifting preferences within the Council should in turn be seen in the context of the 'neo-mercantilist' 'battle' among different financial centres within the EU to attract financial firms relocating from London (Howarth and Quaglia 2018). The changing attitude of the German government is particularly telling in this regard. While, on the one hand, Germany favoured the establishment of a centralised supervisory framework for UK-based CCPs as this would lead them to relocate within the EU, on the other hand, by retaining ample supervisory powers over domestic CCPs Germany could still tailor its regulatory framework to the demands of prospective financial investors.

3.5   DISCUSSION OF HYPOTHESES AND CONCLUSION

In this chapter we have shown how the emergence of a differentiated supervisory framework for intra-EU and extra-EU CCPs in the context of the 2019 reform of EMIR can be explained by looking at the preferences of five decisive actors: the European Commission, the European Parliament, the ECB, France and Germany. We have argued that two interrelated factors were decisive in leading to the differentiated supervisory framework emerging as a result of the EMIR 2019 reform: an alignment of preferences between France and Germany generated by a 'neo-mercantilist' dynamic of competition to attract financial investment from the UK (Quaglia and Howarth 2018, p. 1118); and the Brexit referendum. First, even if the EMIR did not require unanimity, centralisation would only have been possible if it was compatible with the preferences of France, Germany and the European Parliament. While such preference alignment came about in the case of extra-EU CCPs, in the case of EU-based CCPs, resistance by Germany and other Member States within the Council prevented supervisory centralisation. As a result, the supervisory framework for intra-EU CCPs remains decentralised at the domestic level, with centralised EU agencies only playing an auxiliary role in supervision. Second, the Brexit process and the consequent prospect of a departure of the largest provider of CCP services to the EU acted as a regulatory shock with a profound impact on the CCP regulatory framework. However, it allowed for a greater alignment of preferences with regard to the centralisation of supervision of extra-EU CCPs. In this final section, we evaluate the level of supervisory and regulatory centralisation achieved from the point of view of two of the perspectives presented in the theoretical chapter: the horizontal international and the vertical international perspectives.

3.5.1   CCP Regulation and the Vertical International Perspective

The EU regulatory structure for CCPs was first established in response to a joint agreement reached at the G20 level in Pittsburgh in 2009. Coherently with the vertical international perspective, this common international pressure played out differently at the EU level and at the domestic level of each Member State. In this regard, our analysis is particularly relevant to assessing the plausibility of hypotheses 3 and 5.

Our findings are relevant to hypothesis 3 in that we find that the preferences of large Member States had a decisive impact on regulatory and supervisory outcomes. However, unlike in *H3*, we do not find compatibility with the *formal* domestic regulatory structures of Member States to be the decisive factor in the formation of such preferences. In fact, if hypothesis 3 were accurate we would expect large Member States to support the designing of supranational regulatory institutions matching their domestic regulatory frameworks. In the case of CCP regulation and supervision there is a great deal of heterogeneity between Member States in terms of their domestic structures. In some Member States CCPs are regulated by the central bank, in others by domestic financial regulators and yet in others there is a more dispersed supervisory system with both the financial regulators and the central bank sharing competences. Looking in more detail at the domestic regulatory structures of France and Germany, we see that the former has a diffused supervisory framework in which the Banque de France shares competences with two regulators (Autorité des Marchés Financiers and Autorité de Contrôle Prudentiel), whereas in Germany the domestic market watchdog BaFIN has the core of the competences, with a more marginal role for the Bundesbank. If hypothesis 3 were to apply to our case we would expect Germany to strongly support an uploading of supervisory authority over EU-based CCPs to ESMA, as this would closely match its domestic supervisory architecture. Instead, we would expect the French position to be more ambiguous. However, the preferences of both countries do not seem to align with these expectations. In fact, Germany strongly opposed supervisory centralisation for intra-EU CCPs in the EU-level supervisor, while France was more positive about a centralised solution, specifically including strengthening the role of the central bank. Concerning the supervision of extra-EU CCPs, the positions of these two countries seem to match hypothesis 3 more closely. In fact, both countries supported a centralised framework with a strengthening of ESMA that was compatible with their domestic regulatory frameworks, as it would not require any modification of the existing supervisory structures. However, our analysis has also allowed us to highlight that Member States' preferences are not solely influenced by the formal design of their domestic regulatory structures. Instead, other factors related to their domestic economies, like the desire to foster the competitiveness of their financial sectors, seem to play a more decisive role in shaping Member States' preferences. In fact, France and Germany also supported the centralisation of the supervisory framework for extra-EU CCPs within ESMA in the hope that the creation of a centralised supervisory framework for UK-based CCPs would lead them to relocate part of their activity in the EU, with Paris and Frankfurt set to profit from this dynamic.

Our findings also refine hypothesis 5, which posits that the Commission might exploit international agreements to increase its own institutional role in financial regulation, thereby leading to centralisation. To the extent that ESMA is an EU agency exercising power delegated by the European Commission and over which the latter exercises oversight, a strengthening of ESMA equates to a strengthening of the Commission. In line with the argument developed in the introduction to this volume, we have found that the Commission was able to strategically use its power of legislative initiative to propose measures leading to supervisory centralisation. This happened in the cases of both the 2012 EMIR and the 2019 EMIR reform. In the case of the 2012 EMIR, which we have briefly touched upon in this chapter, the Commission seized the opportunity created by the international agreement reached by the G20 on the clearing of OTC derivatives to table a legislative proposal giving the newly-established ESMA supervisory powers over CCPs. Even though the proposal did not then succeed in gaining support from the European Parliament and the Council, the swift legislative initiative by the Commission was nevertheless a decisive driver of regulatory centralisation. In the case of the 2019 EMIR reform too, the Commission seized the opportunity created by another exogenous event – the decision by the UK government to withdraw from the EU – to launch another legislative proposal to centralise the supervisory structures for both intra-EU and extra-EU CCPs. Again, even though centralisation was resisted by the EU Council, the legislative initiative allowed the European Commission to pursue supervisory centralisation in the context of Brexit, allowing for a profound reform of the supervisory regime for extra-EU CCPs.

However, the Commission was not the only EU institution playing a decisive role in shaping financial regulation and neither did it only pursue centralisation in areas which it formally controls. In fact, in our case study covering the internal dimension of supervisory centralisation we have shown how bureaucratic competition might ensue between different EU institutions seeking to gain supervisory powers over specific market segments (James and Quaglia 2019).

In the case of EMIR, two alternative projects did emerge, one giving supervisory powers to the ECB and the other to ESMA. In the end, quite puzzlingly, the newly-created ESMA ended up acquiring more supervisory powers than the all-powerful ECB. The European Parliament played a decisive role in determining this outcome, as it supported strengthening ESMA rather than the ECB (on the role of the European Parliament, also see Chapter 2 of this volume). This preference can be explained by the fact that under EU law the Parliament can exercise greater oversight over ESMA (an EU body) than over the ECB (an independent and institutionally insulated EU institution). Such powers of oversight include specific accountability arrangements relating to appointments and to the institutional budgets. In fact, although the regime for intra-EU CCPs would *prima facie* appear to be decentralised (formal powers remain with the national competent authority), as a result of bureaucratic competition and diverging views regarding accountability within the regulatory structure, we have identified a diffused regulatory structure which combines elements of decentralisation (formal powers) with centralisation (expertise, auxiliary advice). We argue that intra-EU agency competition is decisive in explaining this fragmented outcome (Busuioc 2016). This allows for a refinement of hypothesis 5, which suggests that the European Commission is the primary EU-level policy entrepreneur supporting centralisation, as it would lead to its institutional empowerment. Instead, we have shown that multiple EU agencies might engage in this process, supporting alternative models of centralisation. Furthermore, we have found the European Commission to be the only EU institution with a general preference for centralisation, even if it does not directly lead to an enhancement of its own powers.

3.5.2   CCP Regulation and the Horizontal International Perspective

The fact that the CCP industry is heavily concentrated in the UK makes the study of its post-Brexit regulation particularly relevant for the horizontal international perspective, which focuses on the impact that competition with other global financial centres has on EU regulatory structures. In fact, by potentially turning the largest financial centre in Europe from a member of the EU into an extra-EU financial centre, the Brexit referendum could increase the horizontal competition between the EU and the UK.

The uncertainties related to the Brexit process provide a particularly interesting assessment of hypothesis 6, which argues that growing regulatory competition between financial powers prompts regulatory centralisation in other actors' *internal* regulatory structures. We find this claim to be disconfirmed by our empirical analysis. In fact, once the Brexit process is brought to completion, the UK will become a (regulatory) financial power in direct competition with the EU, even if its CCPs may remain an essential component of the EU financial infrastructure. Following hypothesis 6, the close interconnection between the two financial centres would create strong incentives for the centralisation of supervisory and regulatory structures within the EU. However, our analysis of the *internal* dimension of supervisory centralisation shows an opposite outcome, which can be explained as follows. Despite the fact that the Commission, the Parliament and the ECB all supported the establishment of a centralised regulatory and supervisory framework for EU-based CCPs, explicitly citing the threat of growing regulatory competition from the UK as a reason for this centralisation, resistance by Member States within the Council prevented the establishment of a centralised framework. This resistance is in turn explained by the desire to attract financial investment outflows from the UK. Where we observe centralisation, however, is with regard to the CCPs which provide services in the EU market but which are established in third countries (like the UK CCPs, which will become extra-EU once the Brexit process is brought to completion).

This latter observation allows us to assess the plausibility of hypothesis 7, according to which a high degree of transnational regulatory arbitrage by financial firms will lead to more coordination of supervisory and regulatory structures in order to reduce the scope for arbitrage. We find that the regulatory preferences of the Commission align with this hypothesis. In fact, the Commission justified its legislative initiative to centralise the supervisory framework for both intra-EU and extra-EU CCPs on the ground that Brexit increases the scope for regulatory and supervisory arbitrage, and therefore called for the establishment of a more centralised framework. However, reducing regulatory and supervisory arbitrage did not seem to be a concern for Member States within the Council, at least in the case of intra-EU CCPs. Instead, Member States supported a decentralised supervisory framework for two reasons: first, to protect the prerogatives of domestic regulators; and second, in the hope that this might help them tailor domestic supervisory standards on the needs of potential investors. Rather than reducing the scope for regulatory arbitrage, this 'neo-mercantilist' strategy is further increasing it, potentially leading to a race to the bottom between EU countries in terms of supervisory standards. On the other hand, the centralisation of supervision over extra-EU CCPs confirms hypothesis 7, as growing concern with regulatory arbitrage between the EU and the UK led to the establishment of a centralised structure with regard to third-country CCPs providing services in the EU market.

NOTE

1. By 'neo-mercantilism' we mean any activist effort by governments or other state actors to favour the international competitiveness of domestic sectors or firms deemed strategic.

BIBLIOGRAPHY

Arriba-Sellier, N.D. (2019), 'The Brexit reform of European financial supervision: lost in transition?' *European Business Law Review*, **30** (4), 695–719.

Batsaikhan, U., R. Kalcik and D. Schoenmaker (2017), 'Brexit and the European financial system: mapping markets, players and jobs,' Bruegel Policy Contribution.

Brunsden, J. and Jones, C. (2019), 'ECB attacks EU plans for boosting supervision of clearing houses,' *Financial Times*. Accessed 4 January 2020 at: https://www.ft.com/content/74ddbdb0-4735-11e9-a965-23d669740bfb.

Brunsden, J. and Stafford, P. (2017), 'EU clearing plans for City run into resistance across bloc,' *Financial Times*. Accessed 4 January 2020 at: https://www.ft.com/content/62d54b38-d396-11e7-a303-9060cb1e5f44.

Busch, Danny (2018), 'A stronger role for the European Supervisory Authorities in the EU27,' in Danny Busch, Emiliano Avgouleas and Guido Ferrarini (eds), *Capital Markets Union in Europe*, Oxford: Oxford University Press, 29–54.

Busuioc, E.M. (2016), 'Friend or foe? Inter-agency cooperation, organizational reputation, and turf,' *Public Administration*, **94** (1), 40–56.

City of London (2016), 'Shaping legislation: UK engagement in EU financial services policy-making.' Accessed 15 November 2019 at: https://www.cityoflondon.gov.uk/business/economic-research-and-information/research-publications/Documents/research-2016/shaping-EU-legislation-2.pdf.

Deutsche Börse Group (2017), 'Deutsche Börse Group response to the public consultation on the operations of the European Supervisory Authorities.' Accessed 12 September 2019 at: https://www.deutsche-boerse.com/resource/blob/59518/2264e7df68d43a5e3264ebccdb26ba86/data/20170321-response-to-operations-of-the-european-supervisory-authorities.pdf.

Deutsche Bundesbank (2014), 'Deutsche Bundesbank's reply to the European Commission's Green Paper "Building a Capital Markets Union".' Accessed 15 September 2019 at: https://www.bundesbank.de/resource/blob/666796/2c7871a875437fd1a8e3422d04560cab/mL/2015-05-21-statement-capital-market-union-answers-data.pdf.

Draghi, M. (2018), 'Risk-reducing and risk-sharing in our Monetary Union,' Speech delivered at the European University Institute, 11 May.

EMIR 2012 (2012), Regulation (EU) No 648/2012 of the European Parliament and of the Council of 4 July 2012 on OTC derivatives, central counterparties and trade repositories text with EEA relevance, OJ L 201, 27 July 2012, pp. 1–59; amended multiple times. Accessed 4 January 2020 at: https://eur-lex.europa.eu/legal-content/EN/TXT/?uri=CELEX:02012R0648-20190617.

EMIR 2019 (2019), Regulation (EU) 2019/834 of the European Parliament and of the Council of 20 May 2019 amending Regulation (EU) No 648/2012 as regards the clearing obligation, the suspension of the clearing obligation, the reporting requirements, the risk-mitigation techniques for OTC derivative contracts not cleared by a central counterparty, the registration and supervision of trade repositories and the requirements for trade repositories, OJ L 141, 28 May 2019, pp. 42–63 and Regulation (EU) 2019 of the European Parliament and of the Council of 23 October 2019 amending Regulation (EU) No 648/2012 as regards the procedures and authorities involved for the authorisation of CCPs and requirements for the recognition of extra-EU CCPs [awaiting publication in the Official Journal].

ESMA (2015), 'Guidelines and recommendations regarding written agreements between members of CCP colleges.' Accessed 15 September 2019 at: https://www .esma.europa.eu/sites/default/files/library/2015/11/2013-661_report_gr_on_college _written_agreement_-_final_for_publication_20130604.pdf.

ESMA (2019a), 'List of competent authorities designated for the purposes of Regulation (EU) No. 648/2012 on OTC derivatives, central counterparties and trade repositories (EMIR).' Accessed 4 January 2020 at: https://www.esma.europa.eu/sites/default/ files/emir.pdf.

ESMA (2019b), 'Annual Statistical Report on EU Derivatives Markets.' Accessed 20 September 2019 at: https://www.esma.europa.eu/sites/default/files/library/esma50 -165-639_esma-rae_asr-derivatives_2018.pdf.

European Central Bank (2017), Recommendation for a Decision of the European Parliament and of the Council amending Article 22 of the Statute of the European System of Central Banks and of the European Central Bank.

European Central Bank (2019), Withdrawal of the Recommendation for the ECB for a Decision of the European Parliament and the Council amending Article 22 of the Statute of the European System of Central Banks and of the European Central Bank, Letter to Antonio Tajani, President of the European Parliament, 20 March 2019.

European Commission (2017a), Communication on responding to challenges for critical financial market infrastructures and further developing the Capital Markets Union, No. COM/2017/0225.

European Commission (2017b), Proposal for a Regulation of the European Parliament and of the Council amending Regulation (EU) No 1095/2010 establishing a European Supervisory Authority (European Securities and Markets Authority) and amending Regulation (EU) No 648/2012 as regards the procedures and authorities involved for the authorisation of CCPs and requirements for the recognition of third-country CCPs. Procedure 2017/0136/COD. Accessed 4 January 2020 at: https://eur-lex .europa.eu/procedure/EN/2017_136.

European Commission (2017c), Communication on the mid-term review of the Capital Markets Union action plan, No. 292 final.

European Commission (2017d), Proposal for a Regulation of the European Parliament and the Council amending Regulation (EU) No 1095/2010 establishing a European Supervisory Authority (European Securities and Markets Authority) and amending Regulation (EU) No 648/2012 as regards the procedures and authorities involved for the authorisation of CCPs and requirements for the recognition of third-country CCPs, Procedure No. 2017/0136 (COD).

European Commission (2018), Commission Implementing Decision (EU) 2018/2031 of 19 December 2018 determining, for a limited period of time, that the regulatory framework applicable to central counterparties in the United Kingdom of Great Britain and Northern Ireland is equivalent, in accordance with Regulation (EU) No 648/2012 of the European Parliament and of the Council C/2018/9139, OJ L 325, 20 December 2018, pp. 50–52.

FIA (2017), Letter to Vice-President Valdis Dombrovskis, 6 June.

Financial Times (2011a), 'EU states in clearing houses authorisation push,' 9 May. Accessed 4 January 2020 at: https://www.ft.com/content/15e6b066-7a4a-11e0-bc74 -00144feabdc0.

Financial Times (2011b), 'UK gets best of compromise on Emir,' 4 October. Accessed 4 January 2020 at: https://www.ft.com/content/b51054d8-eeaf-11e0-959a -00144feab49a.

Financial Times (2016), 'François Hollande rules out City's euro clearing role,' 29 June. Accessed 4 January 2020 at: https://www.ft.com/content/e8e0c44a-3d89-11e6 -9f2c-36b487ebd80a.

Financial Times (2018a), 'Germany's Olaf Scholz suggests euro clearing be moved to Frankfurt.' Accessed 4 January 2020 at: https://www.ft.com/content/d8b0e782-6b1b -11e8-8cf3-0c230fa67aec.

Financial Times (2018b), 'Bank of France governor pushes Paris as post-Brexit clearing hub,' 23 November. Accessed 4 January 2020 at: https://www.ft.com/content/ 088ad4b0-ef09-11e8-8180-9cf212677a57.

Friedrich, J. and M. Thiemann (2017), 'Capital Markets Union: the need for common laws and common supervision,' *Vierteljahrshefte zur Wirtschaftsforschung*, **86** (2), 61–75.

Genito, L. (2019), 'Mandatory clearing: the infrastructural authority of central counterparty clearing houses in the OTC derivatives market,' *Review of International Political Economy*, **26** (5), 938–962.

German Federal Government (2014), 'Green Paper of the European Commission on a Capital Markets Union, German Comments.' Accessed 15 July 2018 at: https://ec .europa.eu/eusurvey/publication/capital-markets-union-2015.

Grossule, E. (2019), 'Risks and benefits of the increasing role of ESMA: a perspective from the OTC derivatives regulation in the Brexit period,' *European Business Organization Law Review*, 1–22.

House of Lords (2017), 'Supervision of central counterparties,' 22 November. Accessed 4 January 2020 at: https://publications.parliament.uk/pa/cm201719/cmselect/ cmeuleg/301-ii/30123.htm.

House of Lords (2018), 'Brexit: EU supervision of UK-based central counterparties.' Accessed 18 September 209 at: https://publications.parliament.uk/pa/cm201719/ cmselect/cmeuleg/301-xlv/30115.htm.

Howarth, D. and Lucia Quaglia (2018), 'Brexit and the battle for financial services,' *Journal of European Public Policy*, **25** (8), 1118–1136.

ISDA (2017), Letter to Commissioner Valdis Dombrovskis, 8 June. Accessed 5 September 2019 at: https://www.isda.org/a/i8iDE/isda-final-response-to-ec -communication-8-june-2017.pdf.

James, S. and Lucia Quaglia (2019), 'Brexit and the political economy of euro-denominated clearing,' *Review of International Political Economy*, 1–23.

Marjosola, H. (2015), 'Missing pieces in the patchwork of EU financial stability regime? The case of central counterparties,' *Common Market Law Review*, **52** (6), 1491–1527.

Moloney, N. (2017), 'Brexit and EU financial governance: business as usual or institutional change?' *European Law Review*, **42** (1), 112–128.

Quaglia, L., David Howarth and Moritz Liebe (2016), 'The political economy of European capital markets union,' *Journal of Common Market Studies*, **54**, 185–203.

Reuters (2017), 'France wants right to veto euro clearing in UK after Brexit,' 6 September. Accessed 4 January 2020 at: https://www.reuters.com/article/us-britain -eu-clearing-idUSKCN1BH1EL.

Smoleńska, A. (2017), 'Connecting and disconnecting critical financial market infra-structures: oversight and regulation of CCPs after Brexit,' in Franklin Allen, Elena Carletti, Joanna Gray and Mitu Gulati (eds), *The Changing Geography of Finance and Regulation in Europe*, Florence: Florence School of Banking and Finance, 141–151.

UK HM Treasury (2018), Letter to Sir William Cash MP, 21 November. Accessed 4 January 2020 at: http://europeanmemoranda.cabinetoffice.gov.uk/files/2018/11/EST_to_HOC_EU_Committee_-_EMIR_211118.pdf.

4. The choice of instrument for EU legislation: mapping the system of governance under MiFID II and MiFIR

Magnus Strand[1]

4.1 INTRODUCTION

Centralisation is a coat of many colours, and as is shown in this book it can be studied from many perspectives. Perhaps the broadest stripes in the pattern are those of the legal instruments governing the field at issue – in this case financial markets in the EU. This study focuses particularly on governance of EU markets in financial instruments under Directive 2014/65/EU of the European Parliament and of the Council of 15 May 2014 on markets in financial instruments [MiFID II], and Regulation (EU) No 600/2014 of the European Parliament and of the Council of 15 May 2014 on markets in financial instruments [MiFIR].

In this chapter the results of an empirical legal study are presented. It should be pointed out that legal studies are usually not empirical but hermeneutical.[2] However, this is not a hermeneutical study of what one ought or ought not to do according to the texts comprising financial market law, and consequently not a study of the normative content of this law. Instead the study focuses on whether, and if so how, the governance of financial markets in the EU has been centralised at the EU level and more particularly whether, and if so to what extent, the choice of legal instrument is relevant to the degree of centralisation.

The study is thus focused on EU legislation and the governing effects of EU rulemaking, and more specifically on comparing the degree of centralisation achieved through the different forms of regulatory acts adopted by the EU. Consequently, the effects of international treaties and agreements on EU legislation are not covered here. In other words, the overarching subject of study is how the EU institutions have used their normative powers to adopt rules creating rights and obligations for the various agents involved in transactions in EU markets in financial instruments, together with the powers of and obligations on the agencies at both the EU and national levels which have been entrusted with the monitoring and enforcement of compliance with these rules.

In this context it should be further clarified that the results of the study are only formally valid for the instruments compared, which are those governing trade in financial instruments in the EU. It is nonetheless open for discussion whether some of the results have broader implications for EU rulemaking in general. In fact, this study was designed partly to test a method that may be more generally useful to analyse EU rulemaking, using rulemaking for the financial markets as a pilot study. The precise research question will now be presented.

4.2   RESEARCH QUESTION AND MAIN RESULTS

This study was designed to explore the level and character of EU centralisation resulting from MiFID II and MiFIR in order to investigate whether there is variation in the regulatory intensity (defined below) of the two instruments, whether or not any such variation seems to be attributable to the characters of regulations and directives, and finally to ascertain whether or not the results allow a hypothesis on the deliberations that prompt the EU legislator to put certain rules in a regulation and others in a directive. Essentially, it has been tested whether a case study on MiFID II and MiFIR will falsify the common preconceptions concerning the respective characters of regulations and directives, but the study also yields some interesting ancillary results, which will be discussed below.

The relevance of regulatory intensity to this study is related to a certain aspect of law that needs to be briefly explained. The legal point of departure with regard to businesses such as investment firms and the other actors involved in the financial markets is the freedom to conduct business enshrined in Article 16 of the Charter of Fundamental Rights of the European Union and the more specific fundamental freedoms of free movement in the internal market protected by the TFEU (those most relevant here being the right of establishment (Article 49 TFEU), the free movement of services (Article 56 TFEU) and the free movement of capital (Article 63 TFEU)). These rights and freedoms are subject to limitations by law, but as a general legal point of departure any absence of legal rules governing the exercise of them means that the actors are, in principle, free to conduct their businesses as they see fit. It follows that an introduction of new rules shifts power in these markets from the businesses involved to the rulemakers, which can be described as a centralisation of power by legislative pre-emption. Rulemaking can take place in various ways and traditionally does so in national parliaments. The object of this study is, however, rulemaking in the EU. If the rulemakers at issue are at the EU level, it means centralisation of power in the EU. Therefore, a higher level of regulatory intensity in principle means a higher level of EU govern-ance through the legislative and non-legislative instruments employed and consequently a higher degree of centralisation. This legal point of departure has guided the design of this study.

On the basis of this study, it is concluded below that at a general level the choice of legislative instrument adopted by the EU legislator (a regulation or directive) did not in this case seem to have any significant impact on the level of centralisation achieved using the instrument. Instead, the rules in the instrument seem to address different agents. MiFIR mainly governs the EU levels of administration and MiFID II mainly governs the national levels of administration and the rights of and obligations on private parties. However, it is further demonstrated that the activities of national authorities are also governed through the adoption of non-legislative acts. With few exceptions, these are regulations. This means that powers conferred on EU institutions under MiFID II and MiFIR entail a possibility of pre-emption of Member State discretion, which can be described as at least potential centralisation. Moreover, the Commission has used this possibility extensively, adopting non-legislative acts constituting real centralisation. With regard to MiFID II and MiFIR, the overarching legislative acts, the common preconceptions concerning the respective characters of regulations and directives are not falsified, but the results suggest that the use of a directive to govern national administrations and private parties may conceal the fact that they are to a large extent governed through non-legislative acts in the form of regulations. This form of normative governance through non-legislative acts is perhaps the most conspicuous aspect of EU centralisation in the legal governance of financial markets found in this study.

Another legal factor deserving mention is that elements of legal uncertainty and fragmentation are inevitable in any new set of legislation. The system of governance adopted for trade in financial markets is no exception. Over time, at least some of these elements will be addressed by the European Court of Justice in the context of preliminary rulings under Article 267 TFEU. Through such rulings, legal uncertainties can be straightened out and gaps filled, grad-ually forming a more coherent set of rules. This process serves to align inter-pretations of the applicable legal acts in order to achieve uniformity in their application. Of course, the process also adds further elements of centralisation to the legislation thus addressed.

As this summary has highlighted, there are a number of aspects of EU law that need to be explained in order to allow the reader to understand this study. Therefore, before presenting the research question and the method used in more detail, it is necessary to provide some background information on the EU legal system. The focus will be on EU rulemaking.

4.3   BACKGROUND: LEGAL ACTS OF THE EU

4.3.1   The Classes of Legal Acts under Art 288 TFEU

In the EU, legislation intended to harmonise the laws of all Member States can be enacted by the EU institutions in accordance with rules and procedures laid down in the EU Treaties. Most of the details are included in the TFEU. Article 288 TFEU specifies that legal acts of the EU can be regulations, directives, decisions, recommendations or opinions. For the purpose of harmonising the regulatory system controlling financial markets in the EU, the legal acts mainly adopted are regulations and directives. These are the two most common types or classes of legal acts used by the EU legislator to adopt regulatory measures of general application. With regard to regulations and directives, Article 288 TFEU further specifies:

> A regulation shall have general application. It shall be binding in its entirety and directly applicable in all Member States.
> A directive shall be binding, as to the result to be achieved, upon each Member State to which it is addressed, but shall leave to the national authorities the choice of form and methods.

It does not follow from this description that directives are generally valid in all Member States, and historically not all directives have been designed to be binding on all Member States. It has, however, become highly unusual for a directive to not be addressed to all the Member States of the EU. Consequently, the normative content of directives (in other words, 'the result to be achieved') is generally intended to be transposed into the national legal systems of all the Member States.

The EU legislator has generally had a preference for regulations over directives (Bergström 2005: 12), and in the last 20 years this preference has spread in an unprecedented way into legislation concerning the internal market (SOU 2009: 71, 323). It is commonly accepted that this is because, as was explained in the introductory chapter of this book, EU rules are implemented differently in Member States depending on their specific national economic, political, institutional, legal and social conditions. Therefore, the outcome in terms of the regulatory structure and policy substance in the various Member States is not necessarily uniform (e.g. *H1.1*). This generally applies to directives more than to regulations. By contrast, regulations typically take less time to become legally effective (as there is no need to offer Member States a transposition period to convert their rules into national law), are applied directly and so are less vulnerable to national transposition errors, and (as a consequence) do not to the same extent as directives necessitate monitoring and enforcement of their implementation in the Member States by the Commission. A sense of urgency, such as that driving the post-crisis wave of legislation in the area of financial markets, is liable to increase the incentives for the Commission to suggest a regulation and also to lessen resistance in the Council against the choice of a regulation over a directive (de Larosière 2009: 29). This would suggest that urgency may be a factor driving centralisation. It will, however, be explained below that it may be an over-simplification to suggest that regulations per se lead to more centralisation than directives. In this regard it is interesting to notice that for the purpose of regulating trade in financial instruments the EU legislator has opted for the combination of a regulation and a directive. This has inspired the research questions below, which aim to compare and test the degree of centralisation resulting from use of these legal instruments, and to achieve a fuller understanding of EU rulemaking by differentiating between the legal actors and subject matters addressed by the rules in the legal instruments. For instance, was the choice of adding a regulation primarily triggered by a wish to govern the conduct of investment firms and other private actors in the financial markets more closely or instead by a need to regulate institutional interaction between national authorities on the one hand and EU institutions and agencies on the other?

Concerning the other classes of legal acts, it should first be noted that, in contrast to regulations and directives, decisions are usually aimed at specific addressees and are only binding on them. There are nevertheless, and interestingly, decisions of general application, some of which are part of the regulatory system controlling financial markets in the EU. Recommendations and opinions are so-called 'soft-law' instruments that are not generally binding, and they will therefore not be discussed further here.[3]

4.3.2 The Distinction between Legislative and Non-legislative Acts

The legal instruments adopted by the EU legislator can not only be sub-divided into the five classes of legal acts described in Article 288 TFEU. Another and arguably equally important distinction follows from subsequent TFEU Articles: that between legislative and non-legislative acts.

The latter term is somewhat counter-intuitive as non-legislative acts are indeed binding legal acts that are enacted as regulations, directives or any other class of legal act described under Article 288 TFEU. The concepts of 'legislative acts' and 'non-legislative acts' are not intended to indicate any difference in the binding nature of the instruments within these categories. Instead, they indicate the legislative procedure which is used by the EU legislator to adopt the legal acts in question. In this regard, Article 289(3) TFEU specifies that "[l]egal acts adopted by legislative procedure shall constitute legislative acts."

By contrast, legal acts adopted in any other way than by legislative procedure constitute non-legislative acts.

By 'legislative procedure' Article 289 TFEU means the ordinary legislative procedure (see Articles 289(1) and 294 TFEU) and the various special legislative procedures provided for in the EU Treaties to accommodate particular policy areas (see Articles 289(2) and, for example, 86(1) TFEU). With regard to the regulatory system applicable to markets in financial instruments in the EU, there are at present two central instruments that have been adopted by legislative procedure and that are consequently legislative acts: MiFID II and MiFIR.

The TFEU explicitly outlines two sub-categories of non-legislative acts: delegated acts and implementing acts. Under Article 290 TFEU, legislative acts may include provisions on a delegation of power to the Commission to adopt non-legislative acts of general application in order to supplement or amend "certain non-essential elements of the legislative act". Such non-legislative acts adopted by the Commission are delegated acts, and they are subject to special conditions laid down in the legislative acts delegating power to the Commission. Similarly, under Article 291 TFEU, the Commission (or exceptionally the Council) is empowered to adopt non-legislative acts in situations where "uniform conditions for implementing legally binding Union acts are needed". These non-legislative acts are implementing acts and they are subject to control by the Member States under Regulation (EU) No. 182/2011 of the European Parliament and of the Council of 16 February 2011 laying down the rules and general principles concerning mechanisms for control by Member States of the Commission's exercise of implementing powers.

Member States, however, have much less control over non-legislative acts than legislative acts, notwithstanding the conditions for delegation and the control mechanisms in Regulation (EU) No. 182/2011. As non-legislative acts need to pass neither through the European Parliament or the Council, and nor to pass through the procedure for national parliamentary review of new EU acts under Protocol (No 2) on the Application of the Principles of Subsidiarity and Proportionality, there is an absence of strong veto players in the rulemaking process (*H2*). This is liable to drive centralisation by Commission rulemaking, as the Commission will be tempted to increase its institutional power in order to more effectively control the financial markets.

As will be demonstrated below, many provisions in MiFID II and MiFIR include delegations of power to the Commission to adopt non-legislative acts, and these powers have been used to adopt more than 50 non-legislative acts. The adoption of such non-legislative acts by the Commission inevitably involves what in this book we have called 'intentional uploading of formal legislative rule-making and rule supervision to the supranational level'. In order to decide whether this includes real centralisation we would also need to analyse the rules in the non-legislative acts to ascertain whether they are prescriptive in detail (*H4.1* and *H4.2*). While it can be hypothesised that elements in these non-legislative acts adopted by the Commission do meet the definition, it is beyond the scope of this contribution to analyse the content of rules in non-legislative acts. The focus here is instead on the rules in MiFID II and MiFIR themselves. Nonetheless, delegations of powers to the Commission and its use of those powers are mapped.

4.3.3 Non-legislative Acts Adopted by EU Agencies

Legal instruments are not only adopted by EU institutions, however, but also by bodies, offices and agencies of the EU (EU agencies) when they have been empowered to do so by delegation from an EU institution. As will be indicated below, this has occurred under MiFID II and MiFIR, as certain acts have been adopted by the European Securities and Markets Authority (ESMA). Consequently, the ESMA and other EU agencies can have a number of capacities in the governance of financial markets in the EU, including normative capacity, making them a kind of 'regulatory intermediaries' (Abbott et al. 2017). Indeed, among the European supervisory agencies involved in the governance of the financial markets in the EU, the ESMA is the one holding the most comprehensive set of powers, both to directly monitor actors in these markets and to take action to sanction non-compliance with EU law.

The delegation of normative powers by the EU institutions to specialised agencies is not new but dates back to the European Coal and Steel Community. In its classic case law on this matter, including case 9/56 *Meroni*, EU:C:1958:7 and case 98/80 *Romano*, EU:C:1981:4, the European Court of Justice has adopted quite stringent conditions for the delegation of normative powers to EU agencies. The extent and the circumstances under which EU agencies should be able to adopt binding norms – what we would now call non-legislative acts – have continued to be a matter of some legal debate (Lenaerts 1993; Schammo 2011; van Cleynenbreugel 2014; Bergström 2015; Chamon 2016: 185–199). Recent case law, such as case C-270/12 *UK v EP and Council (Short selling)*, EU:C:2014:18, suggests that the Court of Justice has relaxed its previous approach, or at least that it has substituted the conditions for the delegation of powers in its early case law with new conditions and will tolerate the delegation of powers to EU agencies, including the power to adopt non-legislative acts of general application and non-legislative acts that are addressed to, and legally binding on, specific individuals (van Cleynenbreugel 2014; Bergström 2015). The conditions set out in the *Short selling* case are essentially that:

1. There is a legal basis for EU legislation on the matter at issue;
2. The delegation of powers is precisely delineated and amenable to judicial review; and
3. The delegation of powers is confined to an area which requires the deployment of specific expertise.[4]

Arguably, these conditions amount to an expansion of the possibilities for EU institutions to delegate supranational normative power to EU agencies (van Cleynenbreugel 2014: 88). It has therefore been submitted that the new approach of the Court of Justice risks tilting the institutional balance of powers within the EU unless the institutions find a way to arrange for mutual political supervision of their delegations of power (Bergström 2015: 241–242; Chamon 2016: 227 and 246–248).

Regardless of whether this will come to pass, it should be observed for our present purposes that the new approach of the Court of Justice has further enabled the ongoing centralisation of EU rulemaking. Non-legislative acts inevitably involve what we call 'intentional uploading of formal legislative rule-making and rule supervision to the supranational level'. In order to decide whether this includes real centralisation we would also need to analyse the rules in the non-legislative acts to ascertain whether they are prescriptive in detail (*H4.1* and *H4.2*). As with non-legislative acts adopted by the Commission, it can be hypothesised that elements of these non-legislative acts adopted by the ESMA will include centralisation. Nonetheless their normative content will not be analysed here, as the focus is on the rules in MiFID II and MiFIR.

4.3.4   Overview: Non-legislative Acts Adopted under MiFID II and MiFIR

Among the legal acts applicable to markets in financial instruments in the EU, MiFID II (a directive) and MiFIR (a regulation) are both legislative acts and were adopted by the EU legislator under the ordinary legislative procedure. However, these two legislative acts are (at the time of writing and excluding instruments not in force and instruments amending other instruments) complemented by no less than 54 non-legislative acts, 52 of which have been adopted by the Commission. With a few exceptions, these non-legislative acts are regulations and the majority are delegated acts (see Table 4.1).

As is apparent from this simple table, the possibility of delegating normative powers to the ESMA has not been used particularly often under MiFID II and MiFIR. Instead, the non-legislative acts in this field have with only a few exceptions been adopted by the Commission. It is further apparent that the legislative instrument of preference is the regulation, an instrument which, under Article 288 TFEU, is of general application and which is binding in its

Table 4.1   *Non-legislative acts adopted under MiFID II and MiFIR*

Type of non-legislative act	Total no. of acts of this type	Acts adopted by	Classes of legal acts
Delegated acts	40	Commission: 40	Regulations: 39 Directives: 1
Implementing acts	12	Commission: 12	Regulations: 11 Decisions: 1
Other acts based on delegation of normative powers	2	ESMA: 2	Decisions: 2

entirety and directly applicable in all Member States, even where the power to adopt non-legislative acts has been conferred on the Commission by MiFID II, which is a directive. Indeed, the Commission has adopted 50 regulations under MiFID II and MiFIR but only one directive (and one decision). By contrast, under the previous regime, that is under the legislative act Directive 2004/39/ EC of the European Parliament and of the Council of 21 April 2004 on markets in financial instruments (MiFID I, not accompanied by any regulation adopted as a legislative act), which was in force from 30 April 2004 to 2 January 2018, the Commission only adopted a total of four non-legislative acts.

However, the observation that most of these non-legislative acts have been adopted by the Commission risks concealing a central trait shared by most of the non-legislative acts adopted under MiFID II and MiFIR, namely that they have been drafted by the ESMA for adoption by the Commission under the procedure for so-called technical standards. Under Regulation (EU) No 1095/2010 of the European Parliament and of the Council of 24 November 2010 establishing a European Supervisory Authority (ESMA), power is conferred on the ESMA to draft technical standards in the form of implementing (implementing technical standards (ITS), Article 15) or delegated acts (regulatory technical standards (RTS), Articles 10–14). The latter form is the more common under MiFID II and is the only one used under MiFIR. Among the non-legislative acts adopted by the Commission under MiFID II and MiFIR, only two regulations, one directive and one decision are neither RTS nor ITS. Of course, the decisions adopted by the ESMA under MiFID II and MiFIR are neither RTS nor ITS. In essence, this means that the ESMA assists the Commission in joint efforts to effectively control the financial markets. This is likely to further reinforce the impetus towards centralisation.

Under Articles 16(12) and 24 of MiFID II, the delegated directive at issue is designed to "specify the concrete organizational requirements (...) to be imposed on investment firms" and to "ensure that investment firms comply" with certain general principles related to information to clients. Just like the regulations, the directive was drafted in close cooperation with the ESMA, which, as is stated in the preamble (recital 32) of the delegated directive, "has been consulted for technical advice".

The decisions adopted have two distinctive characters. The first category of decisions is where the Commission or the ESMA acts under a specific delegation, for instance to pronounce that trading venues in a certain third country under supervision are to be considered equivalent to those in the EU, or that trade in a certain class of financial instrument is temporarily restricted. Decisions belonging to this first category are published in the Official Journal of the EU. The second category consists of decisions adopted by the ESMA board of directors delegating powers to the ESMA Chair in situations where a large number of decisions of a technical nature must be taken and it would be an administrative burden for the board of directors to do it themselves. Such decisions are not published in the Official Journal of the EU but only on the ESMA website.

4.4 THE PRESENT RESEARCH INTEREST

The study presented in this chapter is focused on the distinctive features of regulations and directives in an attempt to ascertain an indication of the extent to which the choice of legal instrument has an impact on the degree of central-isation. As described above, whereas directives specify a set of rules, and their purposes, to be transposed into national law by the Member States in a manner suitable to their national regulatory contexts, regulations are uniformly worded and cannot be reframed or altered by the Member States in any respect. In the light of these characteristics of regulations and directives it may seem a need-less endeavour to distinguish whether MiFID II (the directive) or MiFIR (the regulation) includes a higher degree of centralisation. Since regulations have general application, are binding in their entirety and are directly applicable in all Member States, while directives are only binding in terms of the result to be achieved, it would seem to follow that a higher degree of centralisation should be achieved through regulations than through directives.[5] This is certainly an important factor in the study, but there are reasons to question whether harmo-nisation of laws in the EU through a regulation necessarily comprises more centralisation than through a directive.

First, experience shows that the binding force of regulations will sometimes prompt the EU legislator to include various exceptions. Such exceptions can be made for specific Member States, exempting them from the scope of applica-tion of the regulation. For instance, Denmark, Ireland and the United Kingdom have opted to stay outside certain aspects of EU harmonisation within the area of freedom, security and justice, and consequently regulations in this area include declarations that these Member States are not included in the scope of the instrument. An example of this can be seen in Regulation (EU) No

1215/2012 on jurisdiction and the recognition and enforcement of judgments in civil and commercial matters, recitals 40–41. Exceptions for the purpose of passing a regulation can also appear in the form of exceptions aimed at a specific issue that is sensitive for a certain Member State. For instance, Regulation (EU) 2016/679 on the protection of natural persons with regard to the processing of personal data (GDPR) includes exceptions designed to allow public access to official documents in Article 86 and recital 154. These were added as some Member States would block the Regulation without them (Bergström and Ruotsi 2018). This tendency to include exceptions, of whatever kind, in order to pass a draft regulation through the Council can give rise to what might be called a 'brittlefication' of regulations, in the sense that they may be binding and directly applicable but only at the cost of a diminished normative force, leaving them a more brittle type of instrument than directives. It may also be described as a form of regulatory fragmentation. Hypothetically, therefore, the choice of legal instrument is not determined bluntly by an endeavour to achieve uniform rules and a uniform application of them, but must be contextualised with a view to specifically understanding the political dynamics of the policy field at issue within and between the EU institutions that partake in the legislative procedure at issue.

Second, it has been demonstrated that an EU dimension to rulemaking can in itself have a negative impact on the legitimacy of new rules (Baldwin 1996). In European constitutional tradition, legal obligations on individuals imposed by the State (in contrast to legal obligations towards other individuals, governed by civil law) should be based on legislation passed by the national parliament. The most obvious example of this is perhaps the criminal law maxim *nulla poena sine lege*. This raises some questions on whether the choice of legal instrument, or more specifically the choice of the type of rules to allocate to MiFID II (a directive) or to MiFIR (a regulation) includes considerations of legitimacy in the European constitutional tradition. The EU legislator is fully constitutionally capable under Article 288 TFEU to adopt regulations including not only rights but also obligations for individuals, and if regulations do this then those rights and obligations are directly applicable before national courts and agencies. By contrast, the legal contents of a directive must be transposed into national law by each Member State, usually by an act of its parliament, thus legitimising their regulatory content under the national constitution. Indeed, this author has a distinct sense that the EU legislator avoids including substantive legal obligations on individuals in regulations (proving this would entail an ambitious big data analysis) and it might bolster the legitimacy of new rules if EU legislation including more substantive legal obligations on private individuals (including commercial enterprises) is adopted in the form of directives. To reconnect again to the example of criminal law, one might notice that the EU has the competence to adopt regulations on the structure and work of the EU agencies Eurojust and EPPO under Articles 85 and 86 TFEU, while rules on the definition of criminal offences and sanctions are to be adopted in directives under Article 83 TFEU. It does not seem far-fetched therefore to suggest that the EU legislator, recognising the sensitivity of constitutional legitimacy connected to passing legislation with legal obligations on individuals, might prefer to do so through directives. A hypothetical consequence of these factors is that the EU legislator's choice of legal instrument depends not so much on the extent to which it wishes to centralise or harmonise rules and policymaking, but rather to whom the rules and policies at issue are aimed. These considerations have inspired the choice of research question addressed in this study.

4.5   METHOD

Against this background, the concept of 'regulatory intensity' is introduced, it being understood that the concept is neutral to whether the EU legislator has opted for a regulation or a directive (or, theoretically, any other form of act) as the instrument containing the rules at issue. By regulatory intensity is meant:

1. A binding character of rules in the application stage (at which point, as regards directives, the regulatory content of the directive should ideally be fully and faithfully transposed into national law with a binding effect matching the intentions of the EU legislator);
2. The level of regulatory detail in rules, including
   a.   the amount of detail in the binding text passed by the EU legislator;
   b.   the inclusion of further guiding details in the preamble to the binding text; and
   c.   a passing of non-legislative acts adding further detail to the binding text of the instrument on which the non-legislative act is based.

In an effort to estimate the regulatory intensity of the legal texts studied here, they have been scrutinised in order to determine the points listed in the definition above.

In order to obtain workable data, the texts have been processed as follows:

1. The rules in the texts have been coded into the following categories:
   a.   Legal obligations (i.e. where it is indicated that an authority or other person 'shall' do something, or other expressions to this effect);
   b.   Discretionary powers (i.e. where it is indicated that an authority 'may' do something, or other expressions to this effect);

c. Substantive rights (i.e. where it is indicated that a private party – a legal person such as a commercial enterprise – 'may' do something, or other expressions to this effect).

When measuring regulatory intensity, it is understood that legal obligations represent imperatives that are binding on the regulatory addressee, that is, on the entity upon which the legal obligation is imposed. Discretionary powers and substantive rights, by contrast, provide leeway for the regulatory addressees to act in accordance with their own interests.

It should be further noticed that many legal obligations on one party have a flipside in the form of a legal right for another. For instance, the duty for a competent authority to do something to the benefit of investment firms can be seen as constituting a right for investment firms that the task at issue is carried out with due diligence. The analysis, however, focuses exclusively on the immediate meaning of the wordings used in the rules analysed, consequently disregarding such implicit legal consequences.

2. The level of detail in the individual rules has been coded as 'low', 'medium' or 'high', where a low level indicates that there is only a short sentence, medium indicates a long sentence or a few sentences, and high indicates several or many sentences. To this end, rules that stretch over several paragraphs in the text, and ones in which the same type of imperative has been repeated to the same regulatory addressee within a paragraph, and combinations of these two, have been regarded as one single rule as long as the general character of the instructions in the legal text remains unchanged.

3. The occurrence of further guiding details in the preamble to the individual rules is coded only as occurring or not occurring, without scrutiny of the amount of detail in the individual preamble recitals. It is noticed that in one instance there is a cross-reference from the MiFIR preamble to a MiFID II rule, but this instance is ignored.

4. The occurrence of further guiding details in non-legislative acts has only been coded as occurring or as not occurring without scrutiny of the content of the rules in the non-legislative acts (such as the amount of detail). Non-legislative acts are identified by using the databases on the ESMA website ('Single rulebook') and EUR-Lex. Only non-legislative acts in force by 1 January 2020 have been included. Non-legislative acts amending or correcting other non-legislative acts have been omitted.

Some rules have been omitted from the study. The omitted rules are on definitions, on the scope of application of the instrument or of certain provisions in the instruments, on amendments or alterations in other instruments, and transitional provisions.

Certain characteristics of EU legislation have also prompted reclassification of the person addressed by rules. Where provisions are phrased so as to be aimed at private parties (e.g. investment firms) they have only been listed if they appear in separate paragraphs. Where they appear in the context of a paragraph aimed at a Member State or competent authority, they have instead been seen as being included in the instructions for the Member State or competent authority to attain a specific objective. Conversely, in MiFID II, rules may be phrased so as to be aimed at the Member States but the instruction may be for the Member States to enact legal obligations on private parties. It has been assumed for the purposes of this study that the regulatory content of a directive has been fully and faithfully transposed into national laws with a binding effect matching the intentions of the EU legislator, and accordingly such rules in MiFIR II have been classified as legal obligations on the private parties at issue in order not to thwart the ability of the study to provide useful answers to the research questions asked.

Because of the relative simplicity of the intended analysis, no statistical tools have been used. Instead, the quantifications of regulatory intensity ascertained for MiFID II and MiFIR, as a whole and in relation to the regulatory addressees (i.e. a public or private entity, the behaviour of which a rule is intended to govern), have been straightforwardly compared.

Table 4.2   *Overview of rules in MiFID II and MiFIR*

Instrument and sum total of rules analysed	No. of rules imposing legal obligations, percentage	No. of rules conferring discretionary powers, percentage	No. of rules conferring substantive rights, percentage	No. of non-legislative acts based on instrument	No. of preamble recitals offering guidance
MiFID II, 427 rules	305, 71%	109, 26%	13, 3%	34	97
MiFIR, 309 rules	227, 73%	71, 23%	11, 4%	21	30

4.6   RESULTS

4.6.1   Observations at the General Level

Table 4.2 is an overview of the results for the entire instruments. Percentages are rounded off to whole numbers. Note that there are two rules in MiFID II and six rules in MiFIR that stipulate joint responsibilities for actors, for example, the ESMA and competent authorities. For the purposes of this study it is necessary to code each of these rules as two separate rules aimed at the two respective regulatory addressees concerned.

This very general comparison of MiFID II and MiFIR reveals little or no significant differences between them. In other words, the two instruments seem to have very similar regulatory intensity. Their respective balances between rules stipulating legal obligations, discretionary powers and substantive rights are quite well matched. The number of non-legislative acts adopted on the basis of the respective instruments also seems proportionate to the number of rules in them, and the same goes for connections between non-legislative acts and the rules in the instruments (a total of 108 connections in MiFID II, and a total of 82 connections in MiFIR, which are data not listed in Table 4.2). Only the numbers of substantively guiding recitals in their preambles seems to differ in any tangible way, although, interestingly, if Table 4.2 had instead displayed the number of connections between recitals and rules (as Tables 4.3–4.8 below do) the difference would be reversed (258 connections in MiFID II but as many as 313 in MiFIR, which are data not listed in Table 4.2). However, this has been considered a random variation that cannot serve as the basis for any conclusions.

In Table 4.3, results are listed for MiFID II and MiFIR distinguished by reference to the level of detail in the rules analysed. All the percentages are of the sum total in the categories (cf. Table 4.2).

With regard to connections between non-legislative acts and rules, on the one hand, and preamble recitals and rules, on the other hand, note that many non-legislative acts and many preamble recitals are connected to more than one of the rules analysed. As a consequence, Table 4.3 does not divulge, for example, that connections may have differing characters. For instance, one rule with a high level of detail connected to 10 recitals will register equally as 10 rules with a low level of detail connected to one single preamble recital.

Table 4.3 further suggests that rules stipulating legal obligations and rules conferring substantive rights have higher regulatory intensity in MiFID II as compared to MiFIR, while on the contrary rules conferring discretionary powers have higher regulatory intensity in MiFIR as compared to MiFID II. This difference has been considered interesting, and it was therefore decided to distinguish further between regulatory addressees in order to ascertain whether the variation in regulatory intensity is in some way distributed between regulatory addressees.

As a first step in this endeavour, the data were re-grouped on the basis of classes of regulatory addressees, that is, eliminating the previous distinction. Table 4.4 therefore lists quantities of MiFID II and MiFIR rules distinguished by their regulatory addressees, that is, the type of entity upon which the rules

Table 4.3   *Overview by level of detail in rules*

Instrument and level of detail in rules analysed	No. of rules imposing legal obligations, percentage of total in Table 4.2	No. of rules conferring discretionary powers, percentage of total in Table 4.2	No. of rules conferring substantive rights, percentage of total in Table 4.2	No. of connections between non-legislative acts and rules analysed, percentage of total in instrument	No. of connections between preamble recitals and rules analysed, percentage of total in instrument
MiFID II, low level of detail	223, 73%	95, 87%	5, 38%	55, 51%	150, 58%
MiFID II, medium level of detail	33, 11%	9, 8%	3, 23%	14, 13%	28, 11%
MiFID II, high level of detail	49, 16%	5, 5%	5, 38%	39, 36%	80, 31%
MiFIR, low level of detail	171, 75%	54, 76%	7, 64%	50, 61%	220, 70%
MiFIR, medium level of detail	38, 17%	3, 4%	1, 9%	13, 16%	54, 17%
MiFIR, high level of detail	18, 8%	14, 20%	3, 27%	19, 23%	39, 12%

analysed impose an obligation or confer discretion/rights. The regulatory addressees named in the texts have been categorised as:

1. EU institutions;
2. EU agencies (e.g. the ESMA);
3. National legislators, governments and competent authorities (shorthand: MS actors);
4. Private parties (e.g. investment firms and market operators, shorthand: private parties).

All the percentages are of the sum total in the categories (cf. Table 4.2). N/A means not applicable.

With regard to rules imposing legal obligations, Table 4.4 suggests that EU institutions and agencies are mostly addressed through MiFIR rules, while Member State actors (e.g. national legislators and authorities) are more often addressed through MiFID II. Concerning discretionary powers and substantive rights, on the other hand, Table 4.4 suggests very few differences in the entities addressed by the rules in the respective instruments. It should, however, be noticed that the balance in the conferral of discretionary powers in both instruments is to the benefit of EU institutions, suggesting a clear element of centralisation.

By contrast, Table 4.4 includes interesting differences with regard to private parties. There is a comparatively larger proportion of rules conferring legal obligations on private parties in MiFIR than in MiFID II, although the reverse situation might have been expected under the constitutional view that legal obligations on individuals should be enacted by national parliaments (which would in the EU law context take place in the process of transposing a directive into national law). This has been seen as a further indication that the variation in regulatory intensity is in some way distributed between regulatory addressees, warranting further study of the details of this distribution. Finally, concerning discretionary powers and substantive rights, it is not possible to identify in Table 4.4 any significant differences between the entities addressed by the rules in the respective instruments.

Below, the rules listed in Table 4.4 are examined in more detail, mapping regulatory intensity in relation to the regulatory addressees.

4.6.2 Observations at the Detailed Level

Tables 4.5–4.8 allow comparison of the regulatory intensity in the two instruments according to the regulatory addressees. At this level, interesting differences appear. First, it is apparent that rules aimed at the EU institutions and EU agencies have a higher regulatory intensity in MiFIR than in MiFID II. Second,

Table 4.4   *Overview by regulatory addressee*

Instrument and regulatory addressee	No. of rules imposing legal obligations, percentage of total in Table 4.2	No. of rules conferring discretionary powers, percentage of total in Table 4.2	No. of rules conferring substantive rights, percentage of total in Table 4.2
MiFID II, EU institutions	15, 5%	59, 54%	N/A
MiFID II, EU agencies	79, 26%	12, 11%	N/A
MiFID II, MS actors	160, 52%	38, 35%	N/A
MiFID II, private parties	51, 17%	N/A	13, 100%
MiFIR, EU institutions	34, 15%	39, 55%	N/A
MiFIR, EU agencies	98, 43%	10, 14%	N/A
MiFIR, MS actors	32, 14%	22, 31%	N/A
MiFIR, private parties	63, 28%	N/A	11, 100%

by contrast, it is apparent that rules aimed at Member State actors have higher regulatory intensity in MiFID II than in MiFIR. These tendencies are perhaps to be expected in view of the respective roles of regulations and directives. Third, however, with regard to the rights and obligations of private parties under the two instruments, it is much more difficult to see any obvious pattern.

Comparing rules aimed at EU institutions

Table 4.5 shows the rules aimed at EU institutions (i.e. the Commission, the Council and the European Parliament, although the last two only appear very scarcely), differentiating between rules creating legal obligations and discretionary powers, and differentiating by the level of regulatory intensity of the rules.

With regard to legal obligations conferred on EU institutions, it must be kept in mind that it further follows from Table 4.4 that EU institutions are more often addressed in MiFIR (34 rules creating legal obligations) than in MiFID II (15 rules to that effect). With this said, it also appears from Table 4.5 that a larger proportion of the MiFID II rules have a high regulatory intensity. The absolute numbers of rules with high regulatory intensity are nevertheless almost the same, five in MiFID II and four in MiFIR, and only the latter have any connection to the preamble, albeit only to one recital. Furthermore, MiFIR includes legal obligations on EU institutions with medium intensity which are also connected to preamble recitals, whereas MiFID II contains no rules with medium intensity.

Rules giving EU institutions discretionary powers are more common, the vast majority being rules with a low regulatory intensity. It was noticed in connection with Table 4.4 that the amount of conferral of discretionary powers to EU institutions suggests a clear element of centralisation. Most of these are short rules to the effect that the Commission has the power to adopt non-legislative acts drafted by the ESMA and/or other EU agencies. This will be discussed further below. Table 4.5 shows that there is a larger ratio of rules with high regulatory intensity in MiFIR than in MiFID II, but the absolute numbers are small and it is therefore difficult to make reliable comparisons.

Overall, Table 4.5 adds little to Table 4.4 but confirms that there are more rules stipulating legal obligations on EU institutions in MiFIR than there are in MiFID II. The regulatory intensity of the two instruments is difficult to compare but it is to be noted that only MiFIR contains legal obligations with medium regulatory intensity. Therefore, the level of regulatory intensity might, in the aggregate, be described as slightly higher in MiFIR than in MiFID II with regard to legal obligations on EU institutions.

Table 4.5   *Rules aimed at EU institutions*

Instrument and level of detail in rules analysed	No. of rules imposing legal obligations, percentage of total in Table 4.4	No. of rules conferring discretionary powers, percentage of total in Table 4.4	No. of connections between non-legislative acts and rules analysed, percentage of total in Table 4.3		No. of connections between preamble recitals and rules analysed, percentage of total in Table 4.3	
			Legal obligations	Discretionary powers	Legal obligations	Discretionary powers
MiFID II, low level of detail	10, 67%	55, 93%	0	0	6, 4%	9, 6%
MiFID II, medium level of detail	0	2, 3%	0	0	0	0
MiFID II, high level of detail	5, 33%	2, 3%	0	0	0	0
MiFIR, low level of detail	23, 68%	34, 87%	0	0	5, 2%	30, 14%
MiFIR, medium level of detail	7, 21%	1, 3%	0	0	4, 7%	0
MiFIR, high level of detail	4, 12%	4, 10%	0	0	1, 3%	7, 18%

Comparing rules aimed at EU agencies

In Table 4.6 rules are assembled that are aimed at EU agencies (predominantly the ESMA, but also the European Banking Authority (EBA), the European Securities Committee and the Agency for the Cooperation of Energy Regulators), with differentiation between rules creating legal obligations and discretionary powers and differentiation by the level of regulatory intensity of the rules.

Going back to Table 4.4, it follows from that table that, as with EU institutions, the legal obligations on EU agencies have more often been enacted through MiFIR (98 rules creating legal obligations) than through MiFID II (74 rules). The difference is even clearer when we focus on the percentages in Table 4.4, where it was shown that as much as 43 per cent of the legal obligations stipulated in MiFIR are aimed at EU agencies. By contrast, legal obligations stipulated in MiFID II only aim at EU agencies in 26 per cent of the instances. Many of the legal obligations on EU agencies in both instruments consist in an instruction to draft non-legislative acts for adoption by the Commission. Other common duties include to interact with and, in various ways, to support national authorities in their monitoring activities. Comparing the regulatory intensity of the two instruments, it does not seem there is much difference but, as with EU institutions, MiFIR contains more legal obligations with medium regulatory intensity, and the rules have served as bases for more non-legislative acts. Consequently, it seems that the regulatory intensity in rules stipulating legal obligations on EU agencies is slightly higher in MiFIR than in MiFID II.

By contrast, there is a clear difference when we look at rules conferring discretionary powers on EU agencies. In this sample, there is a much larger proportion of rules with high regulatory intensity in MiFIR (four rules) than in MiFID II (one rule). Admittedly, the numbers are not large, but it should be further noted that there are four non-legislative acts adopted on the basis of MiFIR rules with high regulatory intensity while there are none based on MiFID II rules with high regulatory intensity. One example of such a rule is Articles 40 and 41 in MiFIR, under which the ESMA and the EBA are granted temporary intervention powers in the event that the agency needs to address "a significant investor protection concern or a threat to the orderly functioning and integrity of the financial markets or to the stability of the whole or part of the financial system in the Union", and the issue has not been and cannot be properly addressed otherwise. Another of the rules concerned, Article 45, is similar in nature, while the last, Article 49, serves similar interests but concerns the activities of third-country firms specifically. It is very interesting in this context to notice that under Articles 40, 41 and 45, the Commission is given the power to adopt delegated acts specifying "criteria and factors to be taken into account" by the EU agencies in their assessment of whether they

Table 4.6   *Rules aimed at EU agencies*

Instrument and level of detail in rules analysed	No. of rules imposing legal obligations, percentage of total in Table 4.4	No. of rules conferring discretionary powers, percentage of total in Table 4.4	No. of connections between non-legislative acts and rules analysed, percentage of total in Table 4.3		No. of connections between preamble recitals and rules analysed, percentage of total in Table 4.3	
			Legal obligations	Discretionary powers	Legal obligations	Discretionary powers
MiFID II, low level of detail	64, 81%	11, 92%	4, 7%	4, 7%	29, 19%	5, 3%
MiFID II, medium level of detail	6, 8%	0	0	0	1, 4%	0
MiFID II, high level of detail	9, 11%	1, 8%	0	0	3, 4%	0
MiFIR, low level of detail	74, 76%	6, 60%	6, 12%	1, 2%	62, 28%	7, 3%
MiFIR, medium level of detail	15, 15%	0	1, 8%	0	28, 52%	0
MiFIR, high level of detail	9, 9%	4, 40%	0	4, 21%	10, 26%	4, 10%

should proceed to use their temporary intervention powers (cf. the afore-mentioned *Meroni* case). The Commission has also done this: the criteria and factors at issue are laid down (for the purposes of all three Articles) in Commission Delegated Regulation (EU) 2017/567. Recitals 29–31 in the pre-amble to MiFIR are, moreover, relevant in this context. Evidently, quite some attention has been devoted to these issues by the EU legislator, seemingly in order to control the use of temporary intervention powers.

In sum, it follows from Tables 4.4 and 4.6 that there are more rules govern-ing EU agencies in MiFIR than in MiFID II, suggesting again that at the EU level of the system of governance in the financial markets, MiFIR offers more centralisation than MiFID II. It was demonstrated through Table 4.6 that there is no significant difference in regulatory intensity between the two instruments as regards the legal obligations of EU agencies but that there is a significant difference concerning their discretionary powers. Analysis of the rules in question has allowed the hypothesis that the reason behind this difference is that the EU legislator has wished to control EU agencies' use of temporary intervention powers.

Comparing rules aimed at Member State actors
In Table 4.7 is displayed the design of rules aimed at one or another emana-tion of the Member States of the EU, commonly the authorities designated to monitor the financial markets but also Member State legislators and govern-ments. All these regulatory addressees have been grouped together as 'Member state actors.' Rules creating legal obligations have been distinguished from rules conferring discretionary powers and the level of regulatory intensity of the rules has been introduced as a variable.

It was concluded from Table 4.4 that legal obligations on Member State actors are mostly stipulated in MiFID II, with such duties for Member States making up 52 per cent of the legal obligations listed in this instrument. Notably, this figure does not include legal obligations on private parties, constituting another 17 per cent of the rules in MiFID II, which are (or should be) listed in the instrument as obligations on the Member States to enact these obligations through national legislation or the like. In any event, the majority of legal obligations in MiFID II are aimed at Member State actors. In MiFIR, the reverse is true, as the legal obligations in the latter instrument are only aimed at Member State actors in 14 per cent of instances, which is the smallest proportion of legal obligations in that instrument. These differences coincide with expectations of the respective functions of regulations and directives.

Contemplating Table 4.7, and focusing first on rules conferring legal obli-gations on Member State actors, it seems that the regulatory intensity of these rules is equivalent in MiFID II and MiFIR. However, a startling difference appears if the focus is turned to the number of connections to non-legislative

Table 4.7   *Rules aimed at Member State actors*

Instrument and level of detail in rules analysed	No. of rules imposing legal obligations, percentage (of total in Table 4.4)	No. of rules conferring discretionary powers, percentage (of total in Table 4.4)	No. of connections between non-legislative acts and rules analysed, percentage of total in Table 4.3		No. of connections between preamble recitals and rules analysed, percentage of total in Table 4.3	
			Legal obligations	Discretionary powers	Legal obligations	Discretionary powers
MiFID II, low level of detail	136, 85%	29, 76%	33, 60%	5, 9%	71, 47%	23, 15%
MiFID II, medium level of detail	14, 9%	7, 18%	2, 14%	0	18, 64%	2, 7%
MiFID II, high level of detail	10, 6%	2, 5%	3, 8%	0	13, 16%	2, 3%
MiFIR, low level of detail	27, 84%	14, 64%	5, 10%	6, 12%	35, 16%	16, 7%
MiFIR, medium level of detail	3, 9%	2, 9%	1, 8%	1, 8%	5, 9%	0
MiFIR, high level of detail	2, 6%	6, 27%	1, 5%	7, 37%	2, 5%	1, 3%

acts based on these rules and the number of connections with preamble recitals. In MiFID II, 60 per cent of the connections to non-legislative acts are in legal obligations with low regulatory intensity. Furthermore, 47 per cent of the connections to preamble recitals are in legal obligations with low regulatory intensity and, moreover, 64 per cent of the connections to preamble recitals are in legal obligations with medium regulatory intensity. No similar emphasis follows from the corresponding MiFIR samples. In rules with high regulatory intensity there are also more connections to both non-legislative acts and to preamble recitals in MiFID II rules than in MiFIR rules, but the difference is less conspicuous. The data do not allow any in-depth analysis of the rules concerned but only of the general tendency, which suggests that legal obligations on Member States laid down in MiFID II with low regulatory intensity are to a comparatively very high degree elaborated in preamble recitals and in non-legislative acts. There is a much lesser tendency to do this in MiFIR. As for the reason why this is so, it is difficult to put forward any hypothesis related to the substantive content of the rules; the picture that emerges from the data is fragmented. It may, however, be worth pointing out that there are 11 non-legislative acts adopted under MiFID II laying down implementing technical standards, but none under MiFIR. If this is taken as an indication, it seems there is a greater degree of hidden centralisation taking place under MiFID II than under MiFIR in the form of non-legislative acts partially pre-empting the margin of discretion for national authorities. This hypothesis warrants further study, for which there is no room here.

Second, with regard to the rules giving Member State actors discretionary powers, Table 4.7 indicates that it is more common for rules in MiFIR to have high regulatory intensity than it is in MiFID II. There are also significantly more connections to non-legislative acts in rules on discretionary powers of Member State actors in MiFIR (14 acts) than in MiFID II (five acts). The rules at issue give power to national authorities to, for example, grant authorisation to private parties and to waive or suspend some of their obligations. It was noted in the course of the study that most if not all such powers for national authorities are coupled with a power for the ESMA and/or the Commission to circumscribe the margin of appreciation for national authorities by adopting non-legislative acts specifying how that power can be used. Consequently, the reason behind the high regulatory intensity is hypothetically the same, in essence, as in the MiFID II rules on legal obligations on Member State actors. This does not seem to have been necessary in the few corresponding MiFID II rules.

To summarise, there seems to be a tendency to control the activities of national authorities through non-legislative acts and through preamble recitals. In MiFID II, the tendency is obvious in relation to legal obligations on Member State actors, while in MiFIR it is comparatively stronger in relation to discretionary powers for Member State actors. The data do not lend themselves to clear conclusions on the reasons behind these tendencies, but it can be hypothesised that the EU legislator wished to create possibilities for the EU institutions and agencies to partially pre-empt the margins of discretion that national authorities enjoy under the frameworks of MiFID II and MiFIR. This opportunity also seems to have been used, and it would be worth studying how this governs work in the national authorities concerned.

Comparing rules aimed at private parties

Table 4.4 would not serve as the basis for any conclusions in relation to rules conferring substantive rights on private parties. As regards legal obligations on private parties, it was mentioned above that the EU legislator may plausibly avoid creating legal obligations on private individuals in regulations, even though under Article 288 TFEU regulations are fully constitutionally capable of generating not only rights but also obligations on individuals. It would seem from Table 4.8 that this hypothesis is falsified by MiFIR, which on the contrary includes more legal obligations aimed at private parties, and a larger ratio of such rules, than MiFID II does.

The details of legal obligations conferred (or to be conferred) on private parties under the two instruments reveal, however, that the legal obligations in MiFIR generally have low regulatory intensity whereas 49 per cent of those in MiFID II have high regulatory intensity. Scrutinising the data, it seems that most of the legal obligations on private parties in MiFIR (but not all) are instructions to provide national and European authorities with information, or to make information publicly available. By contrast, most (but not all) legal obligations on private parties under MiFID II are substantive obligations that are to be enacted by the Member State legislators. This is further evident in the observation that the legal obligations under MiFIR are more often connected to regulatory or implementing standards in non-legislative acts (laying down details for the communication of information) than the corresponding rules in MiFID II. Consequently, it is concluded that the pattern in Table 4.4 can, to a large extent, be explained by reference to the general character of the legal obligations at issue. Indeed, in line with this hypothesis, substantive legal obligations of private parties are generally found in MiFID II while the legal obligations under MiFIR are generally procedural in character. It would be interesting to follow up this result by mapping the extent to which the two instruments provide for legal consequences in the event of a breach of these rules, and what the characters of these legal consequences are.

However, the number of connections between legal obligation rules aimed at private parties and non-legislative acts is significantly higher under MiFID II than under MiFIR. Indeed, of the total number of such connections under MiFID II, 64 per cent are to rules stipulating legal obligations on private parties.

Table 4.8   *Rules aimed at private parties*

Instrument and level of detail in rules analysed	No. of rules imposing legal obligations, percentage (of total in Table 4.4)	No. of rules conferring substantive rights, percentage (of total in Table 4.4)	No. of connections between non-legislative acts and rules analysed, percentage of total in Table 4.3		No. of connections between preamble recitals and rules analysed, percentage of total in Table 4.3	
			Legal obligations	Substantive rights	Legal obligations	Substantive rights
MiFID II, low level of detail	14, 27%	5, 38%	9, 16%	0	6, 4%	1, 1%
MiFID II, medium level of detail	12, 24%	3, 23%	8, 57%	4, 29%	6, 21%	1, 4%
MiFID II, high level of detail	25, 49%	5, 38%	30, 77%	6, 15%	51, 64%	11, 14%
MiFIR, low level of detail	47, 75%	7, 64%	29, 58%	3, 6%	58, 26%	7, 3%
MiFIR, medium level of detail	13, 21%	1, 9%	9, 69%	1, 8%	16, 30%	1, 2%
MiFIR, high level of detail	3, 5%	3, 27%	5, 26%	2, 11%	7, 18%	7, 18%

Some of these are related to the flow of information, as already mentioned, but a significant proportion of these connections are to Commission Delegated Regulation (EU) 2017/565, which specifies organisational requirements for investment firms. This serves to illustrate that the EU is capable of laying down detailed substantive obligations on private parties in non-legislative acts, which must be seen as a clear instance of centralisation.

As regards substantive rights for private parties, the numbers of such rules are small, which has a negative impact on the reliability of comparisons. If a difference can be discerned, it is to indicate that there are slightly more substantive rights rules with high regulatory intensity in MiFID II than in MiFIR, and these are to a slightly higher extent elaborated in preamble recitals.

To summarise, the seeming tendency to create legal obligations on private parties through MiFIR, a regulation, has been demonstrated to relate mostly to procedural matters related to the communication of information, while substantive obligations are generally in MiFID II. It further follows from the study that such substantive obligations can be elaborated in non-legislative acts and it has been submitted that this includes centralisation of rulemaking power to the EU institutions (mainly to the Commission). This raises questions on the specific character and the constitutional legitimacy of these elaborations that deserve further attention.

4.7   CONCLUSIONS

This study has been a quantitative comparison of MiFID II and MiFIR, endeavouring to approximate the level of centralisation of financial market governance in the EU. This has been done by measuring regulatory intensity in the two instruments, including their connections to delegated and implementing instruments. To operationalise the comparison, the rules in the instruments were coded so as to differentiate between four classes of regulatory addressees: EU institutions, EU agencies, Member State actors and private parties. Furthermore, the characters of rules were distinguished into the categories of legal obligations, discretionary powers and substantive rights.

At a general level, it has been possible to conclude that there is no significant difference in regulatory intensity between MiFID II and MiFIR. This falsifies, for the purposes of this limited sample, the expectation that a regulation will necessarily include a higher regulatory intensity – and thereby a higher level of centralisation of normative power to the EU level – than a directive. This conclusion led the inquiry on to an examination of regulatory intensity in the respective instruments with respect to the regulatory addressees involved. These were categorised as EU institutions and agencies, Member State actors, and private parties.

It has been possible to conclude from this study that there are more rules stipulating legal obligations on EU institutions in MiFIR than there are in MiFID II, and more rules governing EU agencies in MiFIR than in MiFID II. It has also been demonstrated that the regulatory intensity in rules conferring discretionary powers on EU agencies is higher in MiFIR than in MiFID II. Other comparisons of rules aimed at the EU institutions or agencies were inconclusive. These results do, however, strengthen the expectation that the EU legislator will address EU institutions and agencies in regulations rather than in directives. The study has also allowed the hypothesis that the EU legislator has wished to control EU agencies' use of temporary intervention powers in the financial markets.

As regards rules addressing Member State actors, it has been demonstrated that legal obligations of Member State actors are stipulated in MiFID II rather than in MiFIR. This is in line with the expectation that the EU legislator will use directives rather than regulations to govern national activities. It has further been demonstrated that there are more legal obligations on private parties in MiFIR than in MiFID II, but that the characters of the rules are different. Substantive obligations on private parties are generally stipulated in MiFID II, reinforcing the expectation that the EU legislator legitimises such obligations through Member State legislation transposing EU rules into national law. These results also seem to suggest that the introduction of MiFIR to accompany MiFID II was primarily triggered by the need to govern institutional interaction between the EU institutions and agencies (mainly the Commission and the ESMA).

Interestingly, however, a tendency has been discerned for the activities of national authorities to be governed to some extent through non-legislative acts and through preamble recitals. This means that the EU legislator has seemingly wished to create possibilities for the EU institutions (and agencies) to partially pre-empt the margins of discretion that national authorities enjoy under the rules of MiFID II and MiFIR, and that this opportunity has been used to some extent. This also applies to legal obligations on private parties. It has also been highlighted that the balance in the conferral of discretionary powers is to the benefit of EU institutions in both instruments, suggesting a clear element of centralisation, and that most of these discretionary powers are given to the Commission in order for it to be able to adopt non-legislative acts. It can therefore be concluded that there is a discrepancy between the main instruments MiFID II and MiFIR (which mainly follow the expected pattern of using directives to be transposed into national law by national legislation for the governance of national authorities and private parties) and centralised EU rulemaking through non-legislative acts (which are almost exclusively regulations but will nevertheless have an impact on the rights and obligations of national authorities and private parties). It should be recalled that non-legislative acts are neither subject to Parliament or Council approval nor to the procedure for national parliamentary review of new EU acts under Protocol (No 2) on the Application of the Principles of Subsidiarity and Proportionality. Consequently, many veto players, or rather veto functions (checks and balances), in rulemaking are by-passed in non-legislative rulemaking. As mentioned above, this is likely to increase centralisation, and furthermore it triggers constitutional tensions (van Cleynenbreugel 2014; Bergström 2015; Chamon 2016) that may surface in legal discourse on financial market rules.

In sum, it has been demonstrated that MiFID II and MiFIR, and the non-legislative acts adopted on the basis of them, constitute an extensive set of rules centralising the system of trade in financial instruments in the EU. At a general level, the choice of a regulation or a directive did not in this case seem to have any significant impact on the level of centralisation achieved through the instrument. Instead, the rules in the respective instruments seem to address different agents. In this respect, the choice of instrument meets expectations in the sense that MiFIR mainly governs the EU level of administration and MiFID II mainly governs the national level of administration and the rights and obligations of private parties. However, it has been further demonstrated that the activities of national authorities are also governed through the adoption of non-legislative acts that are, with few exceptions, regulations. This means powers conferred on the EU institutions under MiFID II and MiFIR entail a possibility of pre-emption of Member State discretion, which must be described as at least potential centralisation, and furthermore, as we have seen, the Commission has used this possibility extensively, which must be described as real centralisation. With regard to MiFID II and MiFIR, the common pre-conceptions concerning the respective characters of regulations and directives have thus not been falsified, but the study has consequently indicated that the use of a directive to govern national administrations and private parties may conceal the fact that they are to a large extent governed through non-legislative acts in the form of regulations. This form of normative governance through non-legislative acts is perhaps the most conspicuous aspect of EU centralisation in the legal governance of the financial markets indicated in this study.

NOTES

1.   The author would like to extend my thanks to the entire team of colleagues involved in this book, and in particular to Heikki Marjosola, Adrienne Héritier and Magnus G. Schoeller. Thanks also go to Professor Daniel Mertens, University of Osnabrück, and to Professor Carl Fredrik Bergström, Associate Professor Malou Larsson Klevhill and Dr Rebecca Söderström, all at Uppsala University. They have all offered very valuable comments on earlier drafts of this contribution. Of course, any flaws in this text are my own responsibility.

2. The study of the content and meaning of the law in any given field consists in the interpretation of texts and the interrelationship of these texts, and only that, while empirical study of, for instance, what people actually do is entirely irrelevant to the normative content of law. One might see this as an instance of 'Hume's law' (Hume 1739 [1896]: 469–470) insofar as empirical studies deal with what is or is not, while traditional legal studies deal with what one ought or ought not to do.
3. The EU institutions and agencies also issue soft-law documents that are not legal acts within the meaning of Art 288 TFEU, notably (in this context) the 'Guidelines' issued by the ESMA. These fall outside the scope of this study.
4. Bergström 2015, at 236, phrases this third criterion more broadly, saying that the delegation of powers is motivated by special needs.
5. Indeed, the interest of centralising certain aspects of the governance of trade in financial instruments, while allowing more flexibility for the Member States in other respects, is the reason put forth by the Commission in its considerations on the choice of legal instrument to be used. See Commission Staff Working Paper, Impact Assessment, SEC (2011) 1226 final (Brussels 20 October 2011): 59–61.

BIBLIOGRAPHY

Abbott, Kenneth W., Levi-Faur, David and Snidal, Duncan. 2017. Introducing regulatory intermediaries. *The ANNALS of the American Academy of Political and Social Science* 670 (1): 6–13.

Baldwin, Robert. 1996. Regulatory legitimacy in the European context: the British Health and Safety Executive, in Majone, Giandomenico (ed.), *Regulating Europe.* London and New York: Routledge, 83–105.

Bergström, Carl Fredrik. 2005. *Comitology: Delegation of Powers in the European Union and the Committee System.* Oxford: Oxford University Press.

Bergström, Carl Fredrik. 2015. Shaping the new system for delegation of powers to EU agencies: *United Kingdom v. European Parliament and Council (Short selling). Common Market Law Review* 52 (1): 219–242.

Bergström, Carl Fredrik and Ruotsi, Mikael. 2018. *Grundlag i gungning? En ESO-rapport om EU och den svenska offentlighetsprincipen.* Swedish Ministry of Finance report: Rapport till Expertgruppen för studier i offentlig ekonomi, 2018:1.

Chamon, Merijn. 2016. *EU Agencies: Legal and Political Limits to the Transformation of the EU Administration.* Oxford: Oxford Studies in European Law, Oxford University Press.

de Larosière, Jacques (chair). 2009. The High-Level Group on Financial Supervision in the EU: Report. https://ec.europa.eu/economy_finance/publications/pages/publication14527_en.pdf. Last accessed 25 March 2020.

Hume, David. 1739 [1896]. *A Treatise of Human Nature.* London: John Noon.

Lenaerts, Koen. 1993. Regulating the regulatory process: "delegation of powers" in the European Community. *European Law Review* 18 (1): 23–49.

Schammo, Pierre. 2011. The European Securities and Markets Authority: lifting the veil on the allocation of powers. *Common Market Law Review* 48 (6): 1879–1913.

SOU 2009:71 (Swedish Government Official Report 2009:71). *EU, Sverige och den inre marknaden – En översyn av horisontella bestämmelser inom varu- och tjänsteområdet.* Stockholm: Fritzes.

van Cleynenbreugel, Pieter. 2014. *Meroni* Circumvented? Article 114 TFEU and EU
    Regulatory Agencies. *Maastricht Journal of European and Comparative Law* 21
    (1): 64–88.

PART II

Horizontal international perspective: rival
financial regulatory powers

5. Sharing global regulatory space: transatlantic coordination of the G20 OTC derivatives reforms[1]

Heikki Marjosola

5.1 INTRODUCTION

The governance of the global market for over-the-counter (OTC) derivatives has undergone a metamorphosis. Set in motion by the Group of Twenty (G20) 2009 summit in Pittsburgh, the regulatory overhaul has transformed what used to be a relatively harmonious and transnational legal regime into a global regulatory space which – like all regulatory spaces (Hancher and Moran 1998) – is highly contested. In the light of the hypotheses developed in Chapter 1 of this book, this chapter evaluates the implementation and coordination of the globally agreed derivatives reforms in and between the United States and the European Union (for earlier research on this topic, see Godwin et al. 2017). The chapter focuses specifically on the possible implications of coordination challenges for regulatory structures. The hypothesis is that, together with the risk of regulatory arbitrage, regulatory competition contributes to regulatory centralisation in internal regulatory structures.

Prompted by the Global Financial Crisis, the G20 initiatives aimed to increase the transparency and stability of derivative markets, particularly by centralising the execution of trading within regulated trading venues and by imposing mandatory clearing, reporting and risk-management requirements. However, instalment of the new governance system has been cumbersome. Much of the consensus reached under the G20 umbrella was lost when soft principles and policy goals were translated into hard rules. As section 5.2 will show, failures in coordination have resulted in an uneven regulatory playing field characterised by jurisdictional conflicts, inconsistencies, regulatory overlaps and gaps (Carney 2013, p. 15). The Financial Stability Board (FSB), mandated by the G20 to oversee and coordinate the implementation of the reforms, has also admitted that due to the unprecedented scale and complexity of the reforms and unforeseen challenges the implementation "has taken longer than originally intended" (FSB 2017, p. 3). Ten years after the Pittsburgh summit, the reforms are still to be completed (FSB 2018).

The delay is partly explained by the fact that the United States and the European Union ended up locking themselves in a "transatlantic regulatory turf war" (Stafford 2014). This chapter analyses this transatlantic conflict as a coordination challenge typical of *shared regulatory spaces*. Situations in which several agencies with overlapping and conflicting mandates are forced to share authority and responsibility are common in national contexts (Freeman and Rossi 2011). This is not often the case in the global context, where regulatory sovereignty continues to be seen as a "territorial prerogative" (Buxbaum 2002, p. 933; see also Brummer 2010). However, the regulatory space for global derivative markets resists neat jurisdictional partitioning. Indeed, the cross-Atlantic dialogues on OTC derivatives regulation have rightly been labelled 'joint jurisdiction' issues (CFTC 2013a).

Two important factors have contributed to the 'shared' nature of the global regulatory space for OTC derivatives. First, unlike rules such as those on capital adequacy, which are entity-specific, many of the new rules target derivative contracts themselves (e.g. mandatory clearing and collateralisation of contracts). Such rules apply to both sides of the contract. The problem is that when the contracting parties are from different jurisdictions it is not always clear which rules apply. For instance, around 80 per cent of credit derivative transactions had a cross-border element in 2012 (Barnier 2013). At the time Lehman Brothers filed for bankruptcy, it had hundreds of thousands of derivative contracts outstanding with around 8,000 different counterparties around the globe (Hull 2011, p. 3).

Second, the shared regulatory space has emerged as a by-product of jurisdictional contestation. Section 5.2 explains how the use of certain unilateral regulatory strategies by the EU and the US – consisting of extraterritoriality, conditional deference and (direct and indirect) protectionism – have contributed to the creation of the global regulatory space. These strategies are key to understanding the emergence and dynamics of this regulatory space and its implications for regulatory structures. Much of the unilateralism has been justified by the need to contain the risks of regulatory competition and regulatory arbitrage, that is, the relocation of regulated activities to jurisdictions with less costly or more accommodating rules.

Section 5.3 analyses how the shared and highly contested nature of this novel regulatory space affects regulatory structures. It argues that the reforms have indeed increased pressure to centralise (vertically) and to consolidate (horizontally) regulatory authority, especially within the EU. Section 5.4 briefly discusses the limits of unilateral regulatory strategies from a more normative perspective, also considering certain future options and trajectories. Section 5.5 concludes.

5.2   OTC DERIVATIVES AND THE REGULATORY REFORM

5.2.1   The Context of the Reform

Derivatives are financial instruments the value of which depends on the performance and price of a reference asset, rate or index, or some other underlying variable. Derivatives can hedge against negative price movements or unfavourable events (such as a rise in fuel prices, or debtor's default) but they may also be used for speculation or arbitrage (see generally Hull 2011, pp. 10–16). Options and forwards provide the ancestral building blocks of all derivatives. A forward agreement simply sets a future time and price for buying or selling an asset, whereas an option holder has the right, but not the obligation, to buy (call option) or sell (put option) the underlying asset at a certain future time. The most common forward-based derivatives are swaps, which involve an exchange of sequential cash flows, such as fixed interest cash flows for floating interest cash flows (interest rate swaps). Credit default swaps (CDS) are a specific type of swap offering protection against default on a loan (Hu 1993; Hull 2011, pp. 5–8). At the most complex end, financial products may be securitised or structured so that derivatives themselves act as the underlying asset (Yen and Lai 2014, pp. 2–3).

OTC derivatives, especially CDSs, were at the centre of the 2007–2009 financial crisis (see, e.g. FCIC 2011, pp. 50–51). In its immediate aftermath, the G20 took decisive action and in 2009 issued the following statement:

> All standardized OTC derivative contracts should be traded on exchanges or electronic trading platforms, where appropriate, and cleared through central counterparties by end-2012 at the latest. OTC derivative contracts should be reported to trade repositories. Non-centrally cleared contracts should be subject to higher capital requirements. (G20 2009)

The reform therefore concerned: (a) the organisation of the entire market (on-exchange vs. OTC); (b) the clearing and settlement of trades (central clearing vs. bilateral settlement); (c) the transparency of the OTC market (trade reporting); and (d) the management of payment and delivery risks for uncleared derivatives. Importantly, the G20 later updated the policy by agreeing that uncleared OTC derivatives should also be subject to mandatory collateralisation rules.

These far-reaching reforms were in particular aimed at the obscure OTC segment of the derivative markets, which had for long avoided public regulation (Partnoy 2001; Carruthers 2013). All derivatives are traded over-the-counter or through regulated exchanges. Derivative exchanges, such as the Chicago

Board of Exchange, offer a limited number of highly standardised products, whereas the private OTC market allows for infinite customisation. In the mid-1980s, the public and exchange-traded derivative market was larger than the private OTC market, but by 2008 the latter had not only surpassed the public market but in fact was worth roughly ten times as much (Carruthers 2013). In June 2013, only 9 per cent of all derivatives were traded on exchanges (Deutsche Börse and Eurex Clearing 2014, p. 7). The G20 reforms aimed to relocate much of the private OTC market in public, transparent and regulated exchanges.

Second, whereas the private OTC market (particularly the CDS market) came close to collapsing in 2008–2009, the derivative clearing houses (central counterparties, or CCPs) navigated through the turmoil relatively unharmed. Instead of public support, the CCPs relied on their sophisticated default management systems. Centralised clearing mitigates payment and delivery risks by centralising it: the role of a CCP is to become a buyer to every seller and a seller to every buyer. CCPs have traditionally cleared all exchange-traded derivatives but only some standardised OTC derivatives. The G20 reforms aimed to expand the scope of derivative-clearing through CCPs by making it mandatory where possible, and also by making it more expensive to enter purely bilateral contracts.

Third, the financial crisis revealed that the private OTC market was prone to systematic under-collateralisation. The fact that 'margining' was left to the parties' commercial judgment meant that market participants with solid credit ratings could effectively trade without committing capital (Singh 2010). In contrast, cleared and exchange-traded derivatives are subject to mandatory margin requirements[2] and CCP participants must also contribute to the CCP's default funds. To diminish the discrepancies between the public and private markets, the G20 reforms expand the scope of mandatory margining also to those OTC contracts that remain uncleared.

Although still unfinished, the reforms have significantly affected market structure. The majority of interest rate derivatives and a significant portion of CDS contracts are now centrally cleared (FSB 2017, pp. 12–13). Mandatory collateralisation of OTC contracts is meant to further push trading towards public exchanges and clearing houses. However, the regulatory push towards centralised clearing has not terminated the competition between public and private derivative markets and the flexibility and lighter cost structure of the OTC market may still trump the safety of exchange-based trading (ISDA 2013, p. 4; Kentz 2014). For instance, in 2015 the Chicago Board Options Exchange submitted a letter to the SEC highlighting the fact that despite regulatory efforts, some markets were moving away from exchanges (McCormick 2015).

5.2.2   From Consensus to Conflict

The transforming market for derivatives represents a stark contrast to the pre-crisis OTC markets, which were primarily based on a transnational self-regulation regime (Braithwaite 2012). As Chapter 6 in this book shows, the terms and standards offered by the International Swaps and Derivatives Association (ISDA) as part of its Master Agreement structure have provided the dominant contractual framework for OTC transactions since the 1980s (see also Feder 2002, p. 741; Choi and Gulati 2006, p. 1140).

The implementation of the G20 initiatives has nevertheless faced several complications. To become effective, the G20 policy commitments needed to be translated into hard rules locally and regionally. For instance, the EU enacted the commitments with two key regulations: Regulation 648/2012 of the European Parliament and Council on OTC derivatives, central counterparties and trade repositories (EMIR) and Regulation 600/2014 on Markets in Financial Instruments (MiFIR). EMIR implements the mandatory clearing obligation (EMIR, Articles 4 and 5) while MiFIR requires that all sufficiently liquid and cleared OTC derivatives must be traded on regulated trading venues (MiFIR, Article 32).

In the United States, the reforms were implemented as part of the Dodd–Frank Wall Street Reform and Consumer Protection Act. The regulatory outcomes in the EU and the US significantly differed in detail and the divergences only grew larger as the reforms moved from the legislative to the executive stage. As a result, for example, one jurisdiction may require mandatory clearing of a certain OTC derivative contract and/or the execution of the trade on a regulated market while the other jurisdiction leaves the choice to the markets. The personal scope of regulations also differ. For instance, the EMIR exempts certain pension scheme arrangements (transitionally) and intra-group trades from the scope of the regulation, which is not the case in the US. The original EMIR rules also captured both financial and certain non-financial counterparties in much the same way, whereas in the US the scope for non-financial counterparties is more tailored. Inconsistencies have also arisen in the context of trade reporting requirements (ESMA 2013, pp. 22–23).

Conflicts concerning transaction-level rules are particularly hard to reconcile. Consider, for instance, the concentration rules, which direct certain standardised contracts into centralised clearing and on organised trading venues. These rules apply to *both* sides of the contract, regardless of the fact that the parties might be located in different jurisdictions. In such a situation one jurisdiction's rules cannot be followed without breaching another's (Carney 2013, p. 15). Collateralisation rules may also lead to such direct conflicts. In so far as they concern the amount of collateral that should be posted, market participants can simply meet the highest requirement, but the rules also concern the division between the initial and variable margins, the classes of collateral eligible and the way collateral must be segregated (Greene and Potiha 2012, p. 281).

Anticipating such conflicts, the G20 tasked the Financial Stability Board (FSB) with overseeing coordination of the reforms among national legislators and regulators. International standard-setting bodies such as the International Organization of Securities Commissions (IOSCO) and the Basel Committee on Banking Supervision (BCBS) have also developed numerous principles and standards to guide implementation. A specific OTC Derivatives Working Group representing a mass of technocratic expertise from national jurisdictions and international organisations was also set up to coordinate implementation (this body was nevertheless short-lived; see Knaack 2015).

The FSB repeatedly urged regulators to identify examples of any regulatory overlaps, inconsistencies and conflicts and to develop options for addressing the issues (FSB 2012). Most importantly, in 2013 the G20 declared that "jurisdictions and regulators should be able to *defer to each other* when it is justified by the quality of their respective regulatory and enforcement regimes" (G20 2013, p. 18, emphasis added). Generally speaking, deference refers to a type of cross-border regulation in which national authorities rely on each other when carrying out the regulation or supervision of participants that operate cross-border. In practice, it may encompass various regulatory mechanisms, such as tailored exemptions, substituted compliance and various recognition and equivalence frameworks (IOSCO 2019, p. 3).

Progress towards a deference-based recognition regime has been slow and uncertain. An FSB progress report (2015, pp. 13–14) summarised the prevailing concerns:

> Several authorities [...] note that unevenness in the pace of implementation of reforms, as well as inconsistencies or gaps in the application of requirements to cross-border transactions, can result in duplicative or overlapping requirements or lead to opportunities for regulatory arbitrage. Some authorities note that this, in turn, could result in market fragmentation and decreased liquidity. In addition, some emerging market and developing economies have indicated that challenges may be presented by the potential cross-border impact of reforms, such as meeting recognition/equivalence requirements of major financial centres in OTC derivatives.

Indeed, the lack of a level playing field and legal uncertainty has had unintended effects on OTC derivative markets. Reports have noted a significant drop in international trading activity and a fragmentation of liquidity along geographical lines (Artamonov 2015; ISDA 2015; FSB 2017, pp. 5–6; IIF 2019). This ongoing market fragmentation illustrates the sensitivity of OTC derivatives to legal uncertainty. Without a level playing field, a predictable system of deference (where market participants can comply with just one jurisdiction's rules) would be needed to stop market fragmentation.

However, such a system might also invite other kinds of strategic behaviour. Derivatives are also known for their ability to reduce the costs of, or capture profit opportunities created by, differing laws, tax rules or accounting requirements (Partnoy 1997, pp. 227–228). Such regulatory arbitrage has been relatively easy. The parties to derivative contracts may simply book transactions in their preferred jurisdiction (see Goodhart and Lastra 2010, p. 715; Riles 2014, p. 88). The dual risks of regulatory arbitrage and market fragmentation have challenged regulators and policymakers, especially in the EU and the US. The following section illustrates how a mix of unilateral regulatory strategies helped create, and later manage, a full-blown regulatory conflict between the Atlantic neighbours.

5.2.3   Managing Regulatory Arbitrage: Between Extraterritoriality and Deference

To counter regulatory arbitrage risks, lawmakers in the US and EU have claimed *extraterritorial* authority for their rules. For instance, certain provisions in EMIR (e.g. the clearing obligation) even apply to contracts between non-EU entities when those contracts would have *a direct, substantial and foreseeable effect in the EU*. The effect of these EMIR rules can also be extended abroad whenever it is considered *necessary or appropriate to prevent the evasion of any EMIR provisions* (see, e.g., Arts. 4(5) and 11(12)).

Similar rules were included in the Dodd–Frank Act. The act provides that its provisions on derivatives (the act uses the term 'swap') apply to any activities outside the United States that either (i) have a direct and significant connection with activities in, or effect on, United States commerce or that (ii) contravene rules or regulations that are necessary or appropriate to prevent the evasion of any of the act's provisions (sections 722(d) and 772(b)).

The similarity between these rules is not a coincidence. The US has a long history of exporting its capital market rules to foreign countries and the extraterritorial reach of its derivative rulebook was just a continuation of this policy motivated by a fear of regulatory arbitrage (and also the risk of losing market share). As Coffee argues, the extraterritorial application of financial regulation cannot be avoided in a world where mobile financial institutions "can easily park their higher-risk operations abroad and beyond the regulatory reach of their home country" (see Coffee 2014, p. 1260). The aggressive US stance nevertheless caused an outcry from European regulators and the financial industry, and the EU checked the US rules with a near-identical approach (Artamonov 2015, p. 12; Knaack 2015, pp. 1226–1227).

A carrot of deference nevertheless complements the stick of extraterritoriality. In the EU, the so-called equivalence regime allows the possibility of disapplying EU rules in favour of another jurisdiction if its regulatory and supervisory regime is considered adequately 'equivalent' to that in the EU. The EU Commission, assisted by ESMA, may adopt implementing acts declaring that the legal, supervisory and enforcement arrangements of a third country are equivalent to the requirements laid down in EMIR (Art. 13(2)). Upon such determination, market participants can comply with EU requirements by being compliant with the requirements of their own, non-EU, jurisdiction (EMIR, Art. 13(3)). An equivalence decision also makes it possible for ESMA to formally recognise a third-country CCP or a third-country trade repository (EMIR Arts. 25(2)(a), 25(6) and 75(1)). Such entity-specific recognition levels the playing field between EU-based entities and foreign entities, allowing the latter to offer their services in the EU single market on equivalent terms. If circumstances change, the ESMA can withdraw its recognition or the Commission can review its equivalence decision. The European Commission has so far adopted 23 equivalence decisions with respect to the regulatory regimes for derivatives and central counterparties of 14 countries (7 June 2019). On the basis of these equivalence decisions, ESMA has recognised more than 30 third-country CCPs from non-EU jurisdictions, thus allowing these CCPs to provide clearing services in the EU.

Much like in the EU, the extraterritorial effect of US regulation can be lifted in the framework of substituted compliance. In its original form, substituted compliance was designed to open up the possibility for foreign actors wishing to conduct business in the US to avoid burdensome and duplicative SEC registration requirements and certain other US rules (Tafara and Peterson 2007). The more recent substituted compliance framework is designed with a view to adjusting the extraterritorial application of the Dodd–Frank Act. Under this regime, certain offshore persons and entities that might come under the scope of US rules can instead comply with regulations in their home jurisdictions (Jackson 2015). The Commodity and Futures Trading Commission (CFTC) has issued 10 comparability determinations which cover the EU, Australia, Canada, Japan, Hong Kong and Switzerland, making favourable determinations in favour of all six. The scope of the comparability determinations has nevertheless been limited, excluding many 'transaction-level' requirements.[3]

Such deference strategies represent an important exception to the traditional *modus operandi* of international financial regulation, where "each state prefers to address cross-border challenges simply by applying its own laws" (Verdier 2013, pp. 1438–1439). However, as the next section will show, getting to the actual decision can be a time-consuming and delicate process.

5.2.4   The Transatlantic Turf Battle Regarding CCPs

Ideally, the stick of extraterritoriality and the carrot of deference should have led to negotiated convergence between the EU and the US, ultimately giving rise to a regime of mutual recognition. Without material differences in rules, there would be fewer risks of regulatory arbitrage and fewer effects on markets. The negotiations appeared to get off to a good start. In 2013, the parties released the so-called Path Forward statement. The agreement laid down a road map towards mutual recognition of derivative rules and outlined a package of measures for approaching common issues concerning cross-border derivatives. According to the statement, the parties would not seek to apply their rules "unreasonably" in the other jurisdiction but instead would "rely on the application and enforcement of the rules by the other jurisdiction" (CFTC 2013a). After the statement, the talks continued in different fora, both official and unofficial. Participants held several meetings in the context of the 'Financial Markets Regulatory Dialogue', which was later renamed the 'Joint EU–US Financial Regulatory Forum'. The purpose of the Forum (which has convened once or twice a year) is, among other things, to "work towards avoiding regulatory arbitrage and towards compatibility […] of each other's standards" (Joint Statement 2016).

Despite comforting declarations and good intentions, the bargain proved to be an exceptionally hard one to strike. By September 2015, the negotiations were locked in a stalemate (Stafford 2015). The range of negotiation issues was extensive, as was detailed in ESMA's September 2013 final technical advice to the European Commission regarding the US regulatory framework (ESMA 2013). One problem concerned the duplicative or conflicting requirements regarding the clearing obligation and risk-mitigation techniques for uncleared OTC derivative contracts. However, the recognition of third-country CCPs was a key concern. The mandatory offloading of derivatives to the perceived safety of centralised clearing creates much new business for CCPs but there is also a risk that the competitive environment pressures CCPs to lower their risk management requirements. These concerns were clearly spelled out in the Commission's EMIR impact assessment, which noted the possibility that regulation could prompt CCPs to compete on risk, that is, compete "through lowering the quality of risk management, more specifically by cutting the margins required from the clearing members" (Commission 2010, p. 68). The deliberations also noted anecdotal evidence supporting this concern:

> A number of market participants seem to fear that this is already happening. They have privately told the Commission services on various occasions that CCPs had started lowering their risk standards in order to lower their costs and attract more clients. Recently, a CCP voiced the same concern in public [footnote omitted].

These claims were never backed with concrete evidence, so the Commission services cannot judge whether they are true or not. Irrespective of whether they are true or not, however, they highlight a potentially dangerous side effect of competition between CCPs.

The EU Commission and the ESMA were therefore reluctant to declare the US regime for CCPs equivalent. Without such a decision, the ESMA could not recognise US-based CCPs and give them unhindered access to EU clearing markets. Failure to reach an agreement risked further reducing the cross-border-derivative activity between the EU and US. The reason is simple: without a deal, trading and clearing at home would become much cheaper than abroad. For instance, EU Capital Requirements Regulation 575/2013 sets higher capital requirements for transactions that are cleared through a 'non-qualified' (i.e. non-authorised or non-recognised) CCP (Art. 382(3)).

ESMA pushed especially adamantly for a harder approach. It criticised the EU's liberal approach to CCP recognition, noting its extreme openness and excessive reliance on third-country rules and supervisory arrangements (ESMA 2015). In contrast, the US authorities required all third-country CCPs to become subject to the direct jurisdiction of the US authorities (ESMA 2013, pp. 20–21). While the EU's original approach arguably presented a "model in terms of mutual reliance", it worsened Europe's position in the transatlantic bargaining process (ESMA 2013, paras 108–109).

Only on 15 March 2016 – four years after the 'Path Forward Agreement' – did the Commission adopt an equivalence decision concerning the US regulatory framework for central counterparties. The ESMA followed suit, recognising several US-based CCPs between June and December 2016. From there on, things ran apparently smoothly. On 13 October 2017, the European Commission adopted an EMIR equivalence decision for derivative transactions in the United States and thus settled the issue concerning the legal, supervisory and enforcement arrangements for non-centrally-cleared OTC derivative transactions. In particular, the decision covered the rules on risk monitoring and the mandatory exchange of collateral for such contracts. Finally, in December 2017 the Commission adopted an equivalence decision under MiFIR concerning US-based derivative trading venues, therefore ensuring that European market participants could continue to trade derivatives on US platforms.

The bargain was far from complete, however. Soon after the EU reached a political agreement on updating the EMIR in March 2019, tensions over the regulation and supervision of overseas CCPs resurfaced. A struggle to control and oversee London-based CCPs in particular risked undermining the fragile transatlantic agreement. London-based CCPs have for long troubled the eurozone and especially the European Central Bank, which has sought more oversight powers and even threatened to limit the access of London-based CCPs to the eurozone under its controversial Location Policy (Marjosola 2015). This issue has re-intensified because of Brexit (Chamorro-Courtland 2019). The EU is anxious to tighten its grip over London's CCPs, which remain the principal destination for the clearing of euro-denominated derivatives. However, London-based CCPs also handle most of the dollar-denominated derivatives. The EU's new proposal effectively provided that if London-based CCPs wished to continue to clear euro-denominated contracts after Brexit, they would either have to move their business within the EU bloc or accept ESMA's oversight and regulation (Tett 2019).

As Bulfone and Smoleńska show in Chapter 3 in this book, the review of EMIR will bring many crucial changes to the ESMA's powers. In the future, the ESMA will have significantly wider regulatory and supervisory powers, particularly as regards third-country CCPs. ESMA will categorise each third-country CCP as either a non-systemically important CCP (Tier 1 CCP) or a systemically important CCP (Tier 2 CCP). In the latter case, the relevant CCPs will become subject to additional requirements and the third-country's regulatory and supervisory framework will have to pass much more intense regulatory scrutiny to maintain the equivalence status.

The review of the CCP supervisory and oversight framework re-intensified the transatlantic conflict. The US policymakers and regulators feared that the second generation of EU extraterritoriality, as introduced in the EMIR reform, was targeted not only at London but also at US-based clearing houses. A political agreement in the form of a joint statement between the European Commission and the CFTC – the US swap regulator – managed to ease the tension, but only temporarily (Brunsden and Stafford 2019; Stafford 2019). Despite the standoff, the CFTC managed to reign in its uncompromising requirements for overseas CCPs, allowing limited deference to third-country regulators such as Japan's (Stafford and Rennison 2019).

The position of London in the transatlantic derivative conflict is also telling of the capacity of the post-Brexit UK to engage in regulatory competition vis-à-vis the US and the EU. Hosting systemically important financial market infrastructure, it will have no choice but to concede significant oversight and supervisory powers to both US and European regulators, at least if it wishes to continue servicing market participants from these jurisdictions.

The regulatory turf war between the US and the EU is disconcerting, given that transatlantic communication channels and collaboration venues have been in place for more than ten years. During 2004–2007, the Committee of European Securities Regulators (which later became ESMA) met several times with the CFTC in the context of a joint work programme which explicitly aimed to facilitate the conduct and supervision of transatlantic derivative business. On the other hand, the dispute is less surprising if considered against the shifting of bargaining power. The power asymmetry between the Atlantic neighbours has been in steady decline, not least because of the institutional evolution and the centralisation of regulatory authority within the EU (Karmel 2007; Posner 2009). The next section examines what role, if any, the new global regulatory space for OTC derivatives has played in centralising regulatory structures.

5.3 THE GLOBAL REGULATORY SPACE AND SHIFTING STRUCTURES OF REGULATION

5.3.1 Centralisation of Regulatory Authority in the EU

The purpose of this section is to examine the book's hypothesis that regulatory competition, together with the risk of regulatory arbitrage, prompts regulatory centralisation in internal regulatory structures.

First of all, from the *vertical international* perspective, the growing importance of global financial regulation constitutes a compelling reason to shift regulatory authority from the Member State level to the EU level. Indeed, the lack of centralised regulatory authority and the inability to speak with one voice have probably held back the development of the European financial markets (Pan 2003). However, as far as the drafting of global financial standards is concerned, the Union is still far from the single representative model, even when it comes to the representation of the eurozone (see De Ryck 2019). The EU is currently a full member of the G20 and so directly represented in the most important standard-setters such as the BSCBs. In addition, the ECB and the SSM (the Banking Union's single supervisory arm hosted by the ECB) are full members of the BSCB[4] whereas ESMA is a full member of IOSCO. However, other European G20 members, and some other Member States with developed financial markets, continue to be represented in these forums too.

What is more interesting for the purpose of this chapter is the case for centralisation when it comes to the *implementation* of international financial standards and G20 policies. The transatlantic turf battle illustrates the formidable task financial regulators face in having to coordinate implementation with their foreign colleagues, whose mandates, reform calendars, priorities and perhaps even incentives are different from their own. As one commissioner from the US Securities and Exchange Commission (SEC) described it:

> [...] at no time in the [SEC's] history have we been more engaged with the international community or more involved in collaborative work streams with our fellow regulators from around the globe. Much of this international work stems from the 2009 G20 initiatives regarding over-the-counter (OTC) derivatives reforms. (Piwowar 2014)

Such international coordination demands are increasing across the spectrum of financial regulations (IOSCO 2015). The need to coordinate the implementation of G20 derivative policy globally first means that implementing powers must be kept at the EU level. It is no surprise that European derivative legislation has been adopted in the form of directly applicable regulations (EMIR and MiFIR). Both acts also include various provisions delegating authority to the European Commission and the ESMA to develop more detailed rules in this area and to deal with the problem of duplicative and conflicting international rules (see, e.g. MiFIR, Article 33). Indeed, in no other area of financial regulation has the ESMA been so active in developing binding technical standards (which the Commission has endorsed without changes) (Moloney 2018, p. 133). To the extent that Member State national authorities have influenced implementation, they have done it through ESMA's governing bodies and working groups.

The need to coordinate implementation internationally therefore provides yet another justification for replacing directives – the EU legislative instrument which by definition leaves implementation of its provisions to Member States – with directly applicable regulations which centralise implementation. On the other hand, as Strand shows in Chapter 4 of this book, there are no significant structural differences between the revised Markets in Financial Instruments Directive (MiFID II) and its sister regulation (MiFIR); MiFID II also centralises implementation by delegating extensive rule-making powers to the Commission and the ESMA, thus narrowing the scope for implementation left to the Member States.

The degree of regulatory centralisation also depends on the *amount of power* delegated to the ESMA and the Commission. The preceding section showed that regulators on both sides of the Atlantic needed to engage in extensive cross-border negotiations on the final content of their rulebooks in order to achieve the necessary convergence. However, the respective regulators' room for manoeuvre was limited by their legislative mandates. Here, the imbalance of power was considerable. The US federal agencies, such as the SEC and CFTC, have historically enjoyed considerable flexibility and discretion to pursue their tasks, including by issuing binding legal acts. In sharp contrast, constitutional restrictions (the so-called *Meroni* doctrine) in the EU require that EU agencies such as the ESMA pursue their mandates without a wide margin of discretion and so with much less flexibility (see Bergström 2015; Marjosola 2015). For instance, whereas the SEC and the CFTC can relatively freely roll back or extend the scope of the Dodd–Frank Act's derivative rules, the EU needed to resort to burdensome and lengthy legislative processes to scale back some of the more strenuous provisions of the EMIR. Regulation 2019/834 (EMIR Refit), which entered into force on 17 June 2019, simplified certain areas covered by the EMIR Regulation and introduced "a more proportionate approach" in line with the Commission's Regulatory Fitness and Performance programme. In certain areas, such as where it comes to the definition of financial and non-financial counterparties for the purposes of determining the scope of the rules, the amendment brought the rules closer to those in force in the US. Some amendments were explicitly motivated by the need to "enable international regulatory convergence" (see, e.g. recital 21 of the EMIR Refit).

This latter finding about legislative delegations is also interesting from the perspective of another of this book's hypotheses. According to one of the hypotheses presented in Chapter 1, vague legislative provisions contribute to decentralisation or fragmentation of regulatory structures. This chapter suggests that the applicability of this hypothesis should be restricted, at least insofar as it concerns areas in which legislative vagueness is filled with Union-level executive acts such as binding technical standards (and non-binding guidelines and other soft law acts issued by European supervisory authorities). For instance, EMIR has been amplified by more than 30 highly detailed regulatory technical standards[5] which concern such crucial issues as the criteria to be used when determining which classes of derivatives should be subject to mandatory clearing. Instead of the EMIR determining which derivatives should be cleared through CCPs (a list that would be very hard to draw up *ex ante*), the EMIR delegates the responsibility to the ESMA and the Commission.[6]

The need to globally coordinate the implementation of financial regulation will pressure the EU legislators to delegate more authority to the European Commission and the ESAs. Indeed, the recent review of the powers and tasks of the European supervisory authorities explicitly referred to both the risk of regulatory arbitrage and the need to coordinate implementation with third-country supervisors as justification for centralising the certain supervisory powers within ESMA. As the recital states, ESMA's role as the Union-wide competent authority "establishes it as the counterpart in the Union for supervisors in third countries, making cross-border cooperation more efficient and effective" (ESA Review, recital 55).

5.3.2 Consolidation of Regulatory Authority – Lessons from the US

Increased inter-agency coordination demands in the global arena may also prompt *consolidation of regulatory authority* horizontally within jurisdictions. As mentioned previously, shared regulatory spaces created by overlapping and duplicative delegations are a common phenomenon in national and regional contexts, for example where multiple agencies are delegated similar functions, or where agencies regulate different products or activities but with a shared purpose (Freeman and Rossi 2011, pp. 1145–1148). The US financial regulatory structure provides a popular example of such a shared regulatory space. In the US, the competence in the field of derivatives is shared between the SEC and the CFTC; the CFTC is the primary regulator for OTC swaps while the SEC regulates security-based swaps, and the agencies regulate 'mixed swaps' jointly. Recognising the functional overlap, the Dodd–Frank Act requires the agencies to coordinate and consult not only with each other but also with other relevant regulators before commencing rulemaking in the area of derivatives (see GAO 2011, p. 23). Such a fragmented regulatory structure with several regulators and overlapping mandates is a historical feature of the entire US financial regulatory structure. For instance, five federal agencies share the responsibility for regulating depository institutions, which can also be regulated by state regulators (Pan 2011, p. 837).

Such overlapping and multiple delegations can result in various weaknesses in terms of efficiency, effectiveness and accountability, alongside certain possible advantages (Freeman and Rossi 2011, pp. 1150–1151). Freeman and Rossi argue that shared regulatory spaces are less problematic than is often thought, and that the case for consolidating 'redundant' agencies under one roof has been significantly oversold in the academic literature. Their argument is that such mergers might simply "convert an interagency coordination problem into an intra-agency problem" (Freeman and Rossi 2011, p. 1154) and that the debate so far has neglected the ability of different *coordination tools* to mitigate inter-agency coordination problems.

A significant blind spot in Freeman and Rossi's analysis, particularly as it concerns the regulation of derivatives, is that it ignores the cross-border context. As this chapter has shown, the regulatory space for financial derivatives post-G20 reforms transcends jurisdictional borders. In these contexts, the lack of clarity as to which of the US government branches, departments or agencies is responsible for implementing policy – and the fact that they often disagree on policy issues – is obviously much more problematic (see also Riles 2014, p. 81). The SEC and the CFTC have traditionally followed very different regulatory philosophies (Markham 2003) and they have a history of engaging in dysfunctional turf battles (Pan 2008, p. 243). Anecdotal evidence suggests that such inter-agency rivalry between the SEC and CFTC has not been absent in the regulatory space for derivatives either (see Piwowar 2014).

More efficient use of coordination tools could no doubt help overcome such coordination problems, as Freeman and Rossi (2011) suggest, but the transatlantic derivative narrative has also shown that multiple and overlapping delegations make it challenging to speak with one voice in cross-border negotiations (Brummer 2013, pp. 13–14). In its equivalence assessment, the ESMA also recognised the challenges arising from the fact that the implementation of derivative rules was not adequately synchronised between the CFTC and SEC.

Therefore, the growing need to also share regulatory space internationally might strengthen the case for agency consolidation.

In the EU, the implementation of derivative reforms lands relatively clearly within the substantive remit of the ESMA, and there has been much less need to coordinate the reforms with the other European agencies and bodies forming the European System of Financial Supervision. Another thing entirely is that the European agencies are executive rather than regulatory in nature. As the preceding section noted, ESMA and the other ESAs are relatively toothless when compared to independent regulatory agencies such as the SEC and the CFTC. Indeed, when it comes to making policy deals such as the 2013 Path Forward agreement, the ESMA has primarily played an advisory role. The European Commission still has the final authority to enter such deals. However, the new EMIR rules will take a significant step forward in both centralising and consolidating authority within the ESMA regarding third-country CCPs. Apart from monitoring equivalence, ESMA's new Supervisory Committee will be vested with *direct supervisory powers* over third-country CCPs. The Supervisory Committee may even withdraw the recognition of a systemically important (Tier 2) CCP and thus force its mandatory relocation to the EU (see also Chapter 3 by Bulfone and Smoleńska in this book).

5.4 FROM UNILATERALISM TO BILATERALISM AND BEYOND

This penultimate section will briefly consider certain drawbacks of the above-examined unliteral regulatory strategies and assess their possible implications for financial regulatory structures. First, deference strategies require regulators to continually vet foreign regulatory structures and monitor foreign supervision and enforcement. This is a complex and costly exercise (Jackson 2015). For instance, ESMA's technical advice about the equivalence of the US regime for derivatives includes a line-by-line comparison table covering more than 200 pages followed by more than 1,000 footnotes. The ESMA has itself noted the "extremely rigid and burdensome" nature of the recognition process for third-country CCPs and the equivalence decision process (ESMA 2015, para. 115). The rigidity of the substituted compliance process in the US has also been criticised. In an opinion on the final rules on the international application of standards, one CFTC commissioner noted that "the Commission has embarked on a cross-border analysis that I fear is taking us down a path of regulatory detail that is overly burdensome, complicated, and unnecessary" (CFTC 2013b, p. 881, dissenting statement by Commissioner Jill E. Sommers). As Chris Brummer (2013, p. 5) has noted, such "check-the-box metrics [...] can become quickly outdated in a fast-paced financial marketplace".

The EU's equivalence regime, which also covers several areas other than derivatives, has produced more than 200 equivalence decisions assessing a total of 32 jurisdictions (European Commission 2017a). There is little indication of how the EU will manage to oversee the developing rulebooks in all these jurisdictions or make sure that the rules that are in place are backed by adequate enforcement and supervision (see also Brummer 2013, p. 5).

A less-intrusive and outcomes-focused approach would demand fewer resources but it would also require *mutual trust*, which in the absence of credible commitment will be hard to kindle. As the transatlantic derivative dispute illustrates, without binding international standards or organisations enforcing them, regulators' commitments are vulnerable to political reconsiderations and compromises (Brummer 2013, pp. 115–116, 136). Indeed, the difficult cross-border politics of derivative regulation reflects the relatively weak status of transnational regulatory institutions in securities and financial regulation (Posner 2018).

On the other hand, such coordination and monitoring costs will probably not prevent achieving the main advantage of unilateral regulatory strategies. Deference strategies, combined with the sticks of extraterritoriality and protectionism, provide an effective way to export regulatory rules and practices to 'weaker' states (see Raustiala 2002, pp. 7–9). Official EU documentation even explicitly acknowledges this purpose, noting that "a possible equivalence finding by the EU is one of the major incentives for third-country regulators to enhance supervisory co-operation and *to seek closer regulatory convergence with the EU*" (European Commission 2017a, p. 4, emphasis added). Indeed, despite the declining importance of the US and the EU as the primary loci of global capital markets (Cox 2012; Brummer 2013, p. 7; Lannoo 2013, p. 21), they together still account for roughly 90 per cent of the market for derivatives (Stafford 2015). Therefore, a deeper transatlantic partnership would force other jurisdictions to converge towards US–EU standards.

However, the coordination problems will not be solved simply by turning a unilateral regulatory strategy into a bilateral one. A joint EU–US leadership would only increase the coordination demands between the Atlantic partners, which would need to act in concert towards the rest of the world. Moreover, as we have already seen, the competitive pressure for market share would constantly risk disintegrating the informal alliance. What such considerations make clear, however, is that when it comes to fields of financial regulation such as derivatives, there are few centrifugal forces affecting the regulatory structures. On the contrary, many have proposed hardening the soft mode of global financial governance with more hierarchical and hard-law structures (see, e.g., Avgouleas 2012; Lastra 2014; Artamonov 2015).

5.5 CONCLUSIONS

The findings in this chapter support the hypothesis that the highly contested global regulatory space for OTC derivatives has contributed to the centralisation of regulatory structures in the European Union. Regulatory competition and the risk of regulatory arbitrage have provided explicit justifications for centralising regulatory and supervisory powers in the Commission and the ESMA. The transatlantic coordination exercise has emphasised the need to be able to negotiate in cross-border dialogues with one voice and with a clear mandate. The need to share regulatory space globally therefore also strengthens the case for consolidating regulatory authority horizontally within jurisdictions.

A number of lessons can be drawn from the regulatory turf battle between the US and the EU. First, global reforms should already be coordinated better when drafting legislation. Second, the executive authorities in charge of coordinating implementation with their foreign colleagues should have broad enough, functional and compatible mandates. In the EU, however, constitutional restrictions limit the delegation of a wide degree of discretion to the executive bodies. This means that more significant fine-tuning – as evidenced by the recently updated EMIR – will have to go through Union legislative bodies also in the future. Closing the transatlantic deal on OTC derivatives would be crucial to stop or at least slow down the ongoing market fragmentation and to counter the immediate regulatory arbitrage threats. For the time being, the EU and the US seem able to use their dominant positions in the markets for derivatives to export their rules overseas. In the longer run, such a 'regulate thy neighbour' model of global financial governance is far from optimal, not least due to its large monitoring and coordination costs. Such problems have increased calls to also centralise regulatory powers globally.

NOTES

1. This chapter is partly based on Marjosola, H. 2016, Regulate thy neighbour: competition and conflict in the cross-border regulatory space for OTC derivatives. Working Paper, EUI LAW, 2016/01, European Regulatory Private Law Project (ERPL-16).
2. Margins comprise an 'initial margin', a fixed component paid up front and a 'variation margin', which is paid periodically based on changes in the value of open positions (Feder 2002, pp. 733–734).
3. For the complex process of developing the respective derivative rules by the CFTC and SEC, see especially Artamonov 2015; Coffee 2014; Greene and Potiha 2012 and Greene and Potiha 2013.
4. The EBA and the Commission have observer status.

5.   See the list of binding technical standards on ESMA's website: https://www. esma
     .europa.eu/convergence/guidelines-and-technical-standards   (last   visited   10
     September 2019).
6.   On the other hand, this 'top-down' approach is complemented by a 'bottom-up'
     approach according to which the scope of clearing is partly based on the classes of
     derivatives already cleared by authorised or recognised CCPs (see EMIR Article
     5(2)). This suggests a level of decentralisation, but one that also sidesteps national
     authorities by relying instead on market participants.

BIBLIOGRAPHY

Artamonov, A 2015, 'Cross-border application of OTC derivatives rules: revisiting the
     substituted compliance approach,' *Journal of Financial Regulation*, vol. 1, no. 2,
     pp. 206–225.
Avgouleas, E 2012, *Governance of Global Financial Markets: The Law, the Economics,
     the Politics*, Cambridge: Cambridge University Press.
Barnier, M 2013, 'International cooperation: a sine qua non for the success of OTC
     derivatives markets reform,' in OTC Derivatives: New Rules, New Actors, New
     Risks; Banque de France, *Financial Stability Review*, no. 17, pp. 41–46.
Beck, T, Coyle, D, Seabright, P and Freixas, X 2010, 'Bailing out the banks: recon-
     ciling stability and competition,' Centre for Economic Policy Research, London,
     18 February. https://voxeu.org/content/bailing-out-banks-reconciling-stability-and
     -competition (last accessed 14 April 2020).
Bergström, CF 2015, 'Shaping the new system for delegation of powers to EU agen-
     cies: United Kingdom v. European Parliament and Council (Short selling),' *Common
     Market Law Review*, vol. 52, no. 1, pp. 219–242.
Braithwaite, JP 2012, 'Standard form contracts as transnational law: evidence from the
     derivatives markets,' *The Modern Law Review*, vol. 75, no. 5, pp. 779–805.
Brummer, C 2010, 'Territoriality as a regulatory technique: notes from the financial
     crisis,' *University of Cincinnati Law Review*, vol. 79, no. 2, pp. 499–526.
Brummer, C (rapporteur) 2013, 'The danger of divergence: transatlantic financial reform
     & the G20 agenda' (a report prepared for the Atlantic Council, Thomson Reuters and
     TheCityUK). Washington: the Atlantic Council. https://www.atlanticcouncil.org/
     in-depth-research-reports/report/the-danger-of-divergence-transatlantic-financial
     -reform-the-g20-agenda/ (last visited 14 April 2020).
Brunsden, J and Stafford, P 2019, 'EU asserts power over City's euro clearing role,'
     The Financial Times, 13 March, FT Trading Room.
Buxbaum, HL 2002, 'Conflict of economic laws: from sovereignty to substance,'
     Virginia Journal of International Law, vol. 42, no. 4, pp. 931–977.
Carney, M 2013, 'Completing the G20 reform agenda for strengthening over-the-counter
     derivatives markets,' in OTC Derivatives: New Rules, New Actors, New Risks;
     Banque de France, *Financial Stability Review*, no. 17, pp. 11–18.
Carruthers, BG 2013, 'Diverging derivatives: law, governance and modern financial
     markets,' *Journal of Comparative Economics*, vol. 41, no. 2, pp. 386–400.
CESR. 2015, Press Release, 'Committee of European Securities Regulators and the US
     CFTC meet to facilitate transatlantic derivatives business and to appoint task force
     to develop further efforts' (Ref. 05-096), 14 February 2005.
CESR-CFTC. 2005, 'Communiqué, CESR-CFTC Common Work Program to Facilitate
     Transatlantic Derivatives Business,' 28 June 2005 (available at https://www.esma

.europa.eu/document/cesr-cftc-common-work-program-facilitate-transatlantic -derivatives-business) (last accessed 14 April 2020).

CFTC. 2012, 'Further definition of "swap dealer," "security-based swap dealer," "major swap participant," "major security-based swap participant" and "eligible contract participant,"' *Federal Register*, vol. 77, no. 100, 23 May 2012, rules and regulations.

CFTC. 2013a 'Cross-border security-based swap activities: re-proposal of Regulation SBSR and certain rules and forms relating to the registration of security-based swap dealers and major security-based swap participants,' *Federal Register*, vol. 78, no. 100, 23 May 2013, proposed rules.

CFTC. 2013b, 'Final exemptive order regarding compliance with certain swap regulations (Dec. 20, 2012),' *Federal Register*, vol. 78, no. 4, Monday 7 January 2013, rules and regulations https://www.govinfo.gov/content/pkg/FR-2013-01-07/pdf/ 2012-31736.pdf (last accessed 14 April 2020).

CFTC. 2013c, Press release, 'The European Commission and the CFTC reach a common path on derivatives,' 11 July 2013, http://www.cftc.gov/PressRoom/ PressReleases/pr6640-13 (last accessed 14 April 2020).

CFTC. 2014, J Christopher Giancarlo, Commissioner of the CFTC, Keynote Address at The Global Forum for Derivatives Markets, 35th Annual Burgenstock Conference, Geneva Switzerland, 24 September 2014.

Chamorro-Courtland, C 2019, 'Brexit scenarios: the future of clearing in Europe,' *Columbia Journal of European Law*, vol. 25, p. 169.

Choi SJ and Gulati GM 2006, 'Contract as statute,' *Michigan Law Review*, vol. 104, no. 5, pp. 1129–1173.

Coffee JC Jr 2014, 'Extraterritorial financial regulation: why ET can't come home,' *Cornell Law Review*, vol. 99, no. 6, pp. 1259–1302.

Cox, J 2012, 'The extraterritorial reach of the US financial laws,' in E Wymeersch, KJ Hopt and G Ferrarini (eds), *Financial Regulation and Supervision: A Post-Crisis Analysis*, Oxford: Oxford University Press, Chapter 15 (Kindle edition).

De Ryck, P 2019, 'Towards unified representation for the euro area within the IMF,' European Parliamentary Research Service, PE 637.969, July 2019.

Deutsche Börse and Eurex Clearing 2014, 'How central counterparties strengthen the safety and integrity of financial markets?' July 2014. https://www.deutsche-boerse .com/resource/blob/78994/37fbffb2a577d8e43d52d19223b49c63/data/how-central -counter-parties-strengthen-the-safety-and-integrity-of-financial-markets_de.pdf (last accessed 14 April 2020).

ESMA. 2013. Final Report: Technical advice on third country regulatory equivalence under EMIR – US, ESMA/2013/115, 1 September 2013.

ESMA. 2014. Report (final) on draft regulatory technical standards on direct, substantial and foreseeable effect in the EU, endorsed by the European Commission on 13 February 2014, Commission Delegated Regulation (EU) No 285/2014.

ESMA. 2015, EMIR Review Report no. 4 (2015/1254), 2015.

European Commission. 2010, EMIR Impact Assessment 2010, EMIR.

European Commission. 2017a, Staff Working Document: EU equivalence decisions in financial services policy: an assessment, p. 4, Brussels, 27 February 2017, SWD (2017) 102 final.

European Commission. 2017b, Press Release, 'Commission adopts EMIR equivalence decision for derivatives transactions in the United States,' Brussels, 13 October 2017.

FCIC. 2011, Financial Crisis Inquiry Commission, Report (The FCIC Report). https://www.govinfo.gov/content/pkg/GPO-FCIC/pdf/GPO-FCIC.pdf (last accessed 14 April 2020).

Feder, NM 2002, 'Deconstructing over-the-counter derivatives,' *Columbia Business Law Review*, vol. 2000, no. 3, pp. 677–748.

Freeman, J and Rossi, J 2011, 'Agency coordination in shared regulatory space,' *Harvard Law Review*, vol. 125, no. 5, pp. 1131–1211.

FSB. 2010, Financial Stability Board, 'Implementing OTC derivatives market reforms,' report, 25 October 2010.

FSB. 2012, Financial Stability Board, meeting in November 2012, joint press statement 'Operating principles and areas of exploration in the regulation of the cross-border OTC derivatives market,' December 2012.

FSB. 2015, Financial Stability Board, OTC derivatives market reforms, tenth progress report on implementation, 4 November 2015.

FSB. 2017, Financial Stability Board, 'Review of OTC derivatives market reforms, effectiveness and broader effects of the reforms,' 29 June 2017.

FSB. 2018, Financial Stability Board, 'Implementation and effects of the G20 financial regulatory reforms,' 4th Annual Report, 28 November 2018.

G20. 2009, G20 Leaders' Statement: The Pittsburgh Summit, 24–25 September 2009, Pittsburgh. http://www.g20.utoronto.ca/2009/2009communique0925.html (Last visited 14 April 2020).

G20. 2013, G20 Leaders' Declaration, St. Petersburg Summit, 5–6 September 2013. https://g20.org/en/g20/Documents/2013-Russia-G20%20Leaders_%20Declaration.pdf (Last visited 14 April 2020).

GAO. 2011, United States Government Accountability Office, 'Financial derivatives, disparate tax treatment and information gaps create uncertainty and potential abuse,' September 2011.

Godwin, A, Ramsay, I and Sayes, E 2017, 'Assessing financial regulatory coordination and integration with reference to OTC derivatives regulation,' *Capital Markets Law Journal*, vol. 12, no. 1, pp. 38–65.

Goodhart, CA and Lastra, RM 2010, 'Border problems,' *Journal of International Economic Law*, vol. 13, no. 3, pp. 705–718.

Greene, EF and Potiha, I 2012, 'Examining the extraterritorial reach of Dodd–Frank's Volcker rule and margin rules for uncleared swaps – a call for regulatory coordination and cooperation,' *Capital Markets Law Journal*, vol. 7, no. 3, pp. 271–316.

Green, EF and Potiha, I 2013, 'Issues in the extraterritorial application of Dodd–Frank's derivatives and clearing rules, the impact on global markets and the inevitability of cross-border and US domestic coordination.' *Capital Markets Law Journal*, vol. 8, no. 4, pp. 338–394.

Hancher, L and Moran, M 1998, 'Organizing regulatory space,' in R Baldwin, C Scott and C Hood (eds), *A Reader on Regulation*, Oxford: Oxford University Press, Chapter 3.

Hu, HTC 1993, 'Misunderstood derivatives: the causes of informational failure and the promise of regulatory incrementalism,' *Yale Law Journal*, vol. 102, no. 6, pp. 1457–1513.

Hull, JC 2011, *Options, Futures, and Other Derivatives*, 8th edition, Pearson College Division.

Institute of International Finance (IIF). 2019, 'Addressing market fragmentation: the need for enhanced global regulatory cooperation,' January 2019. https://www.iif

.com/Portals/0/Files/IIF%20FSB%20Fragmentation%20Report.pdf (last accessed 14 April 2020).

IOSCO. 2015, 'Task force on cross-border regulation final report,' FR 23/2015, September 2015. https://www.iosco.org/library/pubdocs/pdf/IOSCOPD507.pdf (last accessed 14 April 2020)

IOSCO. 2019, 'Market fragmentation & cross-border regulation,' Report. FR07/2019, June 2019. https://www.iosco.org/library/pubdocs/pdf/IOSCOPD629.pdf (last accessed 14 April 2020).

ISDA. 2013, 'Non-cleared OTC derivatives: their importance to the global economy,' March 2013. https://www.isda.org/2013/03/13/non-cleared-otc-derivatives-their -importance-to-the-global-economy/ (last accessed 14 April 2020).

ISDA. 2015, 'Cross-border fragmentation of global derivatives: end-year 2014 update', April 2015. https://www.isda.org/a/EVDDE/market-fragmentation-final.pdf (last accessed 14 April 2020).

Jackson, HE 2015, 'Substituted compliance: the emergence, challenges, and evolution of a new regulatory paradigm,' *Journal of Financial Regulation*, vol. 1, no. 2, pp. 169–205.

Jain, AG 2014, 'Derivatives as a test case for international financial regulation through the WTO,' *Journal of World Trade*, vol. 48, no. 1, pp. 135–165.

Joint Statement. 2016, 'Improvements in EU–US regulatory cooperation,' Brussels, 18 July 2016. https://ec.europa.eu/info/sites/info/files/business_economy_euro/ banking_and_finance/documents/160718-eu-us-joint-financial-regulatory-dialogue -joint-statement_en.pdf (last accessed 14 April 2020).

Karmel, RS 2007, 'The EU challenge to the SEC,' *Fordham International Law Journal*, vol. 31, no. 6, pp. 1692–1712.

Kentz, M 2014, 'Equity derivatives traders warm to OTC,' *Reuters*, 13 April. https:// www.reuters.com/article/markets-derivatives-otc/equity-derivatives-traders-warm -to-otc-idUSL2N0X71ER20150413 (last accessed 14 April 2020).

Knaack, P 2015, 'Innovation and deadlock in global financial governance: transatlantic coordination failure in OTC derivatives regulation,' *Review of International Political Economy*, vol. 22, no. 6, pp. 1217–1248.

Lannoo, K 2013, 'The new financial regulatory paradigm: a transatlantic perspective,' CEPS Policy Brief, no. 287, 21 March 2013.

Lastra, RM 2014, 'Do we need a world financial organization?' *Journal of International Economic Law*, vol. 17, no. 4, pp. 787–805.

Majone, G 1998, 'The rise of the regulatory state in Europe,' in R Baldwin, C Scott and C Hood (eds), *A Reader on Regulation*, Oxford: Oxford University Press, Chapter 5.

Marjosola, H 2014, 'Bridging the constitutional gap in EU executive rule-making: the Court of Justice approves legislative conferral of intervention powers to European securities and Markets Authority: Case C-270/12, UK v. Parliament and Council (Grand Chamber),' *European Constitutional Law Review*, vol. 10, no. 3, pp. 500–527.

Marjosola, H 2015, 'Missing pieces in the patchwork of EU financial stability regime? The case of central counterparties,' *Common Market Law Review*, vol. 52, no, 6, pp. 1491–1527.

Markham, JW 2003, 'Super regulator: a comparative analysis of securities and derivatives regulation in the United States, the United Kingdom, and Japan,' *Brooklyn Journal of International* Law, vol. 28, no. 2, pp. 319–410.

McCormick, L 2015, 'Financial firms move closer to central clearing in repo market,' *Bloomberg*, 13 April 2015. https://www.bloomberg.com/news/articles/2015-04-13/

financial-firms-move-closer-to-central-clearing-in-repo-market (last accessed 14 April 2020).

Moloney, N 2018, *The Age of ESMA: Governing EU Financial Markets*, London: Bloomsbury Publishing.

Pan, EJ 2003, 'Harmonization of US–EU securities regulation: the case for a single European securities regulator,' *Law and Policy in International Business*, vol. 34, no. 2, pp. 499–536.

Pan, EJ 2008, 'Single stock futures and cross-border access for US investors,' *Stanford Journal of Law, Business & Finance*, vol. 12, no. 1, pp. 221–261.

Pan, EJ 2011, 'Structural reform of financial regulation,' *Transnational Law & Contemporary Problems*, vol. 19, no. 3, pp. 796–867.

Partnoy, F 1997, 'Financial derivatives and the costs of regulatory arbitrage,' *The Journal of Corporate Law*, vol. 22, no 2, pp. 211–256.

Partnoy, F 2001, 'The shifting contours of global derivatives regulation,' *University of Pennsylvania Journal of International Law*, vol. 22, no. 3, pp. 421–495.

Piwowar, MS 2014, 'Toward a global regulatory framework for cross-border OTC derivatives activities,' the Harvard Law School Forum on Corporate Governance and Financial Regulation, 22 March.

Posner, E 2009, 'Making rules for global finance: transatlantic regulatory cooperation at the turn of the millennium,' *International Organization*, vol. 63, no. 4, pp. 665–699.

Posner, E 2018, 'Financial regulatory cooperation: coordination of derivatives markets,' in E. Helleiner, S Pagliari and I Spagna (eds), *Governing the World's Biggest Market: The Politics of Derivatives Regulation after the 2008 Crisis*, New York: Oxford University Press, Chapter 2.

Raustiala, K 2002, 'The architecture of international cooperation: transgovernmental networks and the future of international law,' *Virginia Journal of International Law*, vol. 43, pp. 1–92.

Riles, A 2014, 'Managing regulatory arbitrage: a conflict of laws approach,' *Cornell International Law Journal*, vol. 47, no. 1, pp. 63–119.

Singh, M 2010, 'Collateral, netting and systemic risk in the OTC Derivatives Market,' IMF Working Paper 10/99.

Singh, M and Aitken, J 2009, 'Counterparty risk, impact on collateral flows and role for central counterparties,' IMF Working Paper 09/173.

Stafford, P 2014, 'Europe calls on US to recognise overseas clearing rules,' *The Financial Times*, 28 June.

Stafford, P 2015, 'Market calls for US and Europe to end derivatives dispute,' *The Financial Times*, 2 September.

Stafford, P 2019, 'EU plans to tighten derivatives rules rankles in the US,' *The Financial Times*, 27 June, Opinion Tail Risk.

Stafford, P and Rennison, J 2019, 'CFTC agrees to rein in rules for overseas clearing houses,' 12 July, *The Financial Times*, FT Trading Room.

Tafara, E and Peterson, RJ 2007, 'A blueprint for cross-border access to US investors: a new international framework,' *Harvard International Law Journal*, vol. 48, no. 1, pp. 31–68.

Tett, G 2019, 'A transatlantic front opens in the Brexit battle over derivatives: Britain is caught in the middle of a regulatory tussle between the US and the EU,' *The Financial Times*, 19 March.

Verdier, P-H 2013, 'The political economy of international financial regulation,' *Indiana Law Journal*, vol. 88, no. 4, pp. 1405–1474.

Yen, J and Lai, KK 2014, *Emerging Financial Derivatives: Understanding Exotic Options and Structured Products*, London: Routledge.

PART III

Hybrid governance perspective: public and private regulation

6. The emergence of transnational hybrid governance: how private risks trigger public intervention

Johannes Karremans and Adrienne Héritier

6.1 INTRODUCTION

The wave of financial market regulations that followed the financial crisis of 2008 offers new insights for understanding the conditions under which public regulators intervene in privately self-regulated markets and the possible forces containing their actions. The legislative and regulatory initiatives that were taken in the EU between 2009 and 2018, in fact, extended the reach of public regulation into areas that were previously mostly regulated through privately set standards. However, as the new rules and regulations do not affect all aspects of the financial markets in the same way, they provide a considerable degree of within-case variation in terms of the extent to which certain segments of the market are affected by – or remain exempt from – the extension of public oversight. This within-case variation is highly useful in providing a deeper insight into whether – and under which conditions – private self-regulation prompts (centralised) public regulation (*H8*). In this chapter, by investigating the interaction between private and public regulators during the post-crisis regulatory wave, we probe the plausibility of our hypotheses about how systems of hybrid governance emerge and develop.

As anticipated in Chapter 1 (section 1.3), with regard to the emergence and development of systems of hybrid regulatory governance, we expect a sequence of two different causal mechanisms. First, our expectation is that systems of *private self-regulation* develop together with the emergence of new market instruments (*H8.1*) and that private self-regulatory regimes will attract new market actors who will abide by their existing norms and procedures (*H8.2*). Second, systems of *hybrid governance* develop in a subsequent stage and largely rely on the existing structures of the private regimes, but with some surveillance by public actors. More specifically, we expect there to be two conditions under which public authorities may decide to intervene in a private

regulatory regime, thereby creating a mixed public–private system of governance. The first of these conditions (*H8.3*) is that key players in the private regulatory regime are excessively rent-seeking, thereby damaging market players,
customers and consumers. The second condition (*H8.4*) is that the segment
of the market that is privately self-regulated may create system-stability risk,
thereby calling for a centralised regulatory structure. Given the interlinkedness of financial transactions worldwide, the first condition of excessive
rent-seeking may enhance the second condition of system-stability risk if new
financial-instrument markets are important enough in terms of volume.

In this chapter, we probe the plausibility of our argument by looking at
two cases that differ substantially in the extent to which they have been
affected by the post-crisis regulatory wave. These are: (a) the international
over-the-counter (OTC) derivative market; and (b) the Alternative Investment
Market (AIM) of the London Stock Exchange. Both markets emerged and
developed with private self-regulation. However, the extent and the timing
with which public regulators sought to extend their control over them varied
greatly. OTC derivative markets, in fact, came under the spotlight immediately
at the G20 Pittsburgh summit in September 2009. The AIM, by contrast,
remained largely untouched by European legislation until 2016. In two
in-depth case studies, we describe the private self-regulatory regimes that were
put in place in these two markets and analyse how these regimes have been
affected by public regulatory initiatives. In the analysis, we explore the interaction between public authorities and the dominant private actors operating in
the markets.

For the case of OTC derivative markets, we start by describing how the
International Swaps and Derivatives Association (ISDA) was the private
authority regulating these markets between the 1980s and 2008, and how
in the aftermath of the global financial crisis public regulators started to
coordinate their actions at the international level to fill the regulatory gaps
in the markets. Subsequently, by means of a policy document analysis, we
show how ISDA tried to shelter certain segments of the OTC market from the
Commission's regulatory initiatives. The case study thus provides an illustration of how ISDA tried to influence EU regulatory initiatives and sketches the
mix of private and public responsibilities in the current regulatory framework.
As we shall see, in the new hybrid governance framework, the regulatory
quasi-monopoly that ISDA used to have until 2012 has substantially been
curbed by the central clearing obligations introduced by the European Market
Infrastructure Regulation (EMIR). At the same time, however, ISDA main-
tains an important authority not only over those derivatives that are exempted
from central clearing, but also in the definition of the technical terms under
which those exemptions apply.

For the case of the AIM, we start by describing how this market was purposefully established in 1995 to allow small companies to bypass the compliance costs related to British and European legislation, and how it developed a light-touch but controversial regulatory regime. We proceed by examining how an accumulation of malpractices and a record of relatively low returns for investors gradually triggered the attention of public regulators, which, however, limited themselves mostly to pressing the private regulators to monitor misconduct more closely. Subsequently, we show how companies listed in the AIM became directly subject to European transparency rules in 2016, which, however, did not alter the fundamental functioning of the existing regulatory regime. In the case of the AIM, the hybrid regime features limited public intervention and large elements of continuation from the previous private regime.

We conclude the chapter with an assessment of whether these two cases confirm our argument that when market participants are excessively rent-seeking and/or there is potential systemic risk private self-regulation eventually develops into a hybrid system of governance, with public authorities trying to centralise regulation which is, however, based on the existing structures of the private regime.

6.2 THE NEW HYBRID GOVERNANCE OF OTC DERIVATIVE MARKETS

6.2.1 The Emergence of a New Market and its Private Regulation

OTC derivatives constitute a particular sector of the financial market. Backed also by the rise of neoliberal ideas about the benefits of unregulated markets (Mügge 2011), between the 1980s and 2000s they "operated largely within a regulatory vacuum" (Awrey 2010, p. 162). This lack of public regulation was strongly related to the nature of OTC derivatives. Like all other derivatives, these instruments derive their value from another underlying asset (Flanagan 2001) and can therefore be defined as being "nothing more than probabilistic bets on future events" (Stout 2011, p. 304). They include contracts representing the right (and sometimes the obligation) to buy or sell a certain security, commodity, currency or "another financial instrument at some future date at a predetermined settlement rate" (Biggins and Scott 2012, p. 312). Unlike exchange-traded derivatives, however, OTC derivatives are traded 'over-the-counter', directly between buyers and sellers, and therefore do not pass through a central clearing counterparty (CCP) that interposes itself between the buyer and the seller. They are therefore traded via ad hoc agreements between buyers and sellers. Consequently, they are typically more tailor-made for end-users and less standardised. As a result, they are on the one hand considered useful risk management and investment strategies while on the other they are also considered to be riskier than derivatives traded through a CCP (Biggins and Scott 2012, p. 316).

While trades in these types of instrument can be traced back as far as the fifteenth century, the internationalisation of the financial market in the 1980s and the related growth in the use of advanced computer technologies transformed financial markets, and OTC derivative markets came to stand at the centre of modern banking (Schinasi et al. 2000). In this transformation, OTC derivatives became increasingly complex instruments involving multiple payment exchanges, with credit exposures being increasingly associated with time-varying derivatives (Schinasi et al. 2000, pp. 3, 16). Consequently, the flows of liquidity associated with OTC derivative transactions became more difficult to understand and predict, even for experts in the sector. With advanced computer technologies, both the volume and the speed of trades in these instruments increased exponentially (Schinasi et al. 2000). Within just two decades, OTC derivatives became the world's biggest market (Helleiner et al. 2018) and, despite bearing considerable systemic risk, they remained sheltered from public regulation. This shelter was partially provided by the complexity of the market and partially by the private interest group that asserted itself as a private regulatory authority: the International Derivatives and Swaps Association (ISDA).

Ever since its foundation in 1985, ISDA has largely focused its activity on establishing itself as a private actor that ensures stability and predictability in the trading of swaps and derivatives, and in particular of OTC derivatives (Morgan 2008). In the thirty years between the rise of international derivative markets in the 1980s and the financial crash of 2008, ISDA developed a system of private self-regulation in derivative markets that ensured standard practices of derivative trading, providing contractual standards and facilitating transactions. Amongst these, the most important accomplishment was the establishment of a Master Agreement whereby market participants can rely on a standard contract to trade in derivatives. Because of their bespoke nature, at the time of their emergence OTC derivatives lacked a common 'language'. As this shortcoming hampered the expansion of the market, ISDA filled the vacuum by setting standards at which contracts on a global scale could be developed (Rauterberg and Verstein 2013). ISDA's Master Agreement, consequently, became the global standard for trading OTC derivatives and strengthened the association's authority in the eyes of public regulators, and also the idea that the OTC derivative market worked best if self-regulated.[1] In parallel, ISDA played a double guarantee role: towards public regulators it stood as a guarantor of system stability, whereas towards buyers and sellers it facilitated the settling of outstanding obligations. The case of the Lehman Brothers Bank collapse in 2008 is emblematic, as within a week of the collapse all OTC contracts referencing the bank were settled thanks to ISDA's services (Morgan 2009, p. 33).

The establishment of ISDA as a private regulatory authority was in line with the idea that systems of private self-regulation develop together with the emergence of new market instruments (*H8.1*). Even though the practice of OTC derivative trading existed long before the establishment of ISDA, the complexity of the instruments that progressively entered the financial markets in the 1980s was unforeseen. ISDA emerged as an authority that would regulate trading in these complex derivatives and provide common standards internationally. This happened in spite of the growing market share of OTC derivatives and their potential systemic risk. Even though on various occasions trading in OTC derivatives led to big financial losses for high-profile market participants – like Procter & Gamble in 1994 – these risks did not trigger public intervention. On the contrary, such incidents generally resulted in strengthening ISDA's role as a standard-setter and even as an educator of market participants (Flanagan 2001, pp. 224–225).

This brings us to our second hypothesis on the development of private self-regulatory regimes (*H8.2*), namely that they will attract new market participants who will in turn abide by the rules put in place by the existing regulatory regime. This hypothesis finds confirmation not only in the role ISDA played in the market between the 1980s and 2008 but also in the rapid growth and the organisation of its membership. Having been founded by 11 financial institutions, ISDA grew to have 500 members at around the turn of the century and over 900 today, including the world's biggest banks, financial operators and large corporations. It is interesting to note that the members are organised in different categories according to their role in the market: banks dealing in derivatives are Primary Members, service providers that play a key role in the functioning of the market are Associate Members, and end-users are Subscribers. With this organisational structure, ISDA thus provides a forum for all market participants to discuss the rules governing the private regulatory regime. In this forum, however, only the Primary Members develop ISDA's self-regulatory policies and have the final say on the policy-advocacy strategies of the organisation. Table 6.1 illustrates ISDA's organisational structure. The primary members are thus the world's most important commercial banks, most of which have been recognised as having the status of global systemic important banks by international public authorities such as the Financial Stability Board.[2] In parallel, many important public institutions like the European Investment Bank and the European Stability Mechanism are among the Subscriber Members. This is indicative of how a privately born institution like ISDA grew to attract public authorities, which in some cases – like for example the Bank of Italy – even became end-users of the financial instruments sold by ISDA's Primary Members (see also Lagna 2016).

Table 6.1   *ISDA's organisational structure*

	Primary Members	**Associate Members**	**Subscriber Members**
Number	208	311	417
Description	Main global and international dealers of derivatives	Service providers, i.e. key components of the derivative market infrastructure, including exchanges, clearing organisations and repositories, as well as law firms, accounting firms and technology solution providers	End users, i.e. corporations, financial institutions, government entities and others that use derivatives to better manage financial risks
Function	To participate in policy-development and advocacy	To stay up to date with and influence important developments and initiatives	To stay up to date with and influence important developments and initiatives
Examples	ABN AMRO Bank N.V., Banca Monte Dei Paschi di Siena SpA, Barclays, Deutsche Bank AG, Goldman Sachs & Co., Intesa Sanpaolo SpA, JPMorgan Chase & Co., Lloyds Banking Group Plc, Morgan Stanley & Co. International plc, Royal Bank of Canada	Accenture AG, Bloomberg Financial Markets, Chicago Board Options Exchange, Deloitte LLP, Ernst & Young, Eurex Clearing AG, KPMG LLP, NASDAQ OMX Stockholm AB, Satori Consulting, Thomson Reuters	African Development Bank, Banca d'Italia, Bank of England, Eurasian Development Bank, European Investment Bank, European Stability Mechanism, Intel Corporation, McDonald's Corporation, Vodafone Group Services Ltd.

Note: Information retrieved from: https://www.isda.org/membership (accessed 12 September 2019).

The intermingling of the private and public spheres, in turn, is not limited to the use of derivatives by public institutions, but there is also a dependence of private regulatory entities on the enforcing hand of public authorities. As argued earlier, financial contracts rely on private law but – in the case of liquidity crises – they need the guarantee of a central public authority (Pistor 2013). Consequently, private regulators need to engage with public authorities. Therefore, in addition to its self-regulatory activity, since its foundation ISDA also actively engaged in lobbying national governments to make sure that their legislation – particularly in the field of insolvency and bankruptcy – was in harmony with the standards of the Master Agreement. More specifically, ISDA was particularly active in ensuring that OTC derivative transactions remained outside the realm of bankruptcy and gambling legislation (Biggins and Scott 2012). Thus, ISDA ensured that the parties to a derivative exchange would be able to smoothly net out their balances even in the case of the bankruptcy of one of the parties without going through the legal procedures associated with national bankruptcy legislation. Consequently, ISDA also devoted a considerable part of its activity to ensuring that netting (i.e. the clearing of a contract with one single payment combining various streams of payments) was in line with national legal codes (Morgan 2008, pp. 647–651).

Aware of its dependence on the enforcing hand of public authorities, ISDA worked in close collaboration with national governments, which in turn welcomed the expertise provided by market participants. ISDA and public legislators shared an interest in the stability of the financial system. Public legislators therefore trusted the advice of private experts on the most appropriate legislation for the market to function, while the private sector needed a harmonisation of legislation in different national jurisdictions to favour market transactions. In its lobbying activity, ISDA mainly succeeded in leaving derivative markets outside the scope of bankruptcy and gambling laws and also in promoting netting legislation in different countries (Morgan 2008; Biggins and Scott 2012). On a broader scale, the main success of ISDA was probably its capacity to frame how derivative markets were talked and thought of in the public sphere (Morgan 2008, p. 640). Like other business associations, ISDA in fact succeeded in promoting a narrative on the social and economic desirability of derivative markets (Morgan 2008; Bowman et al. 2017; Engelen 2017).

These interactions with public authorities suggest that the possibility of a shift towards a hybrid public–private system of governance was already present in the heyday of ISDA as a private regulatory authority. The interactions between ISDA and public authorities, however, were not triggered by the potential systemic risk in the derivative market or by excessive rent-seeking activities by market participants. Instead, these interactions were the result of a need for the public authorities' enforceable hand, a feature that the private regulatory regime lacked. This suggests that private regulatory regimes are always – at least to some small degree – *hybrid*, in the sense that the private regime needs the recognition and sometimes even the collaboration of a public authority (Pistor 2013) (see Chapter 1 in this volume). In the case of the OTC derivative market, however – up until 2008 – the interactions and collaborations between private and public authorities were generally not initiatives by the latter but instead by the ISDA, aimed at strengthening the enforceability of its contractual standards (Morgan 2008).

This all changed with the global financial crisis of 2008, when the global financial system came close to collapse and public regulators were forced to step in. For the OTC derivative market, this meant an end to almost three decades of being sheltered from public regulation. For ISDA, it meant that probably for the first time it was not taking the initiative in its exchanges with public legislators but instead was forced to react to the latter's initiatives.

6.2.2   Public Intervention and the Establishment of a Hybrid Governance Regime

Following the fall of Lehman Brothers and the consequent financial crisis, between 2008 and 2009 the G20 leaders intensively coordinated their actions to remedy the lack of regulation in the financial market sector. In their common statement after the 2009 Pittsburgh summit, the G20 leaders underlined their commitment to improving and expanding the scope of public regulation and supervision.[3] This commitment particularly regarded OTC derivatives, which were identified as being at the heart of what went wrong during the financial crisis.[4] The package of measures that leaders agreed upon was presented as an effort to tackle excessive risks taken by large global financial firms, like, for example, in the following passage:

> We committed to act together to raise capital standards, to implement strong inter-national compensation standards aimed at ending practices that lead to excessive risk-taking, to improve the over-the-counter derivatives market and to create more powerful tools to hold large global firms to account for the risks they take. Standards for large global financial firms should be commensurate with the cost of their failure. For all these reforms, we have set for ourselves strict and precise timetables.[5]

In the statement, references to the OTC markets always mentioned the excessive risk taken by financial firms. Consequently, the statement presented a number of measures to be implemented by the members of the G20 by the end of 2012. The following passage from the statement indicates the type of measures the G20 leaders agreed on with regard to the OTC derivative market:

> *Improving over-the-counter derivatives markets:* All standardised OTC derivative contracts should be traded on exchanges or electronic trading platforms, where appropriate, and cleared through central counterparties by end-2012 at the latest. OTC derivative contracts should be reported to trade repositories. Non-centrally cleared contracts should be subject to higher capital requirements. We ask the FSB and its relevant members to assess regularly implementation and whether it is sufficient to improve transparency in the derivatives markets, mitigate systemic risk, and protect against market abuse.[6]

The statement explicitly refers to the public regulation of the OTC derivative market as a necessary action to 'mitigate systemic risk' and 'protect against market abuse'. The systemic risk associated with OTC derivatives would later also be underscored by the FSB, which ascribed systemic importance to the large numbers of global financial firms dealing in these instruments.[7] The excessive rent-seeking behaviour and market abuses, in turn, were underscored by the numerous cases of disproportionately high bonuses for managers of financial firms dealing in OTC derivatives (e.g. *The Telegraph* 2009).

As is also discussed in Chapter 3 by Fabio Bulfone and Agnieszka Smoleńska, in Europe the G20 commitments to reform the regulation of the OTC derivatives market translated into the establishment of the European Market Infrastructure Regulation (EMIR) in 2012. The central-clearing and reporting obligations introduced by EMIR can therefore be considered the European extension of the commitments made by the G20 leaders at the 2009 summit in Pittsburgh to tackle excessive risk-taking behaviour by global financial firms.[8] The sequence of events therefore followed the logic of our argument: public authorities step into privately self-regulated markets when they perceive key market players to be becoming excessively rent-seeking (*H8.3*) and when a failure to regulate their activities can cause serious systemic risk (*H8.4*).

At the same time, however, the introduction of European regulation also involved a considerable amount of power politics between member states, with some countries favouring a more light-touch regulation and others strong public intervention (Quaglia 2012). As a result, while EMIR was drafted at the European level, its implementation runs the concrete risk of featuring patterns of de-centralisation, with different countries performing different modalities of market supervision (Helleiner 2014; see also Chapters 2 and 3 in this volume). Nonetheless, in terms of rule-making, EMIR can be considered an effort to centralise regulatory authority at the European level. Under the new regulatory framework, in fact, European institutions such as the European Securities and Markets Authority (ESMA) not only have the authority to decide on the criteria OTC derivatives need to comply with the new reporting and clearing obligations but also have the competence to authorise trade repositories (TRs) and CCPs, which under EMIR have become key players in the derivative market. Following our hybrid governance research perspective, we are interested in exploring how ISDA positioned itself with regard to both the content of the regulation and the centralisation of rule-making.

Thanks to its expertise in the functioning of these markets, ISDA remained a powerful interlocutor for governments and public authorities. For example, ESMA's first chair, Steven Maijoor, gave his first public speech at an ISDA conference[9] and in the speech reasserted the public regulators' view of OTC derivatives as carriers of risk and underscored the market's systemic importance. At the same time, the chairman also acknowledged ISDA's contributions helping to improve the market's resilience. The following passages report Steven Maijoor's statements in this regard:

> The financial crisis we have faced and whose effects are still felt very seriously has no single cause. However, the structure and functioning of the OTC derivatives markets played a major role in amplifying and spreading the risks entrenched in

the financial market by creating an opaque web of interdependencies difficult to
understand and disentangle. [...]
While we all still recognise the importance of OTC derivatives, we have also
become more aware of their limitations and risks. Collective efforts are under way
to make these markets safer.
The industry, in particular ISDA and the major market participants involved in its
activities, have worked to improve the resilience of the OTC derivatives markets
by signing and delivering upon important commitments. The fact that we now have
CCPs clearing OTC derivatives and trade repositories recording the majority of
transactions in certain asset classes is largely due to the efforts of the industry –
although the supervisors have also played a role in guiding those developments.[10]

ISDA, therefore, did not seem to oppose the initiatives towards central clearing
and reporting obligations, but instead promoted itself as the sectoral interlocutor for developing measures that would ensure system stability. In fact, ISDA
started expressing favourable positions towards central clearing as early as
October 2008 in a letter to the American Federal Reserve,[11] and maintained
these positions in the following years. In the run-up to EMIR, ISDA regularly
released policy documents in which it took positions on the EU's legislative
initiatives regarding OTC derivative markets.[12] These documents were often
responses to consultation papers released by the European authorities.[13] In
these exchanges, ISDA confirmed its support for a regulatory framework that
was common to all EU member states and that followed the broader initiative
taken at the global level by the G20 leaders.

Moreover, this development was very much in line with ISDA's traditional
goal of developing common standards for market participants. In addition,
ISDA found itself in a favourable position to influence regulatory initiatives.
In fact, the extension of public oversight – and particularly of central clearing
obligations – required an assessment of the eligibility of specific derivatives
for central clearing. Consequently, public regulators needed the advice of
market insiders to establish such eligibility criteria and ISDA became one of
the main interlocutors (Biggins and Scott 2012, p. 340). The following quota-
tion offers an insight into how ISDA filled this role. The passage is taken from
a comment paper of July 2011 in which ISDA commented on the collateral
requirements for derivatives to be cleared through CCPs.

> Given the importance of this issue, and its technical nature, we favour a solution
> whereby the European Securities and Markets Authority (ESMA) is tasked with
> producing technical standards on collateral at CCPs. That process should be
> designed to allow sufficient time for ESMA to make a decision, with full consulta-
> tion of those operating and using CCPs.[14]

ISDA thus fully accepted ESMA's authority to develop the technical standards
autonomously. At the same time, however, it strongly encouraged ESMA to

consult with market participants, and therefore implicitly with ISDA itself. In the policy documents exchanged with the European authorities, ISDA is always unequivocally positive regarding ESMA's role in the new regulatory framework. Between the lines, however, ISDA has also consistently been advocating a containment of the scope of EMIR (Biggins and Scott 2012; Helleiner et al. 2018).

Despite the fact that the various consultation and policy papers released by ISDA on EMIR mostly regarded technical details of the legislation, they also latently pertained to political disputes on the reach of public regulation. For example, when asked for its opinion on the applicability of EMIR to counter-parties located in a third (non-EU) country, ISDA underlined the importance of having cooperation among jurisdictions in order to "avoid duplication and uncertainty over clearing obligations, and their application regionally".[15] At the same time, ISDA advocated "that a branch or affiliate, based in a third country, of an EMIR-regulated firm dealing with another entity in that third country"[16] should not be subject to EMIR, as this would increase the costs of providing its financial services in the country in which it operates. While on the one hand ISDA favoured international convergence in regulation, at the same time it also tried to influence the content and implementation of the new regulation to favour market participants. With this goal, ISDA also tried – and succeeded – to co-define together with ESMA the reach of the new central clearing obligations.

Even though it repeatedly expressed support for strengthening ESMA's authority and extending central clearing obligations in all the policy docu-ments released between 2009 and 2018, ISDA was also very keen to ensure that certain sections of the market remained sheltered from the new regula-tion (Morgan 2009; Biggins and Scott 2012). For instance, in the following passages taken from a response to the European Commission in 2018, ISDA confirmed its support for international convergence but opposed measures that would touch on the whole market:

> ISDA advocates that EMIR reporting be aligned with similar regimes globally, EMIR should establish a market-wide principle that derivatives transactions, which have been matched via confirmation and reconciliation processes, should only be reported once to supervisors, by one party, not twice.
>
> ISDA cautions against taking a one-size-fits-all approach in deciding on a standard which is to be used for many requirements across disparate product sets and by many different types of entities.[17]

In other words, ISDA consistently advocated for uniform criteria across juris-dictions, but against using uniform criteria in applying the new rules across the whole market. While sponsoring uniformity across the jurisdiction, ISDA advocated against a product-uniformity approach when defining the eligibility criteria for central clearing, underlining that some products are less suitable for clearing than others, and that forcing uniform clearing standards for diverse products could cause market disruptions.

In this policy advocacy, ISDA turned out to be considerably successful. EMIR, in fact, contains two main sources of exemption from the central clearing obligation. The first regards intragroup transactions which consist in OTC contracts established between counterparties that are part of the same group. These transactions still need to go through appropriate centralised risk evaluation, measurement and control procedures yet they are exempt from the obligation to exchange collateral, which, as we mention below, applies to other non-centrally-cleared transactions. The second source of exemption derives from the decisions that ESMA takes regarding clearing eligibility. Under EMIR, in fact, ESMA gains the authority to decide which classes of derivatives should meet the clearing obligation. Both these sources of exemption were explicitly advocated for by ISDA between 2009 and 2012. Intragroup transactions were defined as 'vital to the industry' and ISDA confirmed its advocacy for sheltering certain types of transactions from clearing obligations, as the following passage shows:

> The intragroup transaction exemption (from clearing and/or bilateral margining) is vital to the industry. We appeal to ESMA to use the flexibility afforded it in the EMIR level 1 text to phase Regulatory Technical Standards addressing the exemption in such a way that market participants do not have to collateralise transactions while awaiting regulatory approval of exemptions. If this situation can be avoided – while ensuring regulatory review of validity of application for exemption – it will prevent the creation of a misleading and excessive snapshot of bilateral risk and will also avoid a needless drain of liquidity at a time when liquidity is scarce. We also believe that it would be sensible to grant the exemption for 'kinds' of intragroup transaction (e.g. between certain counterparties) and not on a case-by-case basis (which would seem very demanding for regulators).[18]

The passage is taken from a response to a discussion paper released by ESMA only a few months before EMIR was finally adopted by the EU legislature. In the same document, ISDA also confirms its support for ESMA's autonomy to decide on the exemptions and the reach of central clearing obligations:

> We believe that any clearing obligation must be transparent, clear and publicly disclosed. Furthermore, ESMA should have the flexibility to change the parameters around clearing obligations if required to quickly respond as a result of global discussions and/or market conditions. Again, these changes should be transparent, clear and publicly disclosed.[19]

The 'parameters around the clearing obligations' are precisely the centre of gravity of the interactions between, on the one hand, public authorities stepping into the regulation of the OTC derivative markets and, on the other, ISDA promoting itself as an interlocutor providing sectoral expertise. Once the global financial crisis had changed the public regulators' views on the unregulated status of these markets, ISDA promoted itself as a supporter and an interlocutor for developing public regulation in the OTC derivative market. However, as public regulators needed sectoral expertise to define the reach of the new legislation, ISDA had an opportunity to advocate the sheltering of specific market segments, and so to keep these market segments under its own private regulatory regime.

In sum, when public regulators intervened in the regulation of OTC derivatives, ISDA did not oppose the introduction of central clearing and reporting obligations. On the contrary, in Europe it favoured the authority granted to ESMA about deciding the technical standards to which derivatives should be cleared and reported. In this sense, we can say that ISDA favoured a centralisation of rule-making in Europe (*H8*). As a result, the system of hybrid governance that emerged with the entry into force of EMIR has at least to some extent curbed the control that ISDA's private regulatory regime had over the derivatives market. Today, most derivatives are subject to reporting and central clearing obligations, and it is ESMA rather than ISDA that decides whether certain derivatives are exempt from such obligations. At the same time, however, ISDA still plays an important role in the decisions on these exemptions, as it assists ESMA in its decisions by providing sectoral expertise in defining eligibility criteria. As we will argue more extensively in the conclusion, it is through these channels of expertise-provision that we can expect ISDA to try to maximise its influence on the governance of the derivatives market and has thereby secured itself an important role in the new regulatory structure (*H9*).

6.3 THE REGULATION OF MARKET ABUSES IN THE AIM

6.3.1 The Creation of a Privately Self-regulated Market

Just as the emergence of the unregulated OTC derivatives market happened in conjunction with the rise of neoliberal ideas (Mügge 2011), the establishment of the AIM happened in line with the policy course that the British government was pursuing during the 1990s, namely the adoption of 'light touch' regulations in order to promote capital-raising and economic growth (*Financial Times* 2009). In the following two decades, in turn, the AIM proved to be an important driver of British economic growth, and also after the global financial crisis. In 2015, for example, AIM-listed companies generated over 400,000 jobs in the UK and contributed more than £14 billion to national GDP.[20] The flexibility provided by the AIM regulatory regime is thus not only beneficial to the companies it serves but it also generates revenue for the whole British economy. The AIM is thus not a market operating transnationally[21] but it has a specific location and is an important driver of its host-country's economic performance.

Unlike the OTC derivative market, the AIM is not a market for a particular type of financial instrument but is instead an ad hoc-created market sphere with very flexible rules. As a submarket of the London Stock Exchange (LSE), the AIM was designed as an accessible venue for small companies to raise capital. Its enhanced accessibility is provided by the rules for companies to be listed on the AIM. These rules are in fact much softer and more flexible than those of the main market for initial public offerings. Companies wishing to join the LSE, in fact, need to meet certain criteria, such as providing annual accounts and being valued at £700,000 or more (*Financial Times* 2018). When a company does not or is not able to meet these criteria, it can seek to list itself on the AIM. The AIM rules are relatively few and companies are not necessarily obliged to comply with them. Furthermore, the AIM applies the comply-or-explain mode of financial supervision: if a company fails to comply with AIM's rules, it may simply provide an explanation of why it has failed to do so (Espenlaub et al. 2012).

While the AIM was mainly established to help small companies raise capital, it also provides investors with a number of advantages. Generally, investors are fascinated by cases of fast high returns generated by companies dealing in the latest trending businesses, which are largely present on the AIM (*Financial Times* 2015a). In addition, for investors based in the UK, the AIM provides important tax advantages, such as business property relief and wealth taxes more in general.[22] As we shall see below, however, the rules and the performance of the AIM are at times also investor-unfriendly, in the sense that the rules fail to address malpractices and, often being provided with inaccurate information, inexperienced investors face a relatively high chance of incurring financial losses (*Financial Times* 2015b). At the same time, however, the shadiness of the AIM also provides investors with the advantage of being able to make trades without publicly disclosing their intentions, as they may be required to do on regulated exchanges.[23]

The rules governing the AIM are set by the LSE and are therefore private in nature. More precisely, in European regulatory terms the AIM falls within the category of multilateral trade facilities (MTFs),[24] a term used to refer to markets which are run by either a regulated market (like the LSE) or an investment firm. This terminology was introduced in the European Markets in Financial Instruments Directive (MiFiD) of 2004, which charged Member

States with the responsibility to ensure that firms or exchanges operating an MTF establish transparent rules.[25] As operating an MTF is a regulated activity in the UK, the LSE's opening of the AIM was subject to authorisation by the Financial Conduct Authority (FCA), which is the authority regulating financial services in the UK. The AIM is therefore governed by the privately set rules of the LSE, which in turn was authorised to run the AIM by the British financial authority. This again confirms the insight that private self-regulation is reliant on at least some form of public recognition (Pistor 2013). At the same time, it also highlights that with this structure the LSE is the entity directly subject to national and European legislation, while the AIM operates under the shelter provided by the authority gained by the LSE.

The regulatory framework of the AIM is principle-based rather than rule-based, in the sense that market participants have extensive leeway to interpret and implement a basic set of principles (Espenlaub et al. 2012, p. 429). This system works mainly through the reputational capital that market players build over time. The main actors responsible for ensuring compliance with the market rules are the nominated advisors (Nomads), which follow firms listed in the AIM in their regulatory compliance. Firms listed in the AIM are obliged to be linked to one of the various (currently 34) Nomads, which in turn compete to provide services to as many firms as possible. Nomads are financial companies, including both large international consultation companies such as Deloitte and PricewaterhouseCoopers, and less well-known consultancy companies focusing on specific business areas such as alternative energy, mining or real estate.

In order to operate in the AIM, Nomads must first be approved by the LSE, to which they also remain accountable. The LSE thus delegates the responsibility of market supervision to the Nomads. If a company fails, for example, to comply with AIM regulations, the LSE will fine the Nomad which follows it. Nomads, in turn, can force listed companies to comply with the AIM rules by threatening to cease acting as advisors to them and thus forcing them to leave the AIM. Table 6.2 summarises the scheme whereby the LSE decides the eligibility criteria for becoming a Nomad, and the main responsibilities that the latter has towards the LSE.

In practice, however, a series of malpractices in relation to this regulatory arrangement have been documented (*Financial Times* 2015a). As Nomads not only often receive fees but also may invest in the companies they assist, a conflict of interest regularly emerges between their regulatory function and the earnings they make from assisting specific companies. The LSE relies on fines and sanctions to ensure that the regulatory arrangement works, a threat that has occasionally been implemented in cases in which Nomads and the companies they assist were not able to prove that they had not divulged misleading information. Nomads, in turn, have an incentive to maintain their reputational

Table 6.2   Nomads: eligibility criteria and main responsibilities

Eligibility criteria	Responsibilities
be a firm or company; have practised corporate finance for at least the last two years, with at least three relevant transactions; employ at least four qualified executives; be capable of being effectively supervised by the Exchange; have appropriate financial and non-financial resources; the Exchange is able to exercise discretion as to the application and interpretation of the eligibility criteria as it thinks fit.	to assess the appropriateness of an applicant for the AIM, or an existing AIM company when appointed as its nominated adviser; to advise and guide an AIM company on its responsibilities under the AIM rules for companies, both in respect of its admission and its continuing obligations on an ongoing basis; to liaise with the Exchange when requested to do so by the Exchange or an AIM company for which it acts; to advise the Exchange as soon as practicable if it believes that it or an AIM company has breached the AIM Rules.

Source: London Stock Exchange, AIM Rules for Nominated Advisers, July 2018.

capital and to reduce the chances of an extension of oversight by the LSE and public authorities. Despite various cases of malpractice, sanctions were rarely applied throughout the 2000s (Gerakos et al. 2013). In response to these malpractices, in 2006 the LSE published a handbook containing the basic rules for Nomads. In addition to the responsibilities summarised in Table 6.2, the LSE also added a conflict of interest clause, stating that "a nominated adviser must not have, and must take care to avoid, the semblance of a conflict".[26]

The private regulatory regime of the AIM features both similarities and differences with respect to the case of the OTC derivative market. On the one hand, unlike the OTC derivative market, the AIM is not a market that developed out of the emergence of new financial instruments but was instead purposefully established by the LSE. Compared to the OTC derivative case, therefore, the AIM is a case presenting different drivers behind the establishment of a private regulatory regime, thus disconfirming our hypothesis about self-regulation developing together with new financial instruments (*H8.1*). In the case of the AIM, in fact, there was no particular new financial instrument. The rationale behind the establishment of the AIM was to help small companies to raise capital in financial markets. Listing on the stock exchange and compliance with public regulatory standards can, in fact, be burdensome, particularly for small companies. By creating an alternative market space within the LSE, it became possible for firms to be listed on a stock exchange while at the same time being sheltered from the reach of public regulation and the related compliance costs. In the case of the AIM, this shelter particularly served to escape from the obligations for stock exchange listing defined by European directives (Mendoza 2008, p. 296).

On the other hand, the AIM case confirms our hypothesis about the propensity of private self-regulatory regimes to attract new members. Like the OTC derivative market, in fact, the AIM expanded rapidly. Having been established in 1995 with ten listed British companies, in 2005 the AIM listed more than 1400 companies, both national and international. Between 2004 and 2006, it grew even faster than NASDAQ, raising $55 billion (Mendoza 2008, p. 284) and registering a peak of almost 1,700 listed companies. This number, however, started to gradually fall in the following years, and since 2015 the number of listed companies has been below 1,000 (see Figure 6.1).

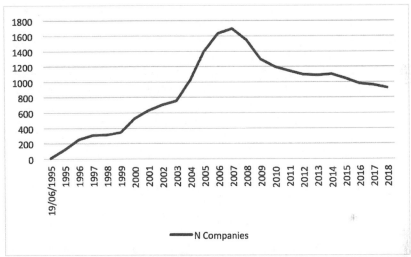

Source: London Stock Exchange data, https://www.londonstockexchange.com/statistics/historic/aim/aim.htm (accessed 27 March 2020).

Figure 6.1   *Number of listed companies in the AIM by year*

This steady decline in the number of companies listed in the AIM and the market's consequent underperformance have attracted a wave of criticism of the functioning of its regulatory framework (*Financial Times* 2017). New light has also been increasingly shed on the overall performance of the AIM in generating returns for investors. While it fascinated investors with cases of fast high returns particularly in the first half of the 2000s, the 20-year record reveals more a story of substantial losses on the part of investors, particularly inexperienced ones who became the victims of misleading information and of the conflict of interests between the Nomads' regulatory function and their relations with listed companies (*Financial Times* 2015a). Even though this underperformance needs to be contextualised against the performance of other markets during these years (Stringham and Chen 2012), these criticisms also triggered the attention of public regulators which have an interest in protecting investors (Gerakos et al. 2013, p. 190).

6.3.2   Public Intervention in an Investor-Unfriendly Market

According to some studies, around 70 per cent of the companies listed on the AIM between 1995 and 2015 caused their investors losses (Dimson et al. 2015; *Financial Times* 2015b). In about a third of these cases, the loss caused by the company amounted to about 95 per cent of the initial investment. Surprisingly, however, not only is there no evidence of substantial action between 1995 and 2015 on structural problems but the LSE was actually found to be acting against efforts by public regulators to make the AIM subject to tougher regulation. More specifically, when in 2013 the British parliament was discussing the Financial Services Bill – which would assign more responsibilities for protecting investors to the FCA – the LSE tried to water down these efforts.[27] Nonetheless, as the LSE was the actor responsible to public authorities for the functioning of the AIM, it came under increased pressure to demonstrate it was tackling malpractices. In parallel, EU legislation was about to expand towards including MTFs, and therefore also the AIM.

In July 2016, the AIM-listed companies became subject to new European legislation. The Market Abuse Regulation (MAR) extended the range of financial instruments covered by EU legislation and also reached out to instruments traded on MTFs. This regulatory approach was confirmed in the renewed version of MiFiD – MiFiD II – which entered into force in January 2018. Under this new regulatory framework, AIM-listed companies are directly subject to EU legislation which obliges them to disclose inside information to the public and to keep that information available for five years. The AIM, in turn, has also been working to adapt its internal rules and to establish new requirements for its listed companies.[28] With the entry into force of first MAR and then MiFiD II, there has therefore been public regulatory intervention in the regulation of the AIM, as AIM-listed companies found guilty of market abuses are no longer fully sheltered by the LSE's private regulatory framework but are directly subject to public legislation. The question, however, is what will happen after the UK leaves the EU? While answering this question goes beyond the scope of this chapter, the process through which MAR was developed may offer some hints.

Similarly to the case of the HFT provisions discussed in Chapter 2, to develop MAR the EU also largely relied on pre-existing national frameworks, taking them from the Member States in which such regulatory frameworks were more developed. As the malpractices of the AIM had already caught the attention of British regulators in the 2000s, Britain had developed a frame-work for tackling abuses taking place in privately regulated trading facilities (Morgan Lewis 2016). First through the Market Abuse Directive (MAD) of 2003 and then through MAR, the British market-abuse framework was largely incorporated in EU legislation, under which national supervisory authorities like the FCA obtained more leverage to sanction market abuses occurring in MTFs. To some extent, while MAR extends the reach of national and European regulators to previously sheltered markets like the AIM, at the same time it features a certain continuity with previously existing legislation. According to some observers (e.g. Morgan Lewis 2016) this continuity offers reasons to believe that – whatever the post-Brexit scenario may be – there will be no rolling back of the current regulatory regime.

Similarly to the case of EMIR, with the MAR the EU regulators also seek to render the organisation requirements of MTFs more similar to those for regulated exchanges. The general aim of the legislation is therefore to extend European public oversight by increasing the amount of information that market participants are required to publicly disclose. The legislation therefore largely keeps in place the existing private regulatory regime but requires more trans-parency regarding what happens within it. The new rules not only apply to the companies listed in the MTF but also to the actors responsible for its internal regulation. Under MiFiD II, in fact, MTFs are also obliged to set up specific arrangements to address conflicts of interests. In the case of the AIM, this meant both introducing a new rule for listed companies to publish a website disclosing information about their business and organisation and new rules for the AIM about disclosing any potential conflicts of interests.[29]

While the scope of MAR is arguably too big to simply consider it a response to the underperformance of the AIM, at the same time its overall objectives were to enhance investor protection, reduce the risks related to disorderly markets, reduce systemic risks, improve efficiency and reduce the risk of unnecessary costs for market participants.[30] The new direct subjection of AIM-listed companies to EU disclosure requirements and the responsibilities of the AIM to address potential conflicts of interest are therefore aimed at these objectives. In the new regulatory configuration, the FCA is charged with the responsibility to develop rules for disclosure with which AIM companies must comply. The FCA, in turn, develops these rules on the basis of technical standards and guidelines issued by ESMA. Therefore, the new European reg-ulatory framework for MTF resembles the centralised structure we previously described for the OTC derivative market. At the same time, the new regulatory framework keeps the existing private regulatory regime in place. The AIM thus remains a self-regulated subset of the LSE – with Nomads still acting as key players in the regime – but with more direct surveillance by the FCA, which must ensure that the European disclosure rules are being followed. Therefore, the AIM case is in line with our argument that private self-regulation prompts a centralisation of rule-making, creating a mix of public–private governance in which the public regulator adds a few additional rules to existing regulatory regimes.

While the available evidence is arguably too thin to fully test our hypotheses on public intervention (*H8.3* and *H8.4*), the case study does allow us to say something about the mechanisms driving public intervention. First, the AIM case probes the plausibility of the idea that widespread malpractices do trigger the attention of public regulators and so increase the possibility of them intervening. The pattern that seems to emerge out of the AIM case, in fact, is that the flaws in the private regulatory regime were widely known already in the 2000s, but pressure for reform only increased when the overall performance of the market started to deteriorate and so cases of malpractice became more disputed. Second, even though the AIM does not bear a systemic risk comparable to that of the OTC derivative market, the objective behind European regulation of MTFs was to reduce the possibility of systemic risk.

6.4   HYBRID GOVERNANCE AND CENTRALISED RULE-MAKING

The two cases analysed in this chapter tell the story of new European rules entering two spheres of the financial markets that were previously almost entirely privately self-regulated (although in the last instance relying on law to enforce contracts). Even though the two cases differ in nature – with OTC derivatives being a global transnational market and the AIM a submarket of the LSE – they share similar patterns of the public regulator stepping into private regimes. In both cases, in fact, the European public regulator intervened by adding new rules to the existing regime. As the new rules are valid for the whole European jurisdiction, in both cases we can speak of a centralisation of rule-making. The general idea set out in Chapter 1 (*H8*), therefore, finds corroboration in our two case studies, as in both cases the failures of the private self-regulatory regimes to tackle systemic risk and excessive rent-seeking prompted intervention. More precisely, in the case of OTC derivatives ISDA favoured the allocation of decision-making authority to European institutions, while in the case of the AIM the new public regulation continues to largely rely on the supervisory responsibilities of the Nomads.

Consequently, in both cases the hybrid regimes maintain important levels of continuity with the previous private regulatory structures. In the case of the OTC derivatives market, the Master Agreement still constitutes an important source of contractual standards and ISDA is still a regulatory reference point. In the case of the AIM, the controversial regulatory regime in which Nomads play a central role is also still in place. What has changed is that transactions happening in these markets are now directly subject to European regulatory requirements, with a few exceptions for OTC derivatives, where a segment of the market is still exempt from public regulation. Public regulators have therefore stepped in by increasing the scope of their market surveillance while at the same time keeping the regulatory structure in place. The centralisation thus mainly consists in certain regulatory standards being defined at the European level (Quaglia 2012). Whether this will also lead to a centralised governance of the markets, however, is still an open question as – as is also discussed in Chapter 2 – different member states have different traditions in carrying out market surveillance (Helleiner 2014).

Together with the case studies presented in Chapter 2, the two *hybrid* regimes discussed in this chapter confirm a general pattern emerging from the EU's financial regulation strategy. As has for example also been seen in the case study on high-frequency trading (Chapter 2), for the OTC derivative market and MTFs the strategy of the EU is to improve regulation by increasing the reporting obligations on market participants. The centralisation of rule-making is thus mainly about creating uniformity in the standards to which information should be disclosed. In this task, ESMA plays a key role, as it defines the standards with which firms operating in the European jurisdiction must comply. These standards define what should and what need not be reported to the public authorities. As we have seen, however, in defining such standards ESMA acts in close cooperation with private organisations, which are particularly keen to provide advice on the viability (and non-viability) of subjecting certain financial products to reporting requirements. In the aftermath of the global financial crisis, therefore, ISDA managed to secure itself an important role in the new European regulatory structure (*H9*).

While the general hypothesis about private self-regulation prompting public regulation finds corroboration in both case studies, a more complex argument needs to be developed for our hypotheses regarding the conditions under which private regulatory regimes emerge and develop (*H8.1* and *H8.2*). On the one hand, the idea that private regimes will attract new members and that these will adapt to the existing regulatory structure (*H8.2*) seems to be highly plausible. In the case of OTC derivatives, in fact, since the 1980s the market has been attracting an exponentially increasing number of participants, all of whom either complied with ISDA's private regulatory regime or even became members of ISDA. Similarly, the AIM quickly grew from having ten listed companies in 1995 to listing over 1,000 companies during the 2000s, all of which were complying with the private regime put in place by the LSE.

On the other hand, our hypothesis about the emergence of private regulatory regimes (*H8.1*) is confirmed as plausible in the first case study but inaccurate in the second. In the first case, even though the trading of derivatives is a practice dating back a few hundred years, the emergence of ISDA's private regulatory authority during the 1980s can be considered to be strongly related to the growing technological complexity of OTC derivatives, which made these instruments somewhat 'new' and difficult to standardise. As a result, the main market participants joined forces and established a private organisation – ISDA – which became the main regulatory authority in the market for these instruments. In a way, therefore, it can be said that ISDA's private regulatory regime emerged in relation to the emergence of 'new' financial instruments.

However, unlike the expectations set out in Chapter 1, the second case study on the AIM shows that private regulatory regimes do not necessarily emerge in relation to new financial instruments but may actually be purposefully created by private actors in order to avoid existing public regulation. In fact, the AIM was established to allow small companies to circumvent the costs related to compliance with public regulation and to provide a venue for investors in which they have lighter information disclosure burdens. The regime regulating the AIM was therefore not established to regulate the trading of a new instrument but simply to regulate a newly established venue.

This requires us to refine our theoretical argument about the emergence of private regulatory regimes by taking into consideration the incentives that private actors have to avoid public regulation. Both the extensive use of new financial instruments and the purposeful establishment of an alternative market can be seen as efforts to circumvent public regulation. The consequent formation of a privately self-regulated regime, in turn, can be seen as an effort to further structure and systematise this sheltering from public regulation. The theoretical framework set out in Chapter 1, therefore, needs to be refined in terms of the conditions under which market participants succeed in avoiding existing public regulation and the incentives they have to systematise such practices with a private regulatory regime. In sum, to understand the emergence and development of private regulatory regimes, a further reflection is needed on the drivers behind the actions of private actors in financial markets.

While our expectations about how private regulatory regimes emerge have turned out to be partially disconfirmed, our theoretical arguments about what drives public intervention instead seem to be highly accurate. Our hypotheses about the conditions under which public regulators step into private regulatory regimes (*H8.3* and *H8.4*) are largely in line with the developments discussed in the two case studies. In both cases, the timing of public regulation is in line with the idea that either excessive rent-seeking or systemic risk plays a prominent role in decisions by public authorities to introduce new legislation. In the case of the OTC derivative market, in fact, the global financial crisis was the main trigger for public intervention. In the case of the AIM, recurring malpractices and the many losses incurred by various investors have kept the market under the attention of public regulators since the mid-2000s. However, in this latter case, strong public intervention only happened in the context of the broader European legislative initiative of MiFID II.

The difference in the timing of public intervention between the two cases can arguably be explained by the different systemic risk that the two markets bear, with OTC derivatives being the 'world's biggest market' (Helleiner et al. 2018) and the AIM being a submarket of the LSE. The systemic risk borne by the OTC derivative market became a central subject of public debate and among policymakers with the outbreak of the global financial crisis in 2008. As a result of the large systemic risk perceived, actions by public regulators were almost immediate, as by 2012 in both the EU and the USA the OTC derivate markets were subject to central clearing and reporting requirements. The AIM, on the other hand, as a submarket of the LSE, bears considerably less systemic risk. Consequently, despite widespread malpractices, intervention by public regulators has been relatively slower.

The final lesson that can be drawn from these two case studies is that private actors are not by definition against a centralisation of rule-making. On the contrary, especially if they operate transnationally, they tend to be in favour of homogenous rules across different jurisdictions. At the same time, private actors may be very keen to shelter particular segments of the market from public regulation. It is on this front that the main struggle between public and private regulation within the EU is currently being fought: who gets control over what. In the process of uploading regulatory competences from the national to the supranational level, therefore, private actors are not necessarily an obstacle but they are taking action in order to contain the reach of regulation. When regulatory competences move from the national to the supranational level, therefore, so does the struggle between private and public authorities.

NOTES

1. For an example of the recognition of ISDA's Master Agreement on the part of public regulators, see the following page on derivative documentation from the Corporate Finance Manual issued by the British government: https://www.gov.uk/hmrc-internal-manuals/corporate-finance-manual/cfm13100 (accessed 28 October 2019).
2. https://www.fsb.org/2018/11/fsb-publishes-2018-g-sib-list/ (accessed 28 October 2019).
3. G20 Leaders' Statement, The Pittsburgh Summit, 24–25 September 2009, Pittsburgh.
4. Benoît Cœuré, Member of the Executive Board of the ECB, Speech at joint Banque de France, Bank of England and ECB conference on OTC derivative reform, Paris, 11 September 2013.
5. Ibid note 4.
6. Ibid note 4. Italics in the original.

7.   Ibid note 3.
8.   See also this press release by the European Commission: https://europa.eu/rapid/press-release_IP-19-848_en.htm (accessed 27 March 2020).
9.   Keynote address of Steven Maijoor, Chair of ESMA, to the ISDA AGM, 13 April 2011.
10. Ibid note 9.
11. See, for example, ISDA, Letter sent to Timothy Geithner, President of the Federal Reserve Bank of New York, 31 October 2008, https://www.isda.org/a/PxoEE/Fed-Letter-Final10-31-08.pdf (accessed 27 March 2020).
12. E.g. ISDA Commentary on Indirect Clearing – Council Text of EMIR (29 July 2011). https://www.isda.org/category/public-policy/europe/ (accessed 30 October 2019).
13. E.g. ISDA, Comments on European Commission Consultation, 14 June 2010, https://www.isda.org/2010/06/14/isda-comments-on-european-commission-consultation-2/ (accessed 27 March 2020).
14. ISDA Comment Paper, A Prudent Approach to Collateral Requirements at CCPs, 29 July 2011, https://www.isda.org/a/zsiDE/02-isda-afme-collateral-at-ccps-jul-201-isda-comment.pdf (accessed 27 March 2020).
15. ISDA, Response to first ESMA discussion paper (dated 16 February 2012), Draft Technical Standards for the Regulation on OTC Derivatives, CCPs and Trade Repositories, 21 March 2012, https://www.isda.org/2012/03/21/isda-afme-bba-response-to-first-esma-discussion-paper-on-emir/ (accessed 27 March 2020).
16. Ibid (note 16).
17. ISDA Responds to EC's Supervisory Reporting Requirements 'Fitness Check', 21 March 2018, https://www.isda.org/2018/03/21/isda-responds-to-ecs-supervisory-reporting-requirements-fitness-check/ (accessed 27 March 2020).
18. ISDA, Response to first ESMA discussion paper (dated 16 February 2012), Draft Technical Standards for the Regulation on OTC Derivatives, CCPs and Trade Repositories, 21 March 2012, https://www.isda.org/2012/03/21/isda-afme-bba-response-to-first-esma-discussion-paper-on-emir/ (accessed 27 March 2020).
19. Ibid (note 19).
20. Grant Thornton, 'Economic Impact of AIM', April 2015, https://www.londonstockexchange.com/companies-and-advisors/aim/publications/documents/gteconomicimpactofaim2015.pdf (accessed 27 March 2020).
21. Even though it has been attracting an increasing number of international investors (*Financial Times* 2015a; 2015b; 2018).
22. Source: London Stock Exchange, 'A guide to AIM tax benefits,' October 2015, https://www.londonstockexchange.com/companies-and-advisors/aim/publications/aimuktaxguide.pdf (accessed 27 March 2020).
23. Source: Investopedia, https://www.investopedia.com/terms/a/alternative-investment-market.asp (accessed 27 March 2020).
24. See HMRC internal manual, Stamp Taxes on Shares Manual: https://www.gov.uk/hmrc-internal-manuals/stamp-taxes-shares-manual/stsm123050 (accessed 5 March 2019).
25. Article 14, Directive 2004/39/EC of the European Parliament and of the Council of 21 April 2004.
26. London Stock Exchange, AIM Rules for Nominated Advisers, July 2018, page 11.
27. RAID (Rights and Accountability in Development) Report, 'Asset laundering and AIM: Congo, corporate misconduct and the market value of human rights,' July 2012.

28. Source: Burges Salmon, Briefing 'AIM companies dealing with inside information,' 23 June 2016, https://www.raid-uk.org/sites/default/files/aim-report.pdf (accessed 27 March 2020).
29. Financial Conduct Authority, https://www.fca.org.uk/mifid-ii/3-multilateral-trading-facilities-mtfs (accessed 27 March 2020).
30. Financial Conduct Authority, https://www.fca.org.uk/mifid-ii/1-overview (accessed 21 December 2019).

BIBLIOGRAPHY

Awrey, D. (2010). 'The dynamics of OTC derivatives regulation: bridging the public–private divide,' *European Business Law Organization Review*, 11, 155–193.
Biggins, J. and Scott, C. (2012). 'Public–private relations in a transnational private regulatory regime: ISDA, the state and OTC derivatives market reform,' *European Business Organization Law Review* (EBOR), 13(3), 309–346.
Bowman, A., Froud, J., Johal, S. and Williams, K. (2017). 'Trade associations, narrative and elite power,' *Theory, Culture & Society*, 34(5–6), 103–126.
Dimson, E., Marsh, P. and Staunton, M. (2015). *Global Investment Returns Sourcebook*, Zurich: Credit Suisse Research Institute.
Engelen, E. (2017). 'Shadow banking after the crisis: the Dutch case,' *Theory, Culture & Society*, 34(5–6), 53–75.
Espenlaub, S., Khurshed, A. and Mohamed, A. (2012). 'IPO survival in a reputational market,' *Journal of Business Finance & Accounting*, 39(3–4), 427–463.
Financial Times (2009). 'Turner to end light-touch regulation,' 19 March.
Financial Times (2015a). 'AIM – 20 years of a few winners and many losers,' 19 June.
Financial Times (2015b). 'Aim is more miss than hit for investors as it marks 20th anniversary,' 19 June.
Financial Times (2017). 'Aim's wild west reputation seems to be deserved,' 15 October.
Financial Times (2018). 'What is AIM and how does its regulation system work?' 10 May.
Flanagan, S.M. (2001). 'The rise of a trade association: group interactions within the International Swaps and Derivatives Association,' *Harvard Negotiation Law Review*, 6, 211–264.
Gerakos, J., Lang, M. and Maffett, M. (2013). 'Post-listing performance and private sector regulation: the experience of London's alternative investment market,' *Journal of Accounting and Economics*, 56(2–3), 189–215.
Helleiner, E. (2014). 'Towards cooperative decentralization? The post-crisis governance of global OTC derivatives'. In: Porter, T. (ed.) *Transnational Financial Regulation after the Crisis*, New York: Routledge: 132–153.
Helleiner, E., Pagliari, S. and Spagna, I. (eds) (2018). *Governing the World's Biggest Market: The Politics of Derivatives Regulation After the 2008 Crisis*, Oxford: Oxford University Press.
Lagna, A. (2016). 'Derivatives and the financialisation of the Italian state,' *New Political Economy*, 21(2), 167–186.
Mendoza, J.M. (2008). 'Securities regulation in low-tier listing venues: the rise of the alternative investment market,' *Fordham Journal of Corporate and Financial Law*, 13, 257–328.

Morgan, G. (2008). 'Market formation and governance in international financial markets: the case of OTC derivatives,' *Human Relations*, 61(5), 637–660.

Morgan, G. (2009). 'Legitimacy in financial markets: credit default swaps in the current crisis,' *Socio-Economic Review*, 8(1), 17–45.

Morgan Lewis (2016). 'UK market abuse extends its reach: implications for market participants,' 11 July 2016, https://www.morganlewis.com/pubs/uk-market-abuse -regime-extends-its-reach-implications-for-market-participants (accessed 27 March 2020).

Mügge, D. (2011). 'From pragmatism to dogmatism: European Union governance, policy paradigms and financial meltdown,' *New Political Economy*, 16(2), 185–206.

Pistor, K. (2013). 'A legal theory of finance,' *Journal of Comparative Economics*, 41(2), 315–330.

Quaglia, L. (2012). 'The "old" and "new" politics of financial services regulation in the European Union,' *New Political Economy*, 17(4), 515–535.

Rauterberg, G. and Verstein, A. (2013). 'Assessing transnational private regulation of the OTC derivatives market: ISDA, the BBA and the future of financial reform,' *Virginia Journal of International Law*, 54(9), 9–50.

Schinasi, G., Craig, R.S., Drees, B. and Kramer, C. (2000). 'Modern banking and OTC derivatives markets,' Occasional Paper 2013, International Monetary Fund.

Stout, L.A. (2011). 'Derivatives and the legal origin of the 2008 credit crisis,' *Harvard Business Law Review*, 1, 1–38.

Stringham, E.P. and Chen, I. (2012). 'The alternative of private regulation: the London Stock Exchange's alternative investment market as a model,' *Economic Affairs*, 32(3), 37–43.

The Telegraph (2009). 'Bankers to receive huge bonuses despite financial crisis', 15 April.

PART IV

Technological innovation perspective

7. The impacts of technological innovation on regulatory structure: Fintech in post-crisis Europe

Agnieszka Smoleńska, Joseph Ganderson and Adrienne Héritier

7.1   INTRODUCTION AND GENERAL ARGUMENT

Specific forms of digitised financial innovation have been the subject of several chapters in this volume: Chapter 2 studied the regulation of high-frequency trading and Chapter 3 the role of clearing houses and central depositories in derivatives trading. In this chapter, we examine technological innovation more broadly and in its own right, considering its impact on European regulatory structures in recent years. How does technological innovation, or 'Fintech',[1] in major financial markets – currencies, payment systems, capital markets, alternative intermediaries and insurance – impact upon regulation?

The dynamic features of financial markets and the innovation of complex financial products and services based on new technologies and business models present regulators with significant challenges. Specifically, how can they effectively scrutinise unprecedentedly large volumes of market data? Is 'Regtech', an instrument developed by private actors, able to ensure compliance with public regulation? Does an alternative approach which institutionalises public–private cooperation offer answers to new regulatory challenges?

New financial technologies and activities often do not fall within the purview of established regulatory regimes, leading to a situation where regulators are playing catch-up with the private sector. At the very least, this necessitates further engagement between public and private actors; at most, it calls for sweeping reforms to regulatory rules and strategies. While it is routine for regulators to encounter asymmetric information problems in interactions with firms (Besanko and Sappington 2001), these are acute in sectors such as finance where disruptive innovation can lead to a state of 'Knightian uncertainty', as was demonstrated by the most recent financial crisis itself (Nelson and Katzenstein 2014). A key lesson drawn from the 2008 crisis was that if regulators do not understand the technology they seek to regulate, they will be unable to assess risks posed to the public. The crisis prompted a reconsideration of regulatory cultures in many countries whilst also coinciding with and partly catalysing the contemporary wave of disruptive financial innovation, often referred to as 'Fintech 3.0' (Arner et al. 2015).[2] This wave has emerged rapidly and exponentially by historical standards: global investment in Fintech firms stood at $111.8bn in 2018, up 120 per cent on the previous year (KPMG 2019); and as of 2017, 20 per cent of all financial services firms had been founded since 2005 (Accenture 2018).

This chapter discusses the dynamics driving regulatory responses to this trend across Europe in the past decade. It examines the steps that public actors (policymakers and regulators) have taken across Europe, teasing out the political and strategic dynamics underlying these moves. In keeping with the broader theme of the volume, we examine these trends with respect to debates over regulatory trends in Europe: centralisation, decentralisation or fragmentation.

Before turning to our empirical analysis, it is necessary to first restate the relevant hypotheses developed in Chapter 1 about the impact of financial technological innovations on national and European financial regulation. Our analysis examines variations in four principal areas of uncertainty linked to new financial instruments and business models: substantive uncertainty, legal uncertainty, uncertainty with respect to risks for public goods; and uncertainty as regards compliance with existing regulation affected by the use of Regtech.

To offer more specific answers to the question of how regulators respond to new financial instruments under specific conditions, we refer to the causal hypotheses developed in the theory chapter about how specific types of new financial instruments based on technology and/or innovative business models linked to specific types of uncertainty are likely to lead to specific regulatory structures. In doing so we outline the underlying causal mechanisms and illustrate the different types of financial innovations and their expected impact upon regulatory structures, focusing on specific examples of innovation.

In line with Chapter 1 on theory, we assume that the nature of uncertainty linked to the newly introduced financial product or service matters most when explaining regulatory outcomes. This assumption was inductively drawn from the scrutiny of the extensive 2017 and 2019 reports from ESMA which provide evidence of regulatory responses to a wide variety of Fintech innovations. From this work, it emerged that these types of uncertainty are crucial in determining regulators' reactions to Fintech. We accordingly propose a systematisation of the nature of uncertainty: (a) unclear substance of the instrument and or the business model introduced; (b) unclear legal nature; (c) the unclear effect regarding cross-sectoral risks that call for a public goods provision by regulation; (d) a degree of uncertainty linked to the use of Regtech offered as a financial regulatory instrument to control rule compliance. These different types of uncertainty trigger different reactions from regulators. Based on the framework established in Chapter 1, we hypothesise as to how they affect the regulatory structure before examining cases in each area:

Hyp 10 If the substantive nature of a new financial instrument and/or a new business model used by a Fintech is unclear, national regulators may take recourse to bespoke regulatory solutions developed in cooperation with Fintechs. The result will be a fragmented regulatory structure.

Hyp 11.1 If the regulator considers a new financial product as a financial instrument falling under existing regulation, fragmentation will be avoided. The resulting regulatory structure will be shaped according to the existing legislation and thus reproduce the existing structure (centralised vs. decentralised).

Hyp 11.2 If the new financial product is not considered a financial instrument falling under existing legislation, locally limited bespoke (self) regulations will emerge, leading to a fragmented regulatory structure.

Hyp 12 If regulators are certain that Fintech activities imply cross-sectoral risks and they can build on pre-existing cross-sectoral rules protecting public goods, they will adopt centralising measures based on these rules.

Hyp 13.1 Low uncertainty about the application of new financial instruments and their compliance with rules due to the use of Regtech offers regulators real time insight in regulatory compliance and triggers automatic enforcement of the relevant rules. This leads to a centralisation of regulatory structures if the relevant rules are strict and precise.

Hyp 13.2 If regulators are endowed with rich material, institutional (competences) and non-material (expertise) resources, they will make use of Regtech, which will result in a centralised regulatory structure if the relevant rules are strict and precise.

7.2   EMPIRICAL ANALYSIS

7.2.1   Substantive Uncertainty: Regulatory Outreach via Facilitator Programmes

Substantive uncertainty refers to a gap between an understanding of technological innovations, with their associated risks and effects, between private firms and public regulators. Substantive uncertainty is manifest across all major areas of financial services, and is generally embodied in specific tools, technologies or product innovations that have hitherto been untested and require regulatory learning processes.[3] This has led to regulators reaching out to certain Fintechs in an attempt to learn about products and assess their regulatory viability.

At the time of writing, the majority of EU Member States have established national 'facilitator' programmes that seek to encourage public–private interaction and information sharing and reduce uncertainty. Facilitators comprise physical infrastructure and resources on the part of the competent national financial services regulator: either innovation hubs, sandboxes or both (see Table 7.1). Among them, the original and most advanced project is run by the UK's Financial Conduct Authority (FCA). The FCA is a relatively new regulator, created in 2013 after the Conservative–Liberal Democrat coalition dissolved its predecessor the Financial Services Authority (FSA) following the financial crisis. Legally, it operates as a non-profit limited company, funded entirely by the firms it regulates, and though it is officially functionally independent of the UK government, it reports annually to the Treasury and bi-annually to Parliament, who appraise its performance. In the UK's post-crisis 'twin peaks' model, it is the regulator responsible for consumer protection, industry standards and promoting competition.[4]

Table 7.1   EU28 Member States and Fintech facilitator programmes (August 2019)

Innovation Hub Only	Austria, Belgium, Bulgaria,* Cyprus, Estonia, Finland, France, Germany, Ireland, Italy, Latvia, Luxembourg, Portugal, Romania, Sweden
Innovation Hub with Sandbox	Denmark, Spain,+ Hungary, Lithuania, Netherlands, Poland, UK
None	Croatia, Czech Republic, Greece, Malta, Slovakia, Slovenia

Notes: *Hub planned but not launched; +Sandbox planned but not launched.

The FCA launched Project Innovate with a 'call for input' and by hosting roundtables with Fintech industry members in summer 2014.[5] The call stated that the FCA sought to "support industry innovation by opening our doors to businesses (large and small) who are developing innovative approaches that can benefit consumers in financial services markets" (FCA 2014, p. 5). The consultations sought to establish recurrent regulatory barriers; the feasibility of establishing an 'incubator' and an 'innovation hub' model long-term; and how best to discern "genuine, ground-breaking innovation" from transitory crazes or false dawns (FCA 2014, pp. 5–6). In October 2014, the FCA responded to feedback by relaunching the Fintech section of its website, establishing criteria for assessing growth potential and, most importantly, formally launching the first dedicated innovation hub. The hub launch was notably receptive to most of the industry respondents' major requests, promising to: proactively assist specific firms with regulatory navigation by assigning a dedicated FCA contact to each case, offer post-authorisation support for up to one year, provide general information and updates on regulation, organise broader outreach events, maintain an informal tone in interactions with firms, and act as a champion of innovation within the FCA itself (FCA 2014, pp. 7–9).[6]

Taken together, these steps represented a receptive and comprehensive environment for Fintech entrepreneurs and firms that was hitherto unmatched across Europe.[7] Objectives such as 'maintaining an informal tone' are indicative of a working relationship founded on respect and mutual understanding rather than deference on the part of firms seeking to please regulators. As far as the FCA is concerned, the project was and remains couched officially within the regulatory remit of stimulating domestic competition for consumers (FCA 2019b). However, Project Innovate also represented a signal of intent to international competitors that the UK was open to investment from Fintech, and placed the country on a stronger institutional footing than other large European economies and the European Union itself in this respect (see below). There were quite transparent political motives underpinning the project. In 2015, Chancellor George Osborne publicly stated his desire for London to become "the global centre for Fintech", stressed that regulators must provide the necessary space for innovation, and acknowledged the international competition explicitly: "the race is on, but we're determined to win it" (Campbell 2015). Indeed, some scholars have suggested that the British regulatory approach even constitutes "large-scale efforts to promote the Fintech industry" (Dorfleitner et al. 2017, p. 15). According to a team member at France's innovation hub, "there has always been a lot of emphasis from the FCA on competitiveness", however this emphasis is not passed down in the same fashion in other financial regulatory regimes, such as France's (Interview 2019a).

This open regulatory philosophy complemented London's pre-existing endowments in finance and technology, and gave the UK a first mover advantage that it has expanded upon in recent years. Whilst Table 7.1 shows the existence of hubs in most other European countries, this belies meaningful differences across borders. Through 2019, eight of the ten largest European institutional Fintech investors by number of deals are based in London, and more investments are made in the UK than the next nine largest countries combined (Fintech Global 2019).

More recently, this British leadership has manifested itself in two strategic directions. Though the FCA has expanded its range of outreach via events programmes and calls for input, more consequential has been its development of a regulatory sandbox and related internationalisation through the development of its Global Financial Innovation Network (GFIN) and bilateral 'Fintech bridges'. These steps respectively represent a simultaneous deepening and widening of its activities. Sandboxes "offer an environment in which Fintech entrepreneurs can conduct limited tests of their innovations with fewer regulatory constraints, real customers, less risk of enforcement action, and ongoing guidance from regulators" (Allen 2019, p. 580). They are thus analogous to clinical trials in pharmaceuticals. The UK was the first country in the world to formally launch its sandbox in April 2016, and referring to it, the FCA's Head of Innovation acknowledged that "as regulators we're under constant pressure to be more pro-innovative" (Kelly 2018). Since then, the sandbox has processed five cohorts, comprising 118 organisations seeking to obtain market access for Fintech products (FCA 2019c).

Sandboxes are viewed as business-friendly regulatory innovations, and the FCA's intervention has sparked a global race of the sort Osborne was referring to. Since April 2016, six other European states have launched or are launching their own sandboxes (see Table 7.1). In addition, in the year following the UK launch, ten other non-European countries, including major financial centres Hong Kong and Singapore, followed suit. Other large economies including Russia, Canada and Indonesia have now also established operations, while the United States is considering a similar initiative.[8]

The FCA has responded by pursuing a strategy of horizontal collaboration through its GFIN initiative and bilateral bridging. In 2018, the FCA stated it wished to pursue a 'global sandbox', which would allow for knowledge pooling between regulators, facilitate joint work on Regtech, and create a cross-border environment for product trials. To date, this network is chaired by the FCA and comprises ten other members in its coordination group, including Hungary, Lithuania, Hong Kong and several smaller states and subnational authorities. A further twenty authorities are members, and seven more have observer status (FCA 2019d). As of September 2019, GFIN is in the process of launching a cross-border pilot with eight firms that will interact with at least two of the seventeen participating regulators, spanning a range of Fintech subsets such as blockchain, Regtech and digital securities. Moreover, the UK has signed five bilateral agreements with Singapore, South Korea, Hong Kong, China and Australia to formally explore expanding market access via controlled trials and collaboration between national innovation hubs (Fintech Alliance 2019). Motivations here are twofold. First, industry has unsurprisingly cited cross-border regulatory collaboration as a priority in a new round of calls for input, calling for cooperation that would allow UK established firms to expand seamlessly. Second, by chairing and coordinating a formal network with a 'hub and spokes' model, the UK expands its influence and becomes an international standard setter.

No other country has yet replicated a comparable network, though the lack of formal collaboration between the UK and other major states hints that others may wish to create their own, rival networks or distinct strategies in the Fintech race. Though currently lagging, intra-European competitive dynamics could be affected by the Brexit process, which may exert pressures on both regulators and private actors. The financial centres of Paris and Frankfurt have actively courted financial services since the UK's 2016 referendum, offering 'passporting' services and prized single market access to Fintechs (Lavery et al. 2018, p. 20). The broader strategies of these two leading economies, and others, merit brief attention here.

Like Osborne, French ministers and authorities have not been shy to admit that they are runners in the race (Lavery et al. 2018, p. 20), though strategy has manifest differently in Paris. France's innovation hub includes dedicated teams at both the Banque de France and Autorité des Marchés Financiers (AMF). However, rather than focusing on formal sandboxing, France has instead established physical infrastructure in the form of 'incubators' in strategic Parisian locations, in partnership with but not formally part of regulators themselves. The central bank has established Le Lab, an incubator space on its premises exclusively dedicated to experimentation and bringing together diverse stakeholders (Banque de France 2019). Another major flagship incubator project, Le Swave, is dedicated to Fintechs and supported by a mixture of public and private institutional partners. These include public agencies, banks, researchers and Le Lab itself. Le Swave was launched as part of the government's broader start-up agenda and explicitly offered funding for relocation (Boland 2018). The remit of AMF's 'Fintech, Innovation and Competitiveness' team explicitly includes making Paris an attractive destination for investors. AMF has signed 'memorandums of understanding' with leading countries such as Canada, Taiwan, Hong Kong and Singapore (Interview 2019a). However, "there is a huge question of information sharing" between regulators, which limits the extent to which countries such as France can interact with partners, preferring instead informal networking processes, such as organised events and conferences (Interview 2019a). As a French regulatory official stated, "on the horizontal level, the collaboration is nascent and everybody is trying to understand if we can do more than just sign an MoU or organise events" (Interview 2019a).

Equally, Germany's innovation hub is run through the federal financial supervisory authority, BaFin. It provides regulatory information for different subsets of Fintech but has notably been less activist than both France and the UK in its approach towards reaching out to Fintech firms (Dorfleitner et al. 2017). Frankfurt has also invested in physical infrastructure, in the form of its TechQuartier space, which is partnered with Deutsche Bundesbank and is comparable to Le Swave.

While sandboxing and hubs represent an active pursuit of private partners on the part of the UK and other jurisdictions, other countries have taken alternative strategic approaches. In 2016, Switzerland adjusted a longstanding banking law to relax Fintech licensing for deposit taking firms that do not lend to customers up to the value of CHF100m ($100m), effectively lifting the threshold at which regulators must involve themselves. This was designed to make it easier for blockchain and cryptocurrency firms to establish themselves (Labbé 2016), and helped the Swiss Financial Market Supervisory Authority (FINMA) become the first regulator to officially license 'crypto banks' in 2019, while at the same establishing strict anti-laundering rules (RT International 2019). Though the banks in question are not yet fully licensed, this is an example of another approach to attracting market entrants in specific fields. It demonstrates that outreach facilitators are but one of a broader array of policymaking tools to attract investment.

Under conditions of substantive uncertainty, we have seen that untested new technologies have led to a process of competition and fragmentation rather than centralisation and standardisation, as predicted in hypothesis 10. However, subsequent attempts to establish bi- or multi-lateral networks are at a more embryonic stage, and are not readily identifiable across Europe. To date, the imperative for horizontal collaboration appears secondary to states' unilateral desire to establish a strong footing in the global race.

Concomitantly, the EU has yet to establish anything approximating comparable outreach programmes of its own. However, European institutions have not been entirely inactive in this area. ESMA and the EBA had both been collecting relevant data in a purely monitoring and advisory capacity in fields such as cryptocurrency and crowdfunding since 2013–2014, prior to the emergence of the national authorities' facilitator programmes. In March 2018, the European Commission published its more comprehensive 'Fintech Action Plan', which established some progressive objectives for EU institutions while also concluding "the case for broad legislative or regulatory action or reform at EU level at this stage is limited" (European Commission 2018, p. 4). As such, proposed actions in the plan largely eschewed the establishment of new specific regulations or institutions in favour of a process of mapping the private and regulatory landscape, establishing guidelines and best practices, and reviewing the impact of related regulatory frameworks such as the General

Data Protection Regulation (GDPR) and Digital Single Market strategy in the context of Fintech (European Commission 2018, p. 4). The 'Action Plan' does also mandate that European authorities monitor national hubs and perform a coordinative role, but at present this amounts to 'interested observer' status rather than that of an active participant, shaping national strategies.

On the specific issue of facilitators, the Commission focused squarely on establishing best practices through competent national authorities. The ESAs published a report on this subject in January 2019, citing three focus areas for future improvement: (1) consistency of facilitator design; (2) transparency of supervisory outcomes between firms and regulators; and (3) facilitation of cooperation with appropriate authorities, including consumer and data protection agencies (ESAs 2018, p. 6). However, the report also noted three areas of significant variation between hubs and sandboxes: (1) modes of interaction between regulators and firms, such as personal versus digital interactions; (2) the nature of advice provided, binding versus non-binding; (3) record-keeping and disclosure of regulatory outcomes, from the publication of frequently asked questions and, in some cases, nil disclosure. Though innovation hub and sandbox models may be similar by design, these disjunctures clearly reflect a lack of horizontal collaboration or formal cooperation. Currently, hubs and sandboxes are adopting different methodologies, unsurprisingly sharing different regulatory guidance and withholding data on their interactions with industry. This bodes ill for future reconciliation or standardisation at the European level. Equally, though an 'EU network' is mooted as a potential solution to this, the report is clear that this would be ESA-led and there is no mention of any integration of powers. Moreover, though ESAs are starting to accrue certain limited competencies concerning responses on substantive uncertainty, no concrete steps towards outreach have yet been undertaken at the European level.

Taken together, then, the European landscape for facilitators currently chiefly reflects a pattern of fragmentation and competition. The UK has been a clear leader in this respect, both in Europe and globally, but has been closely followed by other countries both within and without Europe. The EU itself has taken steps to try to embrace this competitive dynamic while preventing deleterious fragmentation, but Brussels has to date not attempted to replicate such a proactive embrace of substantive uncertainty. Indeed, there is some appetite for further action among the Member States themselves in this respect. AMF Chairman Robert Ophèle (2019) has called for EU-wide regulations for non-financial instruments, such as crypto-assets, albeit based on the French strategy. This is reflective of the race to establish international standards in a national image in this brave new world of innovative non-financial instruments. Whether any European country will establish singular dominance in this area, and whether the EU ultimately reflects its powerful Member States' preferences or operates independent of them, remains to be seen. However, the prospects for standardisation of Fintech facilitators appear weak at present.

7.2.2　Legal Uncertainty: Purposive Interpretation by Regulators

Legal uncertainty arises where a given financial innovation is not clearly captured by existing legislation, but where it is introduced by already regulated entities or where it arises at the fringes of regulated activities as a corollary of regulatory arbitrage (Carruthers and Lamoreaux 2016). Generic terms for financial innovation – such as 'Fintech' – do little to disperse such uncertainty, even where they are referred to directly by EU documents,[9] since the term in fact relates to the use of technology by financial firms rather than a specific regulated financial activity. 'Fintech' does not appear in EU legislation nor as a distinct regulatory category, even in relatively recent handbooks of EU financial law (Armour et al. 2016).

Authorities can respond differently to doubts as to whether a new financial innovation fits within the existing categories established by law both at the national and European levels. Such different strategies may depend on factors such as their role in the pre-innovation regime (Pacces 2010; Ford 2013). Legal uncertainty therefore, the second type of uncertainty we consider, may cause regulators across governance levels to diverge in their interpretations, resulting in a fragmented regulatory structure.

Authorities may respond to uncertainty about the legal nature of a financial innovation by extending an existing legal category to cover it. In fact, according to a survey conducted by the European Securities and Markets Authority (ESMA) in 2018, 60 per cent of Fintech firms identified in Member States fall under MiFID definitions (as 'investment firms').[10]　Other applicable EU regimes include: the Alternative Investment Fund Managers Directive (AIFMD), which regulates entities such as hedge funds and private equity firms;[11] the European Market Infrastructure Regulation (EMIR), which regulates central counterparties and trade repositories;[12] and collective investment firms (UCITS).[13]　In cases where a given activity falls within the scope of regulation, designated competent authorities at national or EU level authorise, supervise and enforce the rules. When faced with uncertainty, regulators may seek to identify the regulated entity engaging with the financial innovation (e.g. a bank or an investment firm), with no bespoke regime developed to govern the specifics of the technological dimension (Interview 2019b). This subsequently extends the pre-existing regulatory structure to the financial innovation (hypothesis 11). Where such an interpretation is extended for EU level for example by ESMA, this reduces potential fragmentation which occurs if legal uncertainty is left unaddressed.

Many financial innovations, however, do not fall neatly within nor even close to pre-existing categories. In such cases, evidence suggests that regulators at different levels may adopt divergent strategies leading to fragmentation of the regulatory structure and competition both between levels and within it. Specifically, they may adopt different legal interpretations in the face of legal certainty with a view to attaining their distinct regulatory or institutional goals. The example of competition for the prevailing definition of 'cryptocurrency' in the EU provides an example of this dynamic.

So far there is no distinct EU regulation of crypto-assets, which has led to legal uncertainty as to how they should be treated for the purpose of prudential regulation, tax and anti-money laundering legislation. EU regulators have adopted interpretations which extend the existing legal categories of financial instruments – to the extent possible – to crypto-assets in order to safeguard the objectives of legislation, such as financial stability or integrity in the markets. ESMA has used the financial instrument definitions under MiFID to apply existing rules to retail transactions involving cryptocurrencies.[14] Specifically, ESMA has held that some crypto-assets may fall within the scope of 'transferable securities' definitions under Art. 4(1)(44) MiFID2, noting however that such an interpretation excludes crypto-assets which have payment-like qualities, such as Bitcoin. Such a broad interpretation pursued by ESMA allows for an extension of EU centralised frameworks to the specific Fintech activity, with the corollary expansion of the scope of centralised regulatory structure. In such cases, EU agencies further facilitate supervisory convergence across the internal market when issuing further guidance and advice to national authorities.

At the same time, some national authorities have adopted different interpretations of cryptocurrencies under their tax code – leading to horizontal competition for such financial innovation between Member States. As under conditions of substantive uncertainty, here their strategy can be explained by a desire to pursue economic competitiveness and a wish to attract innovative Fintechs into their jurisdictions, for example by exempting cryptocurrencies as a financial asset in this context, elaborating bespoke arrangements to regulate taxation of crypto-trades.[15] Such uncoordinated new rules as a response to legal uncertainty have resulted in fragmentation. However, where legal uncertainty is addressed in a differential way by the national regulators, centralisation may still occur through the activity of EU courts. Specifically, the Court of Justice (CJEU) may be asked to resolve distortions in the internal market arising from such fragmentation. In the case of cryptocurrencies, in fact this was precisely the question asked in the context of applying the VAT Directive.[16] The Court has resolved the legal uncertainty by interpreting the scope of EU law so as to encompass the financial innovation in this case. The judges held that transactions which consist of an "exchange of traditional currency for units of the 'bitcoin' virtual currency and vice versa, in return for payment of a sum equal to the difference between, on the one hand, the price paid by the operator to purchase the currency and, on the other hand, the price at which he sells that currency to his clients, constitute the supply of services for consideration" and therefore transactions in Bitcoin fall within the scope of transactions on which VAT has to be paid pursuant to EU law. In so doing the CJEU rejected the arguments of the Swedish Law Commission which argued that transactions in cryptocurrencies should be exempt from VAT payments to the extent that they constitute means of payment.

Such litigation at the EU and national level shows that though centralised agencies, notably ESMA, may seek to respond to legal uncertainty by broadening existing rules, any unresolved legal uncertainty will bring about a fragmented regime, where legal classifications in other areas of law adopted by national regulators diverge. In other words, different statutory interpretation strategies pursued at a centralised level by ESMA (i.e. a majority of EU national authorities) and a decentralised level by local supervisors result in a fragmented regulatory structure in the face of uncertainty concerning the legal nature of Fintechs. Though the EU courts have had to grapple with the question of extension of specific legal concepts to innovations such as cryptocurrencies (namely 'services' and 'activity linked to the issuance of electronic money'),[17] they have not been able to answer the question in a consistent way and there has not yet been a review of ESMA's treatment of cryptocurrencies under the existing MiFID regime (Gikay 2018). Unresolved legal uncertainty leads to fragmentation by provoking centralised and decentralised authorities to pursue different strategies, even when the existing regulatory structure is extended to the financial innovation.

7.2.3 (Un)certainty about EU Public Goods

When dealing with financial innovation regulators must deal not only with legal or substantive uncertainty about the nature of a new product, but also its possible effects on general public goods already protected by law. Doubts or lack thereof as to the negative externalities which innovation may have on such public goods results in different regulatory strategies adopted by the regulators – subsequently leading to different regulatory structures (centralised, decentralised or fragmented). In this section we consider the response of regulators to financial innovation which affects general public goods protected at EU level, such as privacy or market integrity. Specifically, we show how regulators develop their strategies in the face of dangers which a given financial innovation may pose.

We distinguish such specific 'effects-based' uncertainty from types of uncertainty linked to legal or substantive doubts in the light of prominence of new objectives which have emerged in regulation in the aftermath of the global financial crisis. Such new EU legislation covers a number of European public goods to be protected given the societal impact of financial instability. New rules not only seek to ensure adequate management of systemic risk,[18] they also identify new public goods where delivery must be ensured, for example the integrity of the market system. Further, public goods protected in the context of financial regulation are not limited to sector-specific risks, but extend to cross-sectoral public goods, such as security (pursued via anti-money laundering laws (AML)[19]) or privacy (data protection rules (GDPR)[20]). If such public goods are already regulated at EU level, this necessarily entails a regulatory structure, for example one which is decentralised in the case of AML. Prior to the crisis, societal externalities were insufficiently incorporated into the regulatory framework, but in its aftermath regulators became more attuned to these risks. Consequently, when faced with a financial innovation, they no longer assess it purely from the point of view of impact on systemic stability, but increasingly also from the perspective of other public interest objectives (Black 2012).

Where an incidence of a given financial innovation activity on such general public goods is identified, this provides an avenue for an extension of existing rules thereto – even in the light of legal or substantive uncertainty described above. In other words, even for certain types of Fintech activity where legal and substantive uncertainty leads to a fragmentation of the regulatory structure, certainty about the risks they may entail for public goods, can lead regulators to extend such existing public goods regulation to cover the innovation. Evidence of such causal mechanisms can be found in two Fintech areas where new rules governing technological innovations were established by regulators at both national and EU level in the context of rules other than sector-specific prudential regulations, namely cryptocurrencies and cloud computing. In the case of cryptocurrencies, first binding EU regulations have been adopted in the area of anti-money laundering legislation, which regulates 'virtual currencies' with a view to preventing their use for criminal purposes. The framework for financial innovation in cloud computing, meanwhile, is subject to the GDPR and guidelines of the European Data Protection Supervisor constitute one of the first legal documents of EU bodies governing this type of innovation. Developing a causal argument linking certainty about the incidence of a given financial innovation on a public good protected by generally applicable EU rules requires identifying the process through which regulators acquire knowledge (overcome uncertainty) about the effects of financial innovation.

In the first place, regulators may acquire certainty in exercising their general mandates for the monitoring of emerging market trends and risks (Minto et al. 2017). EU agencies and ESMA in particular, with regard to financial services, have a general competence for market monitoring. However, when such risk monitoring is carried out by EU agencies they are constrained by their specific mandates. ESMA, for example, assesses financial innovation such as cryptocurrencies in terms of financial stability, orderly market conduct and investor protection (ESMA 2018). There is evidence, however, that a political mandate may be given to EU agencies to explore the possible effects of a given financial innovation on EU public goods. For example, when the European Commission presented its action plans which outline EU activities in the area of financial regulation, these required European agencies to assess the causal links between innovation and money laundering. The 2018 Fintech Action Plan mandates European Supervisory Agencies to develop specific proposals or reports (for example, concerning formal guidelines on outsourcing to cloud services), placing requirements not only in the context of existing competences of the financial regulators, but also other pieces of EU legislation protecting specific EU public goods (such as privacy) under the GDPR. The European Commission in fact states there that:

> The General Data Protection Regulation and the Anti-Money Laundering Directive provide fundamental safeguards for the protection of personal data and the integrity of the EU financial system against money laundering and terrorism finance.

and

> The GDPR creates a genuine single market for the free movement of personal data at a high level of personal data protection. Fintech shall be fully compliant with applicable personal data protection rules. (European Commission 2018)

The European Commission, however, has been guided in such cases by both Member States and the European Parliament, supported by evidence from financial regulators such as the EBA and the ECB (ECOFIN 2016; European Parliament 2016). Such consensus around the need to develop an EU-wide regime to reduce money laundering by introducing EU rules on cryptocurrencies informed EU agencies in their calls for a bespoke cryptocurrency regime. For example, in February 2019, ESMA substantiated its recommendation for regulation of initial coin offerings and crypto-assets by specific reference to AML rulebook. Specifically, though ESMA already created its own rules for crypto-assets under the existing MiFID provisions in the light of its investor protection mandate, presumably given the early success in introducing general (not temporary) rules for crypto-assets under AML, strategically the EU agency considered a general EU public good (security, market integrity) a more forceful reason for EU regulation than purely sectoral objectives (such as investor protection) (ESMA 2019). Though the resulting regulatory structure is not yet fully centralised, certainty about the risk for the provision of a public good already regulated for at European level enabled ESMA to argue for the uploading of rule-making to the EU.

Such a precautionary approach can be explained by the global financial crisis, the consequences of which made regulators more attuned to the emerging risks relating to activities which have proven particularly welfare-decreasing, such as financial instability and money laundering. Further, such an embedding of regulatory action in broader objectives pursued by the EU is not without strategic merit. As Member States have already agreed to protect such specific EU public goods, extending these rules to new financial innovations allows the bypassing of the lengthy process of developing a bespoke regulatory structure. In the case of cryptocurrencies, uncertainty of regulators about the impact of such financial innovation on EU public goods (security) is overcome through a specific mandate emerging from political processes. The regulatory structure applied subsequently is identical to that in the general EU regulation.

However, certainty about the incidence of a given financial innovation on an EU public good may as well arise in the context of work carried out by agencies which are not sector-specific. Such EU agencies created for the protection of EU public goods may have the tools to identify the specific risks which financial innovation may pose to society quicker and more precisely than sectoral regulators. One example here is the regulation of cloud computing, for which there is no harmonised rulebook at EU level, and where the first EU body to develop a set of rules has been the European Data Protection Supervisor – the EU institution's controller, whose mandate extends as well to acting as an advisory body in EU legislative processes (EDPS 2019). EDPS in particular focuses its attention on monitoring the emerging technological risks related to data processing innovations. On 16 March 2018, EDPS issued guidelines on the use of cloud computing services by the European institutions and bodies – even though no specific regulation of this activity is in place at EU level (EDPS 2018). The guidelines were developed specifically as a response to queries by EU institutions and developed following a stakeholder and expert consultation process (Interview 2019b). The scope of the guidelines concerns only the use of cloud computing by EU institutions; however, the principles may in principle inform approaches taken by other data protection regulators.

This evidence suggests that certainty about a given technological innovation's incidence on the delivery of specific (EU) public goods protected under a EU general rules, allows EU financial regulators such as ESMA to take centralised action (or for the European Commission to require such action from European agencies). As hypothesis 12 holds, when EU regulators have certainty as to the incidence of a given financial innovation on a public good – attained via a political mandate or regulatory expertise – they will extend the existing structure to the new activity or instrument. As a result, the pre-existing general regulatory structure will be replicated for the innovation.

Consensus attained already by member states in the context of such specific EU public goods regulation explains the limited resistance among national regulators to such centralising strategies. Conversely, where the incidence of a given financial activity on a public good is not certain, regulators will be less willing to regulate such innovation at the European level, much less centralise the regulatory structure.

7.2.4 Little Uncertainty: Regtech

Finally, we explore the impact of innovation which is explicitly designed to decrease uncertainty facing regulatory structures. We consider the response of regulators to innovations which increase the information available, often described as 'Regtech' – that is, the application of technological innovation for compliance purposes. Previous sections have shown that financial innovation generally creates uncertainty for financial regulators at the national and EU levels to the extent they elude existing legal and business structures or raise concerns about the (possible) societal negative impact. However, there are also innovations which operate in the opposite direction, namely they reduce information asymmetries between the market and the regulators by increasing certainty about the levels of compliance with existing rules by regulated financial firms in the market through technological solutions. As this section will show, such technologically-enabled advances not only reduce uncertainty for supervisors, facilitating centralisation through convergence where harmonised rules apply. Even further, in the context of increasingly granular regulatory requirements and progressively increasing use of technology the regulators themselves ('Suptech'), reducing uncertainty through technology has more general centralising effects and an impact on general market oversight functions and regulatory approaches. In this section, we explore how national and EU regulators respond to the reduction of uncertainty about the market offered by technological innovations in data reporting and analysis explore the consequences for regulatory structures.

The principal way through which post-crisis regulation has sought to prevent another financial meltdown has been an increase in the reporting obligations of regulated institutions. Increasing transparency and disclosure of all stages of transactions has been the very objective of post-crisis EU regulations, and MiFID in particular. The new rules specifically seek to reduce asymmetry between market participants and regulators. The reporting compliance burden has been put in place at a time when the developments in data science allow for new ways of collecting, processing and reporting of data. To respond to such market demand, new technologies emerged, and private enterprises specialising in facilitating data collection and processing for compliance, known as Regtech (Arner et al. 2017, p. 383; Micheler and Whaley 2019). As a result,

Regtech firms are heterogenous groups: they comprise a variety of services including account verification, general compliance, monitoring and risk analysis (Virtual Capitalist 2019). They also employ a variety of technologies to this end, including data analytics, AI, machine learning and new interfaces. Regtech allows for greater agility, timely reporting, speed and integration, analytics and management information by the supervised entities. With improved accuracy of reporting better compliance can be achieved (Anagnostopoulos 2018, p. 14).

Regtech has facilitated processes of change in the regulatory relationship by making data point reporting and analysis simpler, cheaper, more efficient and timely – it therefore reduces uncertainty about compliance with the regulatory structure. Before such advancements the supervisory relationship was characterised by significant asymmetry and a time lag between market and supervisory action. In the EU context, such technology-facilitated reporting implies greater certainty about compliance with EU rules, especially for cross-border transactions. However, different Member States observe different levels of Regtech development as a result of varying levels of resource availability, regulator encouragement or in fact regulator digitalisation (Interview 2019b). In jurisdictions where Regtechs are more popular, better quality of information could allow for greater automaticity of regulatory action, if adequate procedural safeguards are in place (Arner et al. 2017). Such regulatory solutions are now employed in pilot programmes in some EU jurisdictions, most notably in the UK where the FCA has been running pilots related to digital regulatory reporting, by translating regulatory requirements into machine readable and executable regulation (FCA 2019d). To the extent that the FCA is a frontrunner in this respect, this confirms the hypothesis that resource-rich supervisors are more willing to use new capital intensive and risky technologies. Though for the moment there is little evidence of greater automaticity being employed at centralised level, ESMA's role as the gate keeper for regulatory market data, coupled with its mandate to facilitate convergence of supervisory activity has meant the EU agency has privileged information about the Regtech (or Suptech) developments across EU jurisdictions, even as different solutions continue to be tested out at national (decentralised) level (Armstrong 2019).

However, Regtech's role in decreasing uncertainty has also been deemed to warrant harmonisation. In the absence of national regimes, a new EU regulatory structure has been established where there have been specific concerns raised by Regtech companies, including with regard to meta-risks (such as data protection) and traditional financial sector problems such as conflicts of interest (Micheler and Whaley 2019). A subset of companies which employ Regtech technology have already been regulated at EU level under Art. 59 MiFID 2, that is the data reporting services providers (DRSP). These entities will be now supervised for the first time at EU level as they were mostly unregulated at national level previously (European Commission 2017). To the extent that market reporting and compliance functions increasingly have a cross-border dimension, and whereas such service providers have only been supervised by national regulators only for a limited period of time, the uploading of competences for their oversight to the centralised authority of ESMA has thus been achieved as part of the 2019 ESA review. Should other Regtech companies become regulated separately in the future (given their increasing role, and common characteristics with auditors such a scenario can be envisaged), a similar logic may well apply, leading to further centralisation of oversight over Regtech companies. There is no consistent evidence of Regtech companies being separately regulated at national level, however; where Regtech allows for greater certainty about compliance it reduces the arguments for centralisation of direct supervisory authority (e.g. forbearance) – an argument which has been raised by national authorities.

Regulation of Regtech companies under MiFID as a response to their role in reducing uncertainty supports the hypothesis that the provision of Regtech services would lead to centralisation of the EU regulatory structure – in this case over the new technological service providers. However, since the adoption rates of Regtech are uneven, and compliance functions and regulatory structures are not technology neutral, the resulting regulatory structure could also be fragmented. This is as the adoption of uncertainty-reducing technology alters the relationship between the regulated firm and the regulator (including through the potential for greater automation).

Furthermore, reducing uncertainty and information asymmetry through technological innovation is not neutral from the point of view of the regulatory structure since it affects centralised and decentralised regulators differently. Specifically, the use of information technology in regulation triggers a shift of the regulatory paradigm from one oriented at using data for ex post verification and enforcement of compliance, to one which is ex ante data-driven, where standardisation and real-time analytics play the defining role (Anagnostopoulos 2018; Berner and Judge 2019). As a result, centralisation occurs within the regulatory structures where data-collection and aggregation facilitated by adoption of supervisory technologies (Suptech) leads to centralisation by increasing information asymmetries between the ESMA as the data gateway and the national regulators.

The enhanced ability of regulators to process and extract data from supervised entities and the market leads to what has been called 'data-driven supervision' as a new regulatory strategy (cf. Black 2015; Berner and Judge 2019). Under this model the distribution of tasks within the regulatory framework is altered: what matters is not who takes the decision vis-à-vis the regulated entity, but who decides the standard for data points to be collected, the technology for data analysis and the language (code) which determines the interoperability between various regimes. In other words, even if the regulation and distribution of competences within the regulatory structure do not change formally, the increasing importance of data as a focal point of regulation changes what it means to take a regulatory decision. Further, the data aggregator – even if not fully competent for taking supervisory decisions – simply becomes better informed (Arner et al. 2018). As a result the regulatory structure centralises due to two factors. First, since data-orientation in a cross-border context begets standardisation, in a highly rule-based system with limited discretion, decisions relating to standard-setting determine the regulatory decision. Second, centralisation in the light of the new 'data gateway' function of ESMA. Such dynamics can be observed in the example of the changing role of ESMA in data-processing under the MiFID rules (Moloney 2018, p. 133).

The EU MiFID rule book for financial markets is heavily reliant on granular data requirements. Information, meanwhile, is the 'lifeblood of finance' (Berner and Judge 2019). This means that even when enforcement and decisions (i.e. challengeable acts taken vis-à-vis the regulated entity) are decentralised, rule-setting decisions become relatively more important in a data-driven regulatory paradigm where technology enables real-time monitoring. Furthermore, setting the standard of information reconciliation (i.e. harmonising how information about cross-border trades can be exchanged) becomes a tool for harmonisation even where such an objective is not directly prescribed under the regulation. This is specifically the case of ESMA's work on data reconciliation for two-sided reporting requirements, where the supervisory difficulties and national level with exacting the regulatory requirements have led ESMA to develop a specific messaging system (ISO 20022 XML) which will allow standardised processing of data by authorities (Risk.net 2019). Such (centralising) innovations are developed by ESMA on the basis of already existing infrastructures, operational processes and formats, where the agency has direct competence for centralised oversight (namely with regard to trade repositories) under MiFID.[21] Standardisation in data reporting meaning sets the standards of interoperability – that is how different national systems are to understand each other and use the data. As a result the regulatory structure is integrated via the data reconciliation practices developed by EU agencies with regard to new technological reporting standards. There is no evidence of such standardisation being driven 'bottom up' by national authorities, since they would not have the competence to impose their own standards on other national authorities in the EU. ESMA's capacity to set standards is, however, facilitated by its material and non-material resources (hypothesis 13.2).

It is not merely, however, the role of ESMA in standardisation of data-collection and interoperability which is proven to have a centralising effect. Centralisation occurs as well with ESMA becoming 'a data gateway', which means in essence that though the uncertainty of the regulators about the market is decreased as a result of the greater precision in reporting enabled by technology, where such market information is aggregated at EU by ESMA, a new type of information asymmetry arises: that is between national regulators who have only part of the picture and ESMA which can base its regulatory decisions authoritatively on the basis of holistic information spanning the entire internal market.[22] Technology-enabled data analytics have already allowed ESMA to combine various databases compiled using data from different national supervisors and supervised entities received pursuant to MiFID II and EMIR. The centralising effects of such asymmetry are reinforced by a general shift towards novel regulatory policy modelling tools and the data standardisation already discussed, elaboration of new systemic risk tools, greater interoperability and integration of monitoring systems enabling first collaboration and data sharing, and the development of uniform compliance tools (Weber 2017).

ESMA has already developed new technologies of combining and reconfiguring the data uniquely available to it. Greater use of advanced data analytics (supported by deep learning and AI) enables centralisation, as the authorities which have such aggregate data at their disposal are able to draw conclusions from such data far beyond their original scope.[23] Through complex data amalgamation, ESMA is further able to identify new emergent risks and deliver specific input into primary legislation, enabling greater reflexivity of regulation (Ford 2013; Anagnostopoulos 2018). As a result, even if it does not have the centralised competence for the implementation of a specific regulatory action related to the data point, ESMA – as the information gateway – is in a position to draw conclusions from a holistic overview of the market and identify systemic concerns and emerging risks. Such explorative empirical findings support the general hypothesis that Regtech's increased efficiency of information processing, resource-intensity and standardisation effects facilitate centralisation of the regulatory structure. However, they provide an alternative explanation as to the specific channel through which this occurs, namely through the transformation of the role of data in supervision of financial activity, and a replacement of market-regulator asymmetry with national regulator-EU-level data aggregator asymmetry.

There is evidence, therefore, of Regtech firms already having a two-fold impact on the regulatory structure. First, these firms themselves perform an activity which warrants distinct regulation as a result of the public-like role they play in ensuring compliance. Providers of Regtech services, that is private companies which use data analytics and IT systems to facilitate the fulfilment of reporting obligations by regulated financial activities, have become a separate regulated activity as their role in reducing regulatory uncertainty becomes a public function which warrants oversight. Where the levels of adoption of the Regtech differ, this may, however, result in a fragmented structure since reduction of uncertainty for the purpose of compliance verification is not technology neutral in this case. At the same time, greater use of technology by supervisors at EU level may lead to centralisation by increasing the information asymmetry between the EU and national levels where regulators are endowed with different resources to implement digitised innovations and where advanced data analytics processing at EU level. As a result, centralisation could occur even in the absence of formal structural reforms.

7.3   CONCLUSION

This chapter has investigated how recent developments in digitised technological innovation in financial products and business models have impacted upon financial regulatory structures in Europe. We have argued that the degree of informational uncertainty given with a new financial instrument exerts a crucial influence on the way regulators react to new financial instruments introduced by Fintech. From this, we derived a number of hypotheses showing how variations in types and levels of certainty – substantive uncertainty, legal uncertainty, uncertainty regarding public goods and a technology based reduction of uncertainty regarding rule compliance – lead to specific regulatory reactions and regulatory structures. Most of our expectations are supported by the cases examined. Substantive uncertainty about a new financial product induces regulators to engage in the collaborative development of regulatory solutions in conjunction with Fintechs, resulting in competitive and fragmented regulatory structures. However, this is not immutable, and a second phase will see state-driven attempts to bridge regulatory regimes, across Europe and in strategic markets around the world.

Given legal uncertainty, if an innovation is defined as a financial product, regulators will seek to incorporate it into existing legal provisions. In the case of MiFID2, this leads to centralisation at the EU level, and decentralisation at the national implementation level. If regulators are convinced that new products imply risks endangering EU public goods (data protection, privacy, security), they will use existing law protecting these public goods, resulting in a centralisation of provisions and a centralised regulatory structure if no discretion is left to Member States in the process of implementation. If regulators dispose of sufficient material resources to apply Regtech controlling the implementation of strict regulations in real time, centralisation will ensue.

However, our empirical analysis reveals an additional factor leading to a centralisation of regulatory structures that was not conceptualised ex ante: the importance of governing masses of trans-border data and the need to reconcile the use of these data by a supranational authority, in our case ESMA. This data gatekeeper function leads to an informal de facto centralisation, independent of formal regulatory structures.

NOTES

1. We use the term 'Fintech' to refer to the entirety of digitised financial product innovation and new business models, and 'a Fintech' or 'Fintechs' for the individual firms using such practices.
2. Though key enablers, notably the smartphone, emerged coincidentally around the same time, indirect effects of the crisis such as a loss of consumer confidence in traditional banks have helped accelerate receptiveness to new products and firms (Arner et al. 2015, pp. 15–16).
3. For example, in 2019 UK regulators examined products in foreign exchange, payments, insurance, retail banking, trading, security and still more subfields (FCA 2019a).
4. The other 'peak', the Bank of England, is responsible for prudential regulation.
5. These two processes elicited 69 and 84 responses respectively.
6. Not all suggestions were taken forward. For example, while acknowledging the utility of behavioural market research in principle, the FCA declined to sponsor any such measures, citing conflict of interest concerns.
7. Deloitte's (2017) comparative report on Fintech hubs rated London and Singapore as joint global leaders among all major global financial centres.
8. In 2018, Arizona became the first US state to start a state-level sandbox modelled on *FCA Innovate*, its representatives citing the tardiness of the federal government and actively courting London companies concerned about uncertainty over Brexit (Kelly 2018).
9. For example, the European Commission's Fintech Action Plan, 18 March 2018.
10. Directive 2014/65/EU of the European Parliament and of the Council of 15 May 2014 on markets in financial instruments and amending Directive 2002/92/EC and Directive 2011/61/EU (recast) (Text with EEA relevance) (OJ L 173, 12 June 2014, p. 349) and Regulation (EU) No 600/2014 of the European Parliament and of the Council of 15 May 2014 on markets in financial instruments and amending Regulation (EU) No 648/2012 (Text with EEA relevance) (OJ L 173, 12 June 2014, p. 84) (2019 amendments).
11. Directive 2011/61/EU of the European Parliament and of the Council of 8 June 2011 on Alternative Investment Fund Managers and amending Directives 2003/41/EC and 2009/65/EC and Regulations (EC) No 1060/2009 and (EU) No 1095/2010 (Text with EEA relevance) (OJ L 174, 1 July 2011, p. 1).
12. Regulation (EU) No 648/2012 of the European Parliament and of the Council of 4 July 2012 on OTC derivatives, central counterparties and trade repositories (Text with EEA relevance) (OJ L 201, 27 July 2012, p. 1).
13. Directive 2009/65/EC of the European Parliament and of the Council of 13 July 2009 on the coordination of laws, regulations and administrative provisions relating to undertakings for collective investment in transferable securities (UCITS) (recast) (Text with EEA relevance) (OJ L 302, 17 November 2009, p. 32).
14. ESMA, Advice Initial Coin Offerings and Crypto-Assets, 9 January 2019.
15. Polish litigation concerning taxation of crypto-trades following an imposition of tax obligations by the Finance Ministry clarified a number of these points: http://orzeczenia.nsa.gov.pl/doc/C07AA79AA3. Accessed 10 January 2020.
16. Case C-264/14 *Skatteverket v David Hedqvist*, ECLI:EU:C:2015:718.

17. On the application of Electronic Money Directive to Bitcoin see: Case C-389/17 'Paysera LT' UAB, formerly 'EVP International' UAB third party: Lietuvos bankas, Opinion of AG Wathelet, delivered on 4 October 2018.
18. See Karremans and Héritier, Chapter 6 in this volume.
19. Directive (EU) 2018/843 of the European Parliament and of the Council of 30 May 2018 amending Directive (EU) 2015/849 on the prevention of the use of the financial system for the purposes of money laundering or terrorist financing, and amending Directives 2009/138/EC and 2013/36/EU, OJ L 156, 19 June 2018, pp. 43–74.
20. Regulation (EU) 2016/679 of the European Parliament and of the Council of 27 April 2016 on the protection of natural persons with regard to the processing of personal data and on the free movement of such data, and repealing Directive 95/46/EC (General Data Protection Regulation) (Text with EEA relevance) OJ L 119, 4 May 2016, pp. 1–88.
21. Under the EU rules, ESMA is tasked with developing standards of convergence and templates for data reporting.
22. "The fact that Europe was able to put together a centralised, fully open, publicly available and accessible system for the reference data of financial instruments is quite an achievement. The fact that Europe is now able to collect data from more than 200 trading venues on a daily basis, consolidate information on each and every financial instrument, and make that data publicly available is unique" (Risk. net 2019).
23. "For example, if we think about clearing obligations under Emir, those classes of OTC derivatives which fall into the clearing obligation would have been identified and prescribed on the basis of our analysis of EMIR data" (Risk.net 2019).

BIBLIOGRAPHY

Accenture. 2018. 'Banks' Revenue Growth at Risk Due to Unprecedented Competitive Pressure Resulting from Digital Disruption, Accenture Study Finds', 17 October 2018. /news/banks-revenue-growth-at-risk-due-to-unprecedented-competitive-pre ssure-resulting-from-digital-disruption-accenture-study-finds.htm. Accessed 13 April 2020.

Allen, Hilary J. 2019. 'Regulatory Sandboxes'. *The George Washington Law Review* 87.

Anagnostopoulos, Ioannis. 2018. 'Fintech and Regtech: Impact on Regulators and Banks'. *Journal of Economics and Business* 100(July): 7–25. https://doi.org/10 .1016/j.jeconbus.2018.07.003.

Armour, John, Awrey, Dan, Davies, Paul Enriques, Luca Gordon, Jeffrey N., Mayer, Colin and Payne, Jennifer. 2016. *Principles of Financial Regulation*. Oxford: Oxford University Press, 2016.

Armstrong, Patrick. 2019. 'Regtech and SupTech – Change for Markets and Authorities'. *ESMA Report on Trends, Risks and Vulnerabilities* 1: 42–46. https:// doi.org/10.2856/824070.

Arner, Douglas W., Janos Barberis and Ross P. Buckley. 2015. 'The Evolution of Fintech: A New Post-Crisis Paradigm?' *UNSW Law Research Paper No. 2016-62.* https://doi.org/10.2139/ssrn.2676553.

Arner, Douglas W., Janos Barberis and Ross P. Buckley. 2017. 'Fintech, Regtech and the Reconceptualization of Financial Regulation'. *Northwestern Journal of International Law and Business* 37: 371–414.

Arner, Douglas W., Janos Barberis and Ross P. Buckley. 2018. 'The Emergence of Regtech 2.0: From Know Your Customer to Know Your Data'. *Journal of Financial Transformation*: 79–86.

Banque de France. 2019. 'Le Lab Banque de France'. Banque de France. 2019. https://www.banque-france.fr/en/banque-de-france/about-banque-de-france/le-lab-banque-de-france. Accessed 13 April 2020.

Berner, Richard and Kathryn Judge. 2019. 'The Data Standardization Challenge'. ECGI *Working Paper Series in Law*, January.

Besanko, David and David Edward Michael Sappington. 2001. *Designing Regulatory Policy with Limited Information*. London: Routledge.

Black, Julia. 2012. 'Restructuring Global Financial Regulation: Capacities, Coordination and Learning' in: Wymeersch, E., Hopt, K.J. and Ferrarini, G. (eds) *Financial Regulation and Supervision: a Post-crisis Analysis*. Oxford: Oxford University Press, 3–47.

Black, Julia. 2015. 'Regulatory Styles and Supervisory Strategies' in: Moloney, N., Ferran, E. and Payne, J. (eds) *The Oxford Handbook of Financial Regulation*. Oxford: Oxford University Press, 217–253. https://doi.org/10.1093/oxfordhb/9780199687206.013.10.

Boland, Hannah. 2018. 'France Plans to Lure "Thousands" of UK Fintech Jobs, Says Minister'. *The Telegraph*, 18 September 2018. https://www.telegraph.co.uk/technology/2018/09/18/france-plans-lure-thousands-uk-Fintech-jobs-says-minister/. Accessed 16 December 2019.

Campbell, Peter. 2015. 'Osborne Wants London to Be "Global Centre for Fintech"'. *Financial Times*, 11 November 2015. https://www.ft.com/content/1f24a25e-886f-11e5-90de-f44762bf9896. Accessed 16 December 2019.

Carruthers, B.G. and Lamoreaux, N.R. (2016) 'Regulatory Races: The Effects of Jurisdictional Competition on Regulatory Standards'. *Journal of Economic Literature* 54(1): 52–97.

Cook, N. 2017, Intervention, Webinar 'Regulating Regtech. Powering Innovation in Financial Services', 17 October 2017. https://www.youtube.com/watch?v=uu9YHDID6hI. Accessed 13 April 2020.

Deloitte. 2017. 'The Connecting Global Fintech: Interim Hub Review 2017', https://www2.deloitte.com/uk/en/pages/innovation/articles/a-tale-of-44-cities-global-fintech-hub-federation-gfhf-connecting-global-fintech-hub-report-review.html. Accessed 16 December 2019.

Dorfleitner, Gregor, Lars Hornuf, Matthias Schmitt and Martina Weber. 2017. *Fintech in Germany*. New York, NY: Springer.

ESAs. 2018. 'Fintech: Regulatory Sandboxes and Innovation Hubs'. Paris, France: EBA. https://eba.europa.eu/documents/10180/2545547/JC+2018+74+Joint+Report+on+Regulatory+Sandboxes+and+Innovation+Hubs.pdf. Accessed 16 December 2019.

ECOFIN. 2016. 'Council Conclusions on the Fight Against the Financing of Terrorism', 12 February 2016. https://www.consilium.europa.eu/en/press/press-releases/2016/02/12/conclusions-terrorism-financing/. Accessed 16 December 2019.

EDPS. 2018. 'Guidelines on the Use of Cloud Computing Services by the European Institutions and Bodies', March 2018. https://edps.europa.eu/data-protection/our-work/publications/guidelines/guidelines-use-cloud-computing-services-european_en. Accessed 16 December 2019.

EDPS. 2019. 'Leading by Example: EDPS 2015–2019', December 2019. https://edps
.europa.eu/data-protection/our-work/publications/strategy/leading-example-edps
-2015- 2019_en. Accessed 16 December 2019.

ESMA. 2018. 'ESMA, Report on Risks, Trends and Vulnerabilities', 2018. https://
www.esma.europa.eu/sites/default/files/library/esma50report_on_trends_risks_and
_vulnerabilities_no1_2019.pdf. Accessed 16 December 2019.

ESMA. 2019. 'Advice Initial Coin Offerings and Crypto-Assets, January 2019'. https://
www.esma.europa.eu/sites/default/files/library/esma50-157-1391_crypto_advice
.pdf. Accessed 16 December 2019.

European Commission. 2017. 'Commission Staff Working Document – Impact
Assessment', 20 September 2017. https://eur-lex.europa.eu/legal-content/EN/TXT/
?uri=SWD:2017:308:FIN. Accessed 16 December 2019.

European Commission. 2018. 'Fintech Action Plan: For a More Competitive and
Innovative European Financial Sector'. Brussels: European Commission. https://eur
-lex.europa.eu/resource.html?uri=cellar:6793c578-22e6-11e8-ac73-01aa75ed71a1
.0001.02/DOC_1&format=PDF. Accessed 16 December 2019.

European Parliament. 2016. 'Report on Virtual Currencies', 3 May 2016, https://www
.europarl.europa.eu/doceo/document/A-8-2016-0168_EN.html?redirect. Accessed
16 September 2019.

European Parliament. 2019. *Blockchain and the General Data Protection Regulation
Can Distributed Ledgers Be Squared with European Data Protection Law?*
Brussels: European Parliament.

FCA. 2014. 'Project Innovate: Call for Input – Feedback Statement'. London,
UK: FCA. https://www.fca.org.uk/publication/feedback/fs-14-2.pdf. Accessed 16
December 2019.

FCA. 2019a. 'Regulatory Sandbox – Cohort 5'. https://www.fca.org.uk/firms/
regulatory-sandbox/cohort-5. Accessed 16 December 2019.

FCA. 2019b. 'Regulatory Sandbox'. https://www.fca.org.uk/firms/regulatory-sandbox.
Accessed 16 December 2019.

FCA. 2019c. 'The Impact and Effectiveness of Innovate'. London, UK: FCA. https://
www.fca.org.uk/publication/research/the-impact-and-effectiveness-of-innovate.pdf.
Accessed 16 December 2019.

FCA. 2019d. 'Global Financial Innovation Network (GFIN)'. https://www.fca.org.uk/
firms/global-financial-innovation-network. Accessed 16 December 2019.

Fintech Alliance. 2019. 'UK–Australia Fintech Bridge', 9 June 2019. https://fintech
-alliance.com/government/single/fintech-bridges/uk-australia-fintech-bridge.
Accessed 13 January 2020.

Fintech Global. 2019. 'Fintech Investment in Europe Has a Strong Start to the Year –
Fintech Global', 3 April 2019. https://Fintech.global/Fintech-investment-in-europe
-has-a-strong-start-to-the-year/. Accessed 16 December 2019.

Ford, Cristie. 2013. 'Financial Innovation and Flexible Regulation: Destabilising the
Regulatory State'. *North Carolina Banking Institute* 18(27): 27–38. https://doi.org/
10.3366/ajicl.2011.0005.

Gikay, A.A. (2018) 'European Consumer Law and Blockchain Based Financial Services:
A Functional Approach Against the Rhetoric of Regulatory Uncertainty'. *Tilburg
Law Review* 24(1): 27–48.

Interview. 2019a. Representative at a French financial regulator. Telephone, 5 August
2019.

Interview. 2019b. Former Polish supervisory authority official. Warsaw, 2 December
2019.

Kelly, Jemima. 2018. 'Arizona Sandbox Gives Fintech Start-Ups a Regulatory Path to US'. *Financial Times*, 12 November 2018. https://www.ft.com/content/aac62a22 -c196-11e8-84cd-9e601db069b8. Accessed 16 December 2019.

KPMG. 2019. 'Global Fintech Investment Rockets to \$111.8bn', 20 February 2019. https://home.kpmg/ie/en/home/media/press-releases/2019/02/pulse-of-fintech-2018 .html. Accessed 14 November 2019

Labbé, Amelie. 2016. 'Race for EU Fintech Lead Is On'. *International Financial Law Review*, November. http://search.proquest.com/openview/574aa9c26a43 db28e8b960766cae2875/1?pq-origsite=gscholar&cbl=36341. Accessed 13 April 2020.

Lavery, Scott, Sean McDaniel and Davide Schmid. 2018. 'New Geographies of European Financial Competition? Frankfurt, Paris and the Political Economy of Brexit'. *Geoforum* 94 (August): 72–81. https://doi.org/10.1016/j.geoforum.2018.03 .021.

Micheler, Eva and Anna Whaley. 2019. 'Regulatory Technology – Replacing Law with Computer Code'. *European Business Organization Law Review*. https://doi.org/ 10.2139/ssrn.3210962.   https://link.springer.com/article/10.1007%2Fs40804-019 -00151-1#citeas

Minto, Andrea, Moritz Voelkerling and Melanie Wulff. 2017. 'Separating Apples from Oranges: Identifying Threats to Financial Stability Originating from Fintech'. *Capital Markets Law Journal* 12(4): 428–465. https://doi.org/10.1093/cmlj/kmx035.

Moloney, N. (2018) *The Age of ESMA: Governing EU Financial Markets*. London: Bloomsbury Publishing.

Murphy, Dale D. 2004. 'The Business Dynamics of Global Regulatory Competition', in: Vogel, D. and Kagan, R.A. (eds) *Dynamics of Regulatory Change: How Globalization Affects National Regulatory Policies*, 84–117. Berkeley, CA: University of California Press.

Nelson, Stephen C. and Peter J. Katzenstein. 2014. 'Uncertainty, Risk, and the Financial Crisis of 2008'. *International Organization* 68(2): 361–392. https://doi .org/10.1017/S0020818313000416.

Ophèle, Robert. 2019. 'Innovation and Regulation: The French Approach to Crypto'. presented at the 3rd Annual Fintech Conference, Brussels, 27 February.

Pacces, Alessio M. 2010. 'Consequences of Uncertainty for Regulation: Law and Economics of the Financial Crisis'. *European Company and Financial Law Review* 7(4): 479–511. https://doi.org/10.1515/ecfr.2010.479.

Radaelli, Claudio M. 2004. 'The Puzzle of Regulatory Competition'. *Journal of Public Policy* 24(1): 1–23.

Risk.net. 2019. 'Resented Elsewhere, MiFID Finds Love at About Too Much Data Is Much Air', 5 July 2019.

RT International. 2019. 'World's 1st Crypto Banks Get Licenses in Switzerland', 29 August 2019. https://www.rt.com/business/467539-worlds-first-cryptobanks -licenses/. Accessed 16 December 2019.

Simmons, Beth A. 2001. 'The International Politics of Harmonization: The Case of Capital Market Regulation'. *International Organization* 55(3): 589–620.

Virtual Capitalist. 2019. 'The Rise of Regtech: How Software Can Help Cut Regulatory Risks'. https://www.visualcapitalist.com/Regtech-regulatory-risks/. Accessed 16 December 2019.

Weber, Rolf H. 2017. 'Regtech as a New Legal Challenge'. *Journal of Financial Transformation* 46: 10–16.

8. Governing finance in Europe: discussion and conclusion

Adrienne Héritier

8.1 INTRODUCTION

In this book we have raised the question of whether and why the governance of financial markets has led to a centralisation, decentralisation or fragmentation of regulatory structures in Europe. In the theory chapter we developed hypothetical answers to this question from four research perspectives: European legislation in the context of international agreements; international competition between regulatory powers; the interaction between private self-regulation and public regulation; and technological (digital) innovation of financial instruments.

In this concluding chapter, we first identify whether the findings of the empirical chapters confirm our hypotheses, and if they disconfirm them, what conclusions need to be drawn on our theoretical explanations. We further draw links between the arguments in the individual chapters and identify whether they reinforce, complement or contradict each other.

Second, we go beyond the strict scope of our present theoretically guided empirical investigation and raise questions concerning the political and legal accountability of the regulatory structures we have found. How do they matter in terms of the effects of regulations and endeavours to hold regulators accountable for their decisions? Since accountability questions mostly arise if they are linked to the policy effects of regulation, we consider these two factors together when formulating preliminary arguments regarding political and legal accountability and the effects of financial regulation in Europe. A systematic empirical investigation of these preliminary findings will constitute an important avenue for future research on this topic.

8.2 GENERAL INSIGHTS AND FINDINGS IN THE CHAPTERS

From the *vertical international research perspective*, that is, European financial market legislation in the context of international agreements, we started from the fact that there is pressure which derives from international agreements and regulatory bodies on regional regulators to harmonise financial regulation. In the EU, this pressure translates into a complex political process at the supranational and Member State levels. Since national economic, political, institutional, legal and social factors vary, the outcomes in Europe's regulatory structure and policy substance are not necessarily uniform and do not automatically lead to a centralisation of rule-making.

In their chapter on the *MiFiD II regulation of high frequency trading*, Jan Karremans and Magnus G. Schoeller found that under the indirect influence of the G20 agenda strong attempts were made by the Commission (*H5*), and also by the EP, to advance a centralisation of HFT regulation. Hence, when also taking into consideration the EP, centralisation endeavours originate from *two* actors at the EU level and not, as we anticipated, only from the Commission. Moreover, the authors show that the EU legislative initiatives were partly built on the corresponding pre-existing national regulation of HFT in Germany. While they find that rule-making at the European level constitutes an instance of centralisation led by the Commission and the EP, thus formally uploading regulatory competences to the EU level, this centralisation is challenged in the course of implementation when the centrally defined technical standards are supervised in Member States using different practices and surveillance structures (*H2*). Hence, we find a centralisation of rule-making at the European level but decentralised modes of implementation at the national level.

From the same vertical international perspective, Fabio Bulfone and Agnieszka Smoleńska focus on *central counterparty (CCP) clearing* in the context of the Capital Markets Union (CMU).[1] They show that the Commission indeed seized the opportunity of international pressure resulting from the G20 to initiate centralising legislation (*H5*). However, they also show that this centralising attempt in favour of the Commission and ESMA at the supranational level was challenged by claims from the ECB, which sought to gain supervisory power over the market. This attempt was successfully opposed by the EP, which, given that it has less power to hold the ECB accountable, was in favour of centralising power in the ESMA.

Supporting Karremans' and Schoeller's findings in Chapter 2, Bulfone and Smoleńska also find that a centralisation of rule-making and a decentralisation of regulatory structures at the implementation level exist alongside each other. Regarding rule-making at the supranational level, they also show that given *de facto* consensus decision-making[2] it was only after the UK's exit decision (*H6* and *H7*) that preferences among the larger countries converged and centralisation initiatives with respect to the regulation of third-country CCPs became successful. By contrast, regarding the internal regulation of CCPs, Member States' competing economic interests in taking over part of the UK CCPs' functions in the internal market prevented moves to centralise intra-EU CCPs (that is, entities authorised in one of the Member States), with Germany acting as a veto player (*H5*), being motivated by internal competition for a higher CCP market share after Brexit. As in Chapter 2 on HFT, the authors find that the supervisory structures at the implementation level in Member States vary to a great extent as a function of pre-existing institutional structures. Moreover, the pressure of internal competition for CCP market shares reinforced differences among Member States. As the authors find a decentralisation of implementing structures in the internal market, they question our hypothesis (*H6*) that competition between different regional regulatory powers, in this case the EU and the UK, strengthens internal coherence within one regional regulatory power, as it is argued by Heikki Marjosola in Chapter 5 on the regulatory competition between EU and the US (see below).

The chapter on the *choice of legal instruments* from the vertical international perspective by Magnus Strand addresses the hypothesis that an increasing use of regulations (rather than directives) implies more centralised control. Strand tests this claim with regard to the regulation of financial instruments under MiFID II. In his empirical analysis he does not find such an impact, thereby disconfirming *H4.1* and *H4.2*. Strand takes an important further analytical step by inquiring into rules that are specifically directed at EU agencies. He finds more 'high density' regulation if rules are addressed to regulatory authorities such as ESMA. This can be explained by the legislator's wish to control the EU agencies. Moreover, Strand also analyses non-legislative acts (delegated acts) directed at other institutional actors such as national authorities. He shows that non-legislative acts adopted on the basis of MiFID and MiFIR created an extensive set of rules centralising financial governance when addressing administrations at both the European and national levels. As a result, we learn that if directives – which give more latitude to implementation through transposition into national legislation – are used, this latitude may subsequently be restricted through delegated legislation.

Here, we find a certain contradiction with the empirical findings in both Chapters 2 and 3. While formal regulatory decisions aim at centralisation and harmonisation, their implementation by Member States is characterised by decentralisation, or even fragmentation, in regulatory practices (i.e. a differential application of formal rules by the Member States). We may explain these contradictory findings by distinguishing time periods. The pattern of centralised formal rules and decentralised implementation may emerge in a first instance (t1). In a second instance (t2), delegated legislation governing the implementation phase counters decentralising tendencies and leads back to more centralised implementation. Moreover, as Carl Fredrik Bergström[3] emphasises, in a longer time perspective fragmented or decentralised regulatory structures in implementation tend to be levelled out by court rulings seeking to establish similar regulatory practices and structures.

From the *horizontal international perspective*, we ask whether regulatory competition between regulatory powers leads to a centralisation of regulatory structure within the EU as a regulatory power. Heikki Marjosola argues that the *regulatory rivalry between the EU and the US in the field of OTC regulation*, specifically the regulation of CCPs, leads to a fragmentation of the regulatory structure internationally and in consequence to regulatory arbitrage by the regulated. Regulatory competition and resulting regulatory arbitrage by the industry may in turn lead to an internal centralisation of regulatory structures within one regulatory power seeking to better coordinate its policies in view of external competition (*H6*).

Moreover, in order to reduce regulatory arbitrage, regulatory powers may refrain from imposing their own regulation on the rest of the world (extraterritorial application) or seek to coordinate their regulatory prescriptions (*H7*) if one party takes the lead in this coordination by using strategies of regulatory equivalence or mutual recognition. Such efforts will lead to a gradual convergence of regulatory prescriptions. Marjosola finds that progress towards a deference-based recognition regime has been slow in bargaining on an agreement between the US and the EU, the negotiations being complicated by the Brexit decision and the issue of how to regulate third-country CCPs. The EU's EMIR legislation in response strengthened the powers of the ESMA, the central EU administrative authority, leading to a centralisation within the EU regarding the regulation of third-country CCPs operating in the EU, confirming our hypothesis *H6*. However, as Bulfone and Smoleńska analysed in Chapter 3, this only holds for the regulation of third-country (extra-EU) CCPs providing services in the EU market, but not for that of CCPs already established in one of the Member States (and therefore supervised by a national competent authority – see above).

From the *public–private interaction perspective* Johannes Karremans and Adrienne Héritier ask whether the *self-regulation of financial services* by private actors and subsequent *public–private co-regulation* lead to a centralisation or fragmentation of regulatory structure in the EU. Self-regulation rules have frequently emerged in new markets, with public actors subsequently intervening step by step, leading to a form of hybrid regulatory governance structure (*H8*). While the initial forms of self-regulation may have given rise to a fragmented structure, one would expect an emergence of more centralising features with increasing intervention by public actors. The two cases analysed in this chapter, the self-regulation of OTC derivatives by the International Swaps and Derivatives Association (ISDA) and the Alternative Investment Market (AIM) of the London Stock Exchange (LSE), tell the story of new European rules entering two spheres of the financial markets that were previously almost entirely self-regulated and that shared similar patterns of public regulatory intervention. In both cases, in fact, the European public regulator intervened by adding new rules that are valid for the EU to the existing regime, thus leading to a partial centralisation of regulatory structure.

In both cases we see that failures of private self-regulatory regimes to tackle systemic risk and excessive rent-seeking prompted intervention (*H8*). While the private regulatory regimes – ISDA's 'master agreement' and the regime governed by 'Nomads' in the AIM – remain in place, financial transactions in these markets are now directly subject to European regulatory requirements. However, as the empirical findings in the chapter on MiFID II show, surveillance structures vary across Member States during the implementation phase of a central rule. Thus, also under hybrid regulation, implementation by private actors may differ and lead to a fragmented regulatory structure.

While the general hypothesis about private self-regulation prompting public regulation, given the risks of micro fraud and system instability, is confirmed, our arguments regarding the causes of the emergence of regulatory regimes (*H8.1* and *H8.2*) are only partly confirmed. On the one hand, the idea that private regimes will attract new members and that these will adapt to the existing regulatory structure (*H8.2*) is confirmed in both cases: ISDA has attracted a rapidly rising number of participants in the case of OTC derivatives, and AIM gathered companies under the LSE private regime. On the other hand, our hypothesis that private regulatory regimes emerge as a result of innovation in financial instruments (*H8.1*) only finds confirmation in ISDA's rise as a private authority linked to the growing complexity and technological progress in derivative trading (also see Chapter 6 on technological innovation in financial transactions and its impact on regulatory regimes). By contrast, the case of AIM, which was created by the LSE in order to avoid the heavy regulation of initial public offerings (IPOs), disconfirms our hypothesis. Indeed, this reaction to strengthened regulation is well-known. The regulated seek to eschew regulation by developing a slightly different financial product which does not correspond to the prescriptions of existing regulation. Hence, the emergence of AIM cannot be traced back to an independent rise of new financial instruments.

As a consequence, our theoretical argument on the rise of self-regulation needs to be refined by including private actors having the goal of avoiding existing regulation. An additional general insight deriving from the empirical findings is that private actors are not *per se* against a centralisation of rule-making. On the contrary, especially if they operate transnationally, they tend to be in favour of homogenous rules across different jurisdictions. At the same time, private actors may be very keen to shelter particular segments of the market from public regulation.

From the *technological innovation perspective*, we ask, given the rapid technological digital innovations of ever more financial products, what the challenges are for regulators in governing these new instruments. To what extent do they effect (de)centralisation or fragmentation in the EU's regulatory structure? Agnieszka Smoleńska, Joseph Ganderson and Adrienne Héritier (Chapter 7) argue that the type and level of uncertainty about risks linked to a new financial product or business model are crucial factors influencing the reaction of regulators. They distinguish between substantive, legal and cross-sectoral uncertainty and also (un)certainty regarding compliance with regulatory prescriptions. The authors show that substantive uncertainty regarding the nature of new financial instruments induces regulators to cooperate with the industry when developing bespoke regulatory requirements, engaging in 'sandboxing' or creating innovation hubs. This leads to fragmentation in a first instance, which in turn is limited by seeking regulatory convergence (*H10*). In the case of legal uncertainty, regulators seek to fit the new risks into pre-existing legal rules (*H11*), which also helps them reduce uncertainty in the case of cross-sectoral risks regarding the provision of public goods (*H12*). This can lead to fragmentation where authorities at the centralised and decentralised levels pursue different strategies in the face of uncertainty. In the case of the application of regtech, which presupposes that the regulator and the regulated market actors have at their disposal the necessary resources, the regulator has no uncertainty regarding real-time financial transactions, which, if the relevant rules are detailed and strict, leads to a centralisation of regulation (*H13*). Empirical cases demonstrate the plausibility of these claims. However, it further emerges that an additional factor may drive centralisation, that is, the collection and processing of large quantities of data on financial transactions in the course of trans-border data conciliation by the competent central authority (here, ESMA). The role of the regulatory agency as a data gatekeeper reinforces a centralisation of regulation, even if formal regulatory structures remain decentralised.

In summary, the theoretically guided empirical insights in the five empirical chapters seen together show that the formulation of rules has led to a partial centralisation of regulatory structures in Europe due to pressure from international agreements, regulatory competition between regulatory powers, an increasing influence of public actors on private self-regulation and digital technological innovations in the use of financial instruments and regulation. At the same time, at the level of the implementation of centralising rules by Member States or private actors, decentralising or even fragmenting forces deriving from diverse economic interests and institutional traditions among the Member States impact on regulatory structures. Technological innovation (fintech) and subsequent self-regulation tend to prompt public regulation with the intention of harmonising rules in a first stage, while decentralised implementation at the national level remains (see above). Only in a second stage may divergences in the implementation of rules become subject to renewed attempts at harmonisation through delegated technical legislation (Chapter 4) and court rulings (Chapter 6). Centralising legislation (Chapters 2 and 3), with its demands of massive amounts of data being provided by financial firms in order to allow for transparency, in turn reinforces technological innovation by fintech in the form of regtech (Chapter 6). Regtech, if widely applied, finally leads to a centralisation of regulatory structures, given the scope for real-time control of rule compliance.

The findings of partial centralisation of regulatory structures in rule-making in almost all the chapters, albeit attenuated by decentralisation or fragmentation during implementation, gives rise to the question of how these regulatory structures can be subject to political accountability mechanisms. European regulations imply a loss of decision-making power of national parliaments and hence less democratic accountability at the national level. In future research steps, we will therefore turn to the question of *political and legal accountability*.

8.3   POLITICAL AND LEGAL ACCOUNTABILITY IN VIEW OF REGULATORY EFFECTS

In explaining the regulatory structures resulting from European regulation of financial markets under MiFID II and CMU, we predominantly found centralised regulatory structures in rule-formulation but decentralised or fragmented regulatory structures in the implementation of these rules. Moving to questions on effects and accountability, we ask how the regulatory decisions produced under these structures are held accountable. This question becomes most relevant when it is linked to regulatory effects which are salient in public attention, that is, causing public discontent and therefore giving rise to a wish to hold regulators accountable. In further research steps going beyond the scope of this book, we will therefore analyse *policy effects and accountability mechanisms in their interlinkedness*.

To start with a brief empirical illustration of institutional accountability channels identified in this volume, we have found that technical standards are defined at the EU level (by national authorities represented in ESMA) while market supervision falls under the responsibility of national authorities. This implies that political accountability runs through two channels (and possibly a third one). The first channel is the national level: national financial authorities are responsible to their governments and parliaments. The second channel is the European level: if technical standards are found to be deficient in their effects, in principle the European Parliament should call the Commission to explain and eventually justify the actions of ESMA. The third channel of accountability is the way ESMA functions. In addition to being a supranational agency with its own permanent staff, ESMA also involves a monthly meeting of national financial authorities. In these meetings, national authorities discuss their differences and try to find common solutions for market supervision. These meetings therefore have a tempering effect on the de-centralisation patterns identified in the empirical chapters in this volume. Moreover, the meetings are a form of horizontal accountability mechanism: the national authorities monitor each other.

From this first illustrative mapping of possible political and administrative accountability channels under MiFiD II and CMU, a range of conceptual questions emerge regarding the effects/accountability link. They will be outlined here and tackled in future research.

A first challenge is to determine the *scope and the nature of the effects* of regulation which is subject to accountability mechanisms. Financial market transactions in their functioning and their regulation are not easily accessible to the wider public and the target groups of regulation. In other words, financial market regulation is an informationally secluded policy area. This does not mean that financial regulation is intentionally secluded,[4] but instead that it is hard to grasp it in its technological and economic complexity and in view of the worldwide interlinkedness of financial transactions, market players and regulators' decisions.[5] In consequence, future research will need to limit its analysis to clearly restricted measures (such as the provisions under MiFID II and CMU) that are accessible to a causal explanation in order to analyse their effects on market actors and investors. For such cases, one can investigate institutional accountability mechanisms that are available to the target groups of regulation and the public at large in order for them to contest these effects. Furthermore, the difference that the use of accountability mechanisms makes regarding the regulatory effects in question will need to be analysed.

With regard to the *concept of accountability*, a second challenge is to define accountability mechanisms. These have proliferated in recent decades, as is described in the large literature on political and legal accountability mechanisms in their various forms (e.g. the *Oxford Handbook on Public Accountability*, Bovens and Schillemans 2014).[6] In political science, political accountability is often defined as a mechanism with which, after the delegation of a task by a political actor (the 'principal') to an executive actor (the 'agent'), the execution of this task can be monitored by the principal if it has sufficient information on the quality of task performance (principal–agent approach). If the execution is considered to be unsatisfactory, the principal must be able to sanction the malperformance by various means, such as imposing fines or withdrawing the delegation of the task (i.e. dismissing the agent). These three elements – that is, task delegation, monitoring of task performance and sanctions in the case of non-performance – form arguably one of the most extensive conceptualisations of the mechanism realising political accountability (e.g. Bovens and Schillemans 2014).[7]

Analytical distinctions in the use of accountability mechanisms may be helpful to analyse the link between regulatory effects and accountability. One distinction reaching back to the distinction between procedural law and substantive law (Jeschek et al. 2017) refers to the procedural and substantive accountability provided by courts (see for instance most recently Dawson and Maricut-Akbik 2019). In political science analysis, this distinction between substantive and procedural accountability is relevant and raises the question of how different existing types of accountability mechanisms play out when used by target groups of regulation which are dissatisfied with the effects of financial regulation. Substantive accountability mechanisms in this context would imply a possibility for actors affected by regulatory decisions to question the very substance of the regulation and possibly obtain a modification of the substance, beyond being (only) based on the procedural correctness of the underlying decision process.

Another relevant question linked to regulatory effects and accountability mechanisms and deriving from this discussion asks about the *type of instrument* used in regulation and its implications for political and legal accountability. Pistor, referring to the dilemma of the regulator, emphasises that soft law is more elusive of accountability requests. If rules are rigid and precise, the public can more easily apply political accountability mechanisms, but rigid rules are difficult for the regulator because in cases of contingencies or crisis a flexibility of rules may be needed to deal with a financial market problem. In turn this means less political accountability to the public (Pistor 2019); see also Dawson and Maricut-Akbik (2019).

Further analytical perspectives from which to examine the effects–accountability link may be gained from the distinction between legal and political *ex ante* and *ex post* accountability mechanisms. Bergström (2019) underlines that the main reference point of legal accountability control consists in checking whether – in a hierarchy of norms – inferior value rules conflict with higher value rules. The monitoring may either be conducted by legal or political bodies. In the case of political accountability mechanisms, an *ex ante* and *ex post* distinction may also apply. However, this would not regard congruence with the hierarchy of norms but instead the regulatory objectives declared for a specific measure. Thus, the distinction between *ex ante* and *ex post* monitoring is also present in the principal–agent approach (see above). By contractually binding the agent to *ex ante* defined procedural controls (e.g. regular reporting) and substantive standards (e.g. keeping regulatory decisions within pre-defined limits), the principal can ensure mechanisms of *ex ante* accountability. By contrast, in the case of *ex post* monitoring, principals may rely on information from third parties ('firebell ringing'), top-down intervention ('police patrol') or reporting to national parliaments and the EP. An *ex ante* political monitoring uploading national competences to the European level would consist, for instance, in an *ex ante* preview of decisions by a parliamentary committee, such as in the case of Sweden's constitutional committee (Bergström 2019). From these considerations a further line of research on regulatory effects and accountability mechanisms in financial markets would analyse institutional mechanisms of ex *ante* and *ex post* monitoring with respect to procedural and substantive political accountability, given initially stated regulatory objectives.[8]

8.4   CONCLUSION

To conclude, this volume has explained the European regulatory structure of financial governance flowing from the perspectives of mandates by international agreements, competition between the large regulatory powers of the EU and the US, the interaction between public and private regulators and digital financial innovation. While many of our hypotheses regarding the drivers of centralisation, decentralisation and fragmentation of regulatory structures have been confirmed, we have also found some disconfirming evidence that requires further theoretical refinement in future research. In particular, if we aim to provide a complete explanation of the centralisation, decentralisation or fragmentation of a regulatory structure – rather than probing the explanatory power of a particular theoretical approach – the evidence provided by our empirical analyses points to additional explanatory factors needing to be included in our explanatory framework.

Once the regulatory structures are identified and explained, however, a further research question arises: what do these structures mean when we examine them with regard to their regulatory effects and the linked mechanisms of accountability? Hence, this book has also revealed the next research steps that follow from its findings. In particular, we will need to analyse the effects of the regulatory measures under MiFID II and CMU that we have focused on in this volume and investigate the conditions under which they have been subject to accountability mechanisms of what nature and with what outcome.

NOTES

1.   More precisely, CCPs have been regulated by the recently reformed European Financial Markets Infrastructure Regulation (EMIR).

2. Although EMIR is governed on a Qualified Majority Voting (QMV) legal basis (Art. 114 TFEU).
3. Carl Fredrik Bergström, oral comment at the 'Governing Finance in Europe' workshop at the Hertie School of Governance, Berlin, 7 and 8 November 2019.
4. Walter Mattli (2019) argues that there is also much intentional obfuscation in financial market transactions in order to obtain a relative advantage over competitors (e.g. 'stuffing'). However, this cannot be said for regulators. See also Karremans (2019).
5. The overall impact of individual regulatory measures on financial transactions in their worldwide interlinkedness, as has been argued for instance by Haldane and Madouros (2012), does not follow a linear causal logic but instead may be subject to a logic of chaos theory, where at some point individual actions in their systemic effect may produce a system stability crisis.
6. One problem is the so-called 'multiple accountabilities disorder' when actors become confused by the conflicting expectations of their different account-holders and can therefore not perform their duties effectively (Koppell 2005).
7. In practice, weaker forms of political accountability are widely used when seeking to hold regulatory authorities accountable. They comprise acts of political delegation to an agent and access to information (transparency) in order to control the agent. The sanctioning element is often missing or very weak in terms of its stringency.
8. Of course, legal and political accountability mechanisms are often linked. Dissatisfied target groups of a regulation in a political accountability conflict may step out of the political institutional channel, as it were, and challenge the measure by turning to a court.

BIBLIOGRAPHY

Bergström, C.F. (2019) Oral comment at the 'Governing Finance in Europe' workshop at the Hertie School of Governance, Berlin, 7 and 8 November 2019.
Bergström, C.F. and M. Ruotsi (2018) 'Grundlag gungning. En ESO-rapport om EU och den svenska offentlighetsprincipen', Report to the The Expert Group on Public Economics 2018:1, Ministry of Finances 2018.
Bovens, M. and T. Schillemans (2014) 'Meaningful Accountability', in M. Bovens, R.E. Goodin and T. Schillemans (eds) *The Oxford Handbook of Public Accountability*, Oxford: Oxford University Press, pp. 673–682.
Dawson, M. and A. Maricut-Akbik (2019) 'Procedural and Substantive Uses of Accountability in Modern Governance: Between Payoffs and Trade-offs'. Paper Workshop 'Theorizing and Assessing Accountability in Post-Crisis EU Economic Governance', 25 November 2019 European University Institute Florence.
Haldane, A. and V. Madouros (2012) 'The Dog and the Frisbee', Speech, 366th Economic Policy Symposium, Federal Reserve Bank of Kansas City. On 'The changing policy landscape', Jackson Hole, Wyoming, 31 August 2012.
Jeschek, H.-H., T. Weigend, G. Hazard and C. Yeazell (2017) *Encyclopedia Britannica*, https://www.britannica.com/.
Karremans, J. (2019) 'Never Again Financial Deregulation … Ten Years After the Pittsburgh Summit', EUIdeas Blog, European University Institute, 3 December, https://euideas.eui.eu/2019/12/03/never-again-financial-deregulation-ten-years-after-the-pittsburgh-summit/. Accessed 18 January 2020.

Koppell, J.G.S. (2005) 'Pathologies of Accountability: ICANN and the Challenge of Multiple Accountabilities Disorder', *Public Administration Review*, 65(1), 84–108.

Mattli, W. (2019) *Darkness by Design, The Hidden Power in Global Capital Markets.* Princeton, NJ: Princeton University Press.

Pistor, K. (2019) *The Code of Capital: How the Law Creates Wealth and Inequality.* Princeton, NJ: Princeton University Press.

Index

accountability, political and legal 196–9
agencies (of the EU) 66, 70, 73, 83,
    85–6, 90, 95, 99, 101, 106–7, 124,
    174, 176–8, 182, 192
AIM (Alternative Investment Market)
    case study introduction 139
    market abuse regulation 149–56
    number of listed companies 153
    privately self-regulated market
        149–54, 158
    public intervention 154–6, 159
    rules for nominated advisers 152
Article 288 TFEU
    classes of legal acts under 82–3
    and EU legislator 82–3, 89, 104
    legislative instrument of preference
        86–7

Brexit
    CCPs
        and horizontal international
            perspective 73–4
        linking with need to centralise
            supervision over 64–5
        London-based 121–2
        and 'no-deal' planning 63
        as potential source of systemic
            risk 53–4
        profound impact on framework
            70–71
        regulation following 68–70
        UK's resistance preventing
            supervisory
            centralisation prior to 58
    complicating agreement between US
        and EU 193
    creating sense of urgency 54
    ESMA 11, 63, 68–70
    EU and financial regulation 57, 68
    European Commission 11, 57, 63,
        68–70

European Parliament's preferences
    reshaped by 57, 64
neo-mercantilist competition
    between financial centres
    after 54–5, 67, 68–70, 170,
    192
pivotal actors in EU legislative
    process 57–8
regulatory arbitrage 11, 65, 68, 74
uncertainty surrounding 56–7, 185

capital markets union (CMU)
    areas of future research 197, 199
    as bringing form of powers shared
        by public and private actors
        13
    centralisation of supervision of
        CCPs as part of 54
    nature and goal of 52
    as one of most important EU
        legislative programmes 3–4,
        25
    reform of CCP regulation as part
        of 52
CCPs (central counterparties)
    contentious nature of operations
        53–4
    definition 53
    EU
        national resistance to
            supervisory
            centralisation 65–8
        regulatory structure for 62
        supervision of 60–62
        and US turf battle 113, 120–23,
            129, 193
    as financial market infrastructure
        52–3, 73–4
    G20
        calling for direct supervision 53
        introduced by 12